Henry St. John Bolingbroke

Letters on the Study and Use of History

Henry St. John Bolingbroke

Letters on the Study and Use of History

ISBN/EAN: 9783742804778

Manufactured in Europe, USA, Canada, Australia, Japa

Cover: Foto ©Andreas Hilbeck / pixelio.de

Manufactured and distributed by brebook publishing software (www.brebook.com)

Henry St. John Bolingbroke

Letters on the Study and Use of History

LETTERS

ON THE

STUDY and USE

OF

HISTORY.

By the late RIGHT HONORABLE

HENRY ST. JOHN,

LORD VISCOUNT BOLINGBROKE.

A NEW EDITION.

BASIL:

PRINTED BY J. J. TOURNEISEN.

MDCCLXXXVIII.

THE CONTENTS.

LETTER I.

Of the study of history.   Page. 1

LETTER II.

Concerning the true use and advantages of it.   7

LETTER III.

1. An objection against the utility of history removed. 2. The false and true aims of those who study it. 3. Of the history of the first ages; with reflections on the state of ancient history, profane and sacred.   32

LETTER IV.

1. That there is in history sufficient authenticity to render it useful, notwithstanding all objections to the contrary. 2. Of the method and due restrictions to be observed in the study of it.   73

LETTER V.

1. The great use of history, properly so called, as distinguished from the writings of mere annalists and antiquaries. 2. Greek and Roman historians. 3. Some idea of a complete history. 4. Further cautions to be observed in this study, and the regulation of it according to the different professions, and situations of men: above all, the use to be made of it (1) by divines, and (2) by those who are called to the service of their country.   92

LETTER VI.

From what period modern history is peculiarly useful to the service of our country, viz. From the end of the fifteenth century to the present. The division of

CONTENTS.

Pag.

this into three particular periods; in order to a sketch of the history and state of Europe from that time. 123

LETTER VII.

A sketch of the state and history of Europe from the Pyrenean treaty, in one thousand six hundred and fifty nine, to the year one thousand six hundred and eighty-eight. 152

LETTER VIII.

The same subject continued from the year one thousand six hundred and eighty-eight. 195

LETTER IX.

A plan for a general history of Europe. 302

OF THE

Study of History.

LETTER I.

Chantelou in Touraine, Nov. 6, 1735.

My Lord,

I HAVE considered formerly, with a good deal of attention, the subject on which you command me to communicate my thoughts to you: and I practised in those days, as much as business and pleasure allowed me time to do, the rules that seemed to me necessary to be observed in the study of history. They were very different from those which writers on the same subject have recommended, and which are commonly practised. But I confess to your lordship, that this neither gave me then, nor has given me since, any distrust of them. I do not affect singularity. On the contrary, I think that a due deference is to be paid to received opinions, and that a due compliance with received customs is to be held; though both the one and the other should be, what they often are, absurd or ridiculous. But this servitude is outward only, and abridges in no sort the liberty of private judgment. The obligations of submitting to it likewise, even, outwardly, extend no further, than to those opinions and customs which cannot be opposed; or from which we cannot deviate without doing hurt, or giving offence, to society. In all these cases, our speculations ought to be free: in all other cases, our practice may be so. Without any regard therefore to the opinion and practice even of the learned world, I am very willing to tell you mine. But, as it is hard to recover a thread of thought long ago laid aside, and impossible to prove some things, and explain others, without the assistance of many books which I have not here; your lordship must be content with such an imperfect sketch, as I am able to send you at present in this letter.

THE motives that carry men to the study of history are different. Some intend, if such as they may be said to study, nothing more than amusement, and read the life of ARISTIDES or PHOCION, of EPAMINONDAS or SCIPIO, ALEXANDER or CAESAR, just as they play a game at cards, or as they would read the story of the seven champions.

OTHERS there are, whose motive to this study is nothing better, and who have the further disadvantage of becoming a nuisance very often to society, in proportion to the progress they make. The former do not improve their reading to any good purpose: the latter pervert it to a very bad one, and grow in impertinence as they encrease in learning. I think I have known most of the first kind in England, and most of the last in France. The persons I mean are those who read to talk, to shine in conversation, and to impose in company: who having few ideas to vend of their own growth, ſtore their minds with crude unruminated facts and ſentences; and hope to ſupply, by bare memory, the want of imagination and judgment.

But theſe are in the two loweſt forms. The next I shall mention are in one a little higher; in the form of thoſe who grow neither wiſer nor better by ſtudy themſelves, but who enable others to ſtudy with greater eaſe, and to purpoſes more uſeful; who make fair copies of foul manuſcripts, give the ſignification of hard words, and take a great deal of other grammatical pains. The obligation to theſe men would be great indeed, if they were in general able to do any thing better, and ſubmitted to this drudgery for the ſake of the public; as ſome of them, it muſt be owned with gratitude, have done, but not later, I think, than about the time of the reſurrection of letters. When works of importance are preſſing, generals themſelves may take up the pick-axe and the ſpade; but in the ordinary courſe of things, when that preſſing neceſſity is over, ſuch tools are left in the hands deſtined to uſe them, the hands of common ſoldiers and peaſants. I approve therefore very much the devotion of a ſtudious man at Chriſt-Church, who was over-heard in his oratory entering into a detail with God, as devout perſons are apt to do, and, amongſt other particular thankſ-givings, acknowledging the divine goodneſs in furniſhing the world with makers of Dictionaries! Theſe men court fame as well as their betters, by ſuch means as God has given them to acquire it:

and LITTLETON exerted all the genius he had, when he made a dictionary, though STEPHENS did not. They deserve encouragement, however, whilst they continue to compile, and neither affect wit, nor presume to reason.

THERE is a fourth class, of much less use than these, but of much greater name. Men of the first rank in learning, and to whom the whole tribe of scholars bow with reverence. A man must be as indifferent as I am to common censure or approbation, to avow a thorough contempt for the whole business of these learned lives; for all the researches into antiquity, for all the systems of chronology and history, that we owe to the immense labours of a SCALIGER, a BOCHART, a PETAVIUS, an USHER, and even a MARSHAM. The same materials are common to them all; but these materials are few, and there is a moral impossibility that they should ever have more. They have combined these into every form that can be given to them: they have supposed, they have guessed, they have joined disjointed passages of different authors, and broken traditions of uncertain originals, of various people, and of centuries remote from one another as well as from ours. In short, that they might leave no liberty untaken, even a wild fantastical similitude of sounds has served to prop up a system. As the materials they have are few, so are the very best, and such as pass for authentic, extremely precarious; as some of these learned persons themselves confess.

JULIUS AFRICANUS, EUSEBIUS, and GEORGE the monk opened the principal sources of all this science; but they corrupted the waters. Their point of view was to make profane history and chronology agree with sacred; though the latter chronology is very far from being established with the clearness and certainty necessary to make it a rule. For this purpose, the ancient monuments, that these writers conveyed to posterity, were digested by them according to the system they were to maintain: and none of these monuments were delivered down in their original form, and genuine purity. The Dynasties of MANETHO, for instance, are broken to pieces by EUSEBIUS; and such fragments of them as suited his design, are struck into his work. We have, we know, no more of them. The Codex Alexandrinus we owe to GEORGE the monk. We have no other authority for it: and one cannot see without amazement such a man as Sir JOHN MARSHAM undervaluing this authority in one page, and building his system upon it in the next. He seems even by the lightness of his expressions, if I remember well, for it is long since I looked into his canon, not to be much concerned what foundation his system had, though he shewed his skill in forming one, and in reducing the immense antiquity of the Egyptians within the limits of the Hebraic calculation. In short, my lord, all these systems are so many enchanted castles; they appear to be something, they are nothing but appearances: like them too, dissolve the charm, and they vanish from the sight. To dissolve the charm, we must begin at the beginning of them: the expression may be odd, but it is significant. We must examine scrupulously and indifferently the foundations on which they lean: and when we find these either faintly probable, or grossly improbable, it would be foolish to expect any thing better in the superstructure. This science is one of those that are " a limine salutandae." To do thus much may be necessary, that grave authority may not impose on our ignorance: to do more, would be to assist this very authority in imposing false science upon us. I had rather take the DARIUS whom ALEXANDER conquered, for the son of HYSTASPES, and make as many anachronisms as a Jewish chronologer, than sacrifice half my life to collect all the learned lumber that fills the head of an antiquary.

OF THE
Study of History.

LETTER II.

Concerning the true use and advantages of it.

LET me say something of history in general, before I descend into the consideration of particular parts of it, or of the various methods of study, or of the different views of those that apply themselves to it, as I had begun to do in my former letter.

THE love of history seems inseparable from human nature because it seems inseparable from self-love. The same principle in this instance carries us forward and backward, to future and to past ages. We imagine that the things, which affect us, must affect posterity: this sentiment runs through mankind, from CAESAR down to the parish clerk in POPE's miscellany. We are fond of preserving, as far as it is in our frail power, the memory of our own adventures, of those of our own time, and of those that preceded it. Rude heaps of stones have been raised, and ruder hymns have been composed, for this purpose, by nations who had not yet the use of arts and letters. To go no farther back, the triumphs of ODIN were celebrated in runic songs, and the feats of our

British ancestors were recorded in those of their bards. The savages of America have the same custom at this day: and long historical ballads of their huntings and their wars are sung at all their festivals. There is no need of saying how this passion grows, among civilized nations, in proportion to the means of gratifying it: but let us observe that the same principle of nature directs us as strongly, and more generally as well as more early, to indulge our own curiosity, instead of preparing to gratify that of others. The child hearkens with delight to the tales of his nurse: he learns to read, and he devours with eagerness fabulous legends and novels: in riper years he applies himself to history, or to that which he takes for history, to authorized romance: and, even in age, the desire of knowing what has happened to other men, yields to the desire alone of relating what has happened to ourselves. Thus history, true or false, speaks to our passions always. What pity is it, my lord, that even the best should speak to our understandings so seldom? That it does so, we have none to blame but ourselves. Nature has done her part. She has opened this study to every man who can read and think: and what she has made the most agreeable, reason can make the most useful, application of our minds. But if we consult our reason, we shall be far from following the examples of our fellow-creatures, in this as in most other cases, who are so proud of being rational. We shall neither read to soothe our indolence, nor to gratify our vanity:

as little shall we content ourselves to drudge like grammarians and critics, that others may be able to study with greater ease and profit, like philosophers and statesmen: as little shall we affect the slender merit of becoming great scholars at the expence of groping all our lives in the dark mazes of antiquity. All these mistake the true drift of study, and the true use of history. Nature gave us curiosity to excite the industry of our minds; but she never intended it should be made the principal, much less the sole, object of their application. The true and proper object of this application is a constant improvement in private and in public virtue. An application to any study, that tends neither directly nor indirectly to make us better men and better citizens, is at best but a specious and ingenious sort of idleness, to use an expression of TILLOTSON: and the knowledge we acquire by it is a creditable kind of ignorance, nothing more. This creditable kind of ignorance is, in my opinion, the whole benefit which the generality of men, even of the most learned, reap from the study of history: and yet the study of history seems to me, of all other, the most proper to train us up to private and public virtue.

YOUR lordship may very well be ready by this time, and after so much bold censure on my part, to ask me, what then is the true use of history? in what respects it may serve to make us better and wiser? and what method is to be pursued in the study of it, for attaining these great ends? I will answer you by quoting what I have read somewhere or other, in DIONYSIUS HALICARN. I think, that history is philosophy teaching by examples. We need but to cast our eyes on the world, and we shall see the daily force of example: we need but to turn them inward, and we shall soon discover why example has this force. " Pauci „ prudentia," says TACITUS, " honesta ab „ deterioribus, utilia ab noxiis discernunt: plures „ aliorum eventis docentur." Such is the imperfection of human understanding, such the frail temper of our minds, that abstract or general propositions, though ever so true, appear obscure or doubtful to us very often, till they are explained by examples: and that the wisest lessons in favour of virtue go but a little way to convince the judgment, and determine the will, unless they are enforced by the same means; and we are obliged to apply to ourselves what we see happen to other men. Instructions by precept have the further disadvantage of coming on the authority of others, and frequently require a long deduction of reasoning. " Homines amplius oculis, quam auribus, „ credunt: longum iter est per praecepta, breve „ et efficax per exempla." The reason of this judgment, which I quote from one of SENECA's epistles in confirmation of my own opinion, rests, I think, on this; that when examples are pointed out to us, there is a kind of appeal, with which we are flattered, made to our senses, as well as our understandings. The instruction comes then upon our own authority: we frame the precept after our own experience, and yield to fact when we resist speculation. But this is not the only advantage of inftruction by example; for example appeals not to our underftanding alone, but to our paffions likewife. Example affuages thefe, or animates them; fets paffion on the fide of judgment, and makes the whole man of a-piece; which is more than the ftrongeft reafoning and the cleareft demonftration can do: and thus forming habits by repetition, example fecures the obfervance of thofe precepts which example infinuated. Is it not PLINY, my lord, who fays, that the gentleft, he should have added the moft effectual, way of commanding, is by example? " Mitius „ jubetur exemplo." The harsheft orders are foftened by example, and tyranny itfelf becomes perfuafive. What pity it is that fo few princes have learned this way of commanding? But again: the force of examples is not confined to thofe alone, that pafs immediately under our fight: the examples, that memory fuggefts, have the fame effect in their degree, and an habit of recalling them will foon produce the habit of imitating them. In the fame epiftle, from whence I cited a paffage juft now, SENECA fays that CLEANTHES had never become fo perfect a copy of ZENO, if he had not paffed his Life with him; that PLATO, ARISTOTLE, and the other philofophers of that fchool, profited more by the example, than by the difcourfe of SOCRATES. (But here, by the way, SENECA miftook; for SOCRATES died two years, according to fome, and four years, according to others, before the birth of ARISTOTLE: and his miftake might come from the inaccuracy of those who collected for him; as ERASMUS obferves, after QUINTILIAN, in his judgment on SENECA.) But be this, which was fcarce worth a parenthefis, as it will; he adds that METRODORUS, HERMACHUS and POLYAENUS, men of great note, were formed by living under the fame roof with EPICURUS, not by frequenting his fchool. Thefe are inftances of the force of immediate example. But your lordfhip knows that the citizens of Rome placed the images of their anceftors in the veftibules of their houfes; fo that, whenever they went in or out, thefe venerable buftoes met their eyes, and recalled the glorious actions of the dead, to fire the living, to excite them to imitate, and even to emulate their great forefathers. The fuccefs anfwered the defign. The virtue of one generation was transfufed, by the magic of example, into feveral: and a fpirit of heroifm was maintained through many ages of that common-wealth. Now thefe are fo many inftances of the force of remote example; and from all thefe inftances we may conclude, that examples of both kinds are neceffary.

THE fchool of example, my lord, is the world: and the mafters of this fchool are hiftory and experience. I am far from contending that the former is preferable to the latter. I think upon the whole otherwife: but this I fay, that the former is abfolutely neceffary to prepare us for the latter, and to accompany us whilft we are under the difcipline of the latter, that is, through the whole courfe of our lives. No doubt fome few men may be quoted, to whom nature gave what art and industry can give to no man. But such examples will prove nothing against me, because I admit that the study of history, without experience, is insufficient; but assert, that experience itself is so without genius. Genius is preferable to the other two; but I would wish to find the three together: for how great soever a genius may be, and how much soever he may acquire new light and heat, as he proceeds in his rapid course, certain it is that he will never shine with the full lustre, nor shed the full influence he is capable of, unless to his own experience he adds the experience of other men and other ages. Genius, without the improvement, at least, of experience, is what comets once were thought to be, a blazing meteor, irregular in his course, and dangerous in his approach; of no use to any system, and able to destroy any. Mere sons of earth, if they have experience without any knowledge of the history of the world, are but half scholars in the science of mankind. And if they are conversant in history without experience, they are worse than ignorant; they are pedants, always incapable, sometimes meddling and presuming. The man, who has all three, is an honour to his country, and a public blessing: and such, I trust, your lordship will be in this century, as your great-grand-father * was in the last.

I have insisted a little the longer on this head, and have made these distinctions the rather, because though I attribute a great deal more, than many will

* Earl of CLARENDON.

be ready to allow, to the study of history; yet I would not willingly even seem to fall into the ridicule of ascribing to it such extravagant effects, as several have done, from TULLY down to CASAUBON, LA MOTHE LE VAYER, and other modern pedants. When TULLY informs us, in the second book of his Tusculan disputations, that the first SCIPIO AFRICANUS had always in his hands the works of XENOPHON, he advances nothing but what is probable and reasonable. To say nothing of the retreat of the ten thousand, nor of other parts of XENOPHON's writings; the images of virtue, represented in that admirable picture the Cyropaedia, were proper to entertain a soul that was fraught with virtue, and CYRUS was worthy to be imitated by SCIPIO. So SELIM emulated CAESAR, whose Commentaries were translated for his use against the customs of the Turks: so CAESAR emulated ALEXANDER; and ALEXANDER, ACHILLES. There is nothing ridiculous here, except the use that is made of this passage by those who quote it. But what the same TULLY says, in the fourth book of his academical disputations, concerning LUCULLUS, seems to me very extraordinary. „ In Asiam factus „ imperator venit; cum esset Roma profectus rei „ militaris rudis; " (one would be ready to ascribe so sudden a change, and so vast an improvement, to nothing less than knowledge infused by inspiration, if we were not assured in the same place that they were effected by very natural means, by such as it is in every man's power to employ) „ partim percontando a peritis, partim in rebus gestis legendis."

LUCULLUS, according to this account, verified the reproach on the Roman nobility, which SALLUST puts into the mouth of MARIUS. But as I difcover the paffion of MARIUS, and his prejudices to the patricians, in one cafe; fo I difcover, methinks, the cunning of TULLY, and his partiality to himfelf, in the other. LUCULLUS, after he had been chofen conful, obtained by intrigue the government of Cilicia, and fo put himfelf into a fituation of commanding the Roman army againft MITHRIDATES: TULLY had the fame government afterwards, and though he had no MITHRIDATES, nor any other enemy of confequence, oppofed to him; though all his military feats confifted in furprizing and pillaging a parcel of Highlanders and wild Cilicians; yet he affumed the airs of a conqueror, and defcribed his actions in fo pompous a ftyle, that the account becomes burlefque. He laughs, indeed, in one of his letters to ATTICUS, at his generalfhip: but if we turn to thofe he writ to COELIUS RUFUS, and to CATO, upon this occafion, or to thofe wherein he expreffes to ATTICUS his refentment againft CATO, for not propofing in his favor the honors ufually decreed to conquerors, we may fee how vanity turned his head, and how impudently he infifted on obtaining a triumph. Is it any ftrain now to fuppofe, that he meant to infinuate, in the paffage I have quoted about LUCULLUS, that the difference between him and the former governor of CILICIA, even in military merit, arofe from the different conjuncture alone; and that LUCULLUS could not have done in Cilicia, at that time, more than he himfelf did?

CICERO had read and questioned at least as much as LUCULLUS, and would therefore have appeared as great a captain, if he had had as great a prince as MITHRIDATES to encounter. But the truth is, that LUCULLUS was made a great captain by theory, or the study of history, alone, no more than FERDINAND of Spain and ALPHONSUS of Naples were cured of desperate distempers by reading LIVY and QUINTUS CURTIUS: a silly tale, which BODIN, AMYOT, and others have picked up and propagated. LUCULLUS had served in his youth against the Marsi, probably in other wars, and SYLLA took early notice of him: he went into the east with this general, and had a great share in his confidence. He commanded in several expeditions. It was he who restored the Colophonians to their liberty, and who punished the revolt of the people of Mytelene. Thus we see that LUCULLUS was formed by experience, as well as study, and by an experience gained in those very countries, where he gathered so many laurels afterwards in fighting against the same enemy. The late duke of MARLBOROUGH never read XENOPHON, most certainly, nor the relation perhaps of any modern wars; but he served in his youth under monsieur de TURENNE, and I have heard that he was taken notice of in those early days, by that great man. He afterwards commanded in an expedition to Ireland, served a campaign or two, if I mistake not, under king WILLIAM in Flanders: and, besides these occasions, had none of gaining experience in war, till he came to the head of our armies in one

thousand

Of the STUDY of HISTORY.

thousand seven hundred and two, and triumphed, not over Asiatic troops, but over the veteran armies of France. The Roman had on his side genius and experience cultivated by study: the Briton had genius improved by experience, and no more. The first therefore is not an example of what study can do alone; but the latter is an example of what genius and experience can do without study. They can do much, to be sure, when the first is given in a superior degree. But such examples are very rare: and when they happen, it will be still true, that they would have had fewer blemishes, and would have come nearer to the perfection of private and public virtue, in all the arts of peace and atchievements of war, if the views of such men had been enlarged, and their sentiments ennobled, by acquiring that cast of thought, and that temper of mind, which will grow up and become habitual in every man who applies himself early to the study of history, as well as to the study of philosophy, with the intention of being wiser and better, without the affectation of being more learned.

THE temper of the mind is formed, and a certain turn given to our ways of thinking; in a word, the seeds of that moral character which cannot wholly alter the natural character, but may correct the evil and improve the good that is in it, or do the very contrary, are sown betimes, and much sooner than is commonly supposed. It is equally certain, that we shall gather or not gather experience, be the better or the worse for this experience, when we come into the world and mingle amongſt mankind, according to the temper of mind, and the turn of thought, that we have acquired beforehand, and bring along with us. They will tincture all our future acquiſitions; ſo that the very ſame experience, which ſecures the judgment of one man, or excites him to virtue, ſhall lead another into error, or plunge him into vice. From hence it follows, that the ſtudy of hiſtory has in this reſpect a double advantage. If experience alone can make us perfect in our parts, experience cannot begin to teach them till we are actually on the ſtage: whereas, by a previous application to this ſtudy, we con them over at leaſt, before we appear there: we are not quite unprepared, we learn our parts ſooner, and we learn them better.

LET me explain what I mean by an example. There is ſcarce any folly or vice more epidemical among the ſons of men, than that ridiculous and hurtful vanity, by which the people of each country are apt to prefer themſelves to thoſe of every other; and to make their own cuſtoms, and manners, and opinions, the ſtandards of right and wrong, of true and falſe. The Chineſe mandarins were ſtrangely ſurpriſed, and almoſt incredulous, when the Jeſuits ſhewed them how ſmall a figure their empire made in the general map of the world. The Samojedes wondered much at the Czar of Muſcovy for not living among them: and the Hottentot, who returned from Europe, ſtripped himſelf naked as ſoon as he came home, put on his bracelets of guts and garbage, and grew ſtinking and loufy as faft as he could. Now nothing can contribute more to prevent us from being tainted with this vanity, than to accuftom ourfelves early to contemplate the different nations of the earth, in that vaft map which hiftory fpreads before us, in their rife and their fall, in their barbarous and civilized ftates, in the likenefs and unlikenefs of them all to one another, and of each to itfelf. By frequently renewing this profpect to the mind, the Mexican with his cap and coat of feathers, facrificing a human victim to his god, will not appear more favage to our eyes, than the Spaniard with an hat on his head, and a gonilla round his neck, facrificing whole nations to his ambition, his avarice, and even the wantonnefs of his cruelty. I might shew, by a multitude of other examples, how hiftory prepares us for experience, and guides us in it: and many of thefe would be both curious and important. I might likewife bring feveral other inftances, wherein hiftory ferves to purge the mind of thofe national partialities and prejudices that we are apt to contract in our education, and that experience for the moft part rather confirms than removes: becaufe it is for the moft part confined, like our education. But I apprehend growing too prolix, and shall therefore conclude this head by obferving, that though an early and proper application, to the ftudy of hiftory will contribute extremely to keep our minds free from a ridiculous partiality in favor of our own country, and a vicious prejudice againft others; yet the fame ftudy will create in us a preference

B 2

LETTER II.

of affection to our own country. There is a story told of ABGARUS. He brought several beasts taken in different places to Rome, they say, and let them loose before AUGUSTUS: every beast ran immediately to that part of the Circus, where a parcel of earth taken from his native soil had been laid. „ Credat Judaeus Apella. " This tale might pass on JOSEPHUS; for in him, I believe, I read it: but surely the love of our country is a lesson of reason, not an institution of nature. Education and habit, obligation and interest, attach us to it, not instinct. It is however so necessary to be cultivated, and the prosperity of all societies, as well as the grandeur of some, depends upon it so much, that orators by their eloquence, and poets by their enthusiasm, have endeavoured to work up this precept of morality into a principle of passion. But the examples which we find in history, improved by the lively descriptions, and the just applauses or censures of historians, will have a much better and more permanent effect, than declamation, or song, or the dry ethics of mere philosophy. In fine, to converse with historians is to keep good company: many of them were excellent men, and those who were not such, have taken care however to appear such in their writings. It must be therefore of great use to prepare ourselves by this conversation for that of the world; and to receive our first impressions, and to acquire our first habits, in a scene where images of virtue and vice are continually represented to us in the colors that belong properly to them, before we enter on another scene, where virtue and vice are too often confounded, and what belongs to one is ascribed to the other.

BESIDES the advantage of beginning our acquaintance with mankind sooner, and of bringing with us into the world, and the business of it, such a cast of thought and such a temper of mind, as will enable us to make a better use of our experience; there is this further advantage in the study of history, that the improvement we make by it extends to more objects, and is made at the expence of other men: whereas that improvement, which is the effect of our own experience, is confined to fewer objects, and is made at our own expence. To state the account fairly therefore between these two improvements; though the latter be the more valuable, yet allowance being made on one side for the much greater number of examples that history presents to us, and deduction being made on the other of the price we often pay for our experience, the value of the former will rise in proportion. " I have recorded these „ things," says POLYBIUS, after giving an account of the defeat of REGULUS, " that they who read „ these commentaries may be rendered better by „ them; for all men have two ways of improve-„ ment, one arising from their own experience, „ and one from the experience of others. Evi-„ dentior quidem illa est, quæ per propria ducit „ infortunia; at tutior illa, quæ per aliena. „ I use CASAUBON's translation. POLYBIUS goes on, and concludes, " that since the first of these ways

LETTER II.

"exposes us to great labour and peril, whilst the second works the same good effect, and is attended by no evil circumstance, every one ought to take for granted, that the study of history is the best school where he can learn how to conduct himself in all the situations of life." REGULUS had seen at Rome many examples of magnanimity, of frugality, of the contempt of riches and of other virtues; and these virtues he practised. But he had not learned, nor had opportunity of learning another lesson, which the examples recorded in history inculcate frequently, the lesson of moderation. An insatiable thirst of military fame, an unconfined ambition of extending their empire, an extravagant confidence in their own courage and force, an insolent contempt of their enemies, and an impetuous over-bearing spirit with which they pursued all their enterprizes, composed in his days the distinguishing character of a Roman. Whatever the senate and people resolved to the members of that common-wealth, appeared both practicable and just. Neither difficulties nor dangers could check them; and their sages had not yet discovered, that virtues in excess degenerate into vices. Notwithstanding the beautiful rant which HORACE puts into his mouth, I make no doubt that REGULUS learned at Carthage those lessons of moderation which he had not learned at Rome; but he learned them by experience, and the fruits of this experience came too late, and cost too dear; for they cost the total defeat of the Roman army, the prolongation of a calamitous war which might have been finished by a glorious peace, the loss of liberty to thousands of Roman citizens, and to REGULUS himself the loss of life in the midst of torments, if we are entirely to credit what is perhaps exaggeration in the Roman authors.

THERE is another advantage, worthy our observation, that belongs to the study of history; and that I shall mention here, not only because of the importance of it, but because it leads me immediately to speak of the nature of the improvement we ought to have in our view, and of the method in which it seems to me that this improvement ought to be pursued: two particulars from which your lordship may think perhaps that I digress too long. The advantage I mean consists in this, that the examples which history presents to us, both of men and of events, are generally complete: the whole example is before us, and consequently the whole lesson, or sometimes the various lessons, which philosophy proposes to teach us by this example. For first, as to men; we see them at their whole length in history, and we see them generally there through a medium less partial at least than that of experience: for I imagine, that a whig or a tory, whilst those parties subsisted, would have condemned in SATURNINUS the spirit of faction which he applauded in his own tribunes, and would have applauded in DRUSUS the spirit of moderation which he despised in those of the contrary party, and which he suspected and hated in those of his own party. The villain who has

imposed on mankind by his power or cunning, and whom experience could not unmask for a time, is unmasked at length: and the honest man, who has been misunderstood or defamed, is justified before his story ends. Or if this does not happen, if the villain dies with his mask on, in the midst of applause, and honor, and wealth, and power, and if the honest man dies under the same load of calumny and disgrace under which he lived, driven perhaps into exile, and exposed to want; yet we see historical justice executed, the name of one branded with infamy, and that of the other celebrated with panegyric to succeeding ages. "Prae-
„ cipuum munus annalium reor, ne virtutes silean-
„ tur; utque pravis dictis factisque ex posteritate
„ et infamia metus sit." Thus, according to Tacitus, and according to truth, from which his judgments seldom deviate, the principal duty of history is to erect a tribunal, like that among the Egyptians, mentioned by Diodorus Siculus, where men and princes themselves were tried, and condemned or acquitted, after their deaths; where those who had not been punished for their crimes, and those who had not been honored for their virtues, received a just retribution. The sentence is pronounced in one case, as it was in the other, too late to correct or recompense; but it is pronounced in time to render these examples of general instruction to mankind. Thus Cicero, that I may quote one instance out of thousands, and that I may do justice to the general character of that great man, whose particular failing I have censured so

freely; CICERO, I say, was abandoned by OCTAVIUS, and massacred by ANTONY. But let any man read this fragment of ARELLIUS FUSCUS, and chuse which he would wish to have been, the orator, or the triumvir? "Quoad humanum genus „ incolume manserit, quamdiu usus literis, honor „ summae eloquentiae pretium erit, quamdiu rerum „ natura aut fortuna steterit, aut memoria dura- „ verit, admirabile posteris vigebis ingenium, et „ uno proscriptus seculo, proscribes Antonium om- „ nibus. „

THUS again, as to events that stand recorded in history, we see them all, we see them as they followed one another, or as they produced one another, causes or effects, immediate or remote. We are cast back, as it were, into former ages: we live with the men who lived before us, and we inhabit countries that we never saw. Place is enlarged, and time prolonged, in this manner; so that the man who applies himself early to the study of history, may acquire in a few years, and before he sets his foot abroad in the world, not only a more extended knowledge of mankind, but the experience of more centuries than any of the patriarchs saw. The events we are witnesses of, in the course of the longest life, appear to us very often original, unprepared, single, and un-relative, if I may use such an expression for want of a better in English; in French I would say isolés: they appear such very often, are called accidents, and looked on as the effects of chance; a word, by the way, which is in constant use, and has frequently no determinate meaning. We

get over the present difficulty, we improve the momentary advantage, as well as we can, and we look no farther. Experience can carry us no farther; for experience can go a very little way back in discovering causes: and effects are not the objects of experience till they happen. From hence many errors in judgment, and by consequence in conduct, necessarily arise. And here too lies the difference we are speaking of between history and experience. The advantage on the side of the former is double. In ancient history as we have said already, the examples are complete, which are incomplete in the course of experience. The beginning, the progression, and the end appear, not of particular reigns, much less of particular enterprizes, or systems of policy alone, but of governments, of nations, of empires, and of all the various systems that have succeeded one another in the course of their duration. In modern history, the examples may be, and sometimes are, incomplete; but they have this advantage when they are so, that they serve to render complete the examples of our own time. Experience is doubly defective; we are born too late to see the beginning, and we die too soon to see the end of many things. History supplies both these defects. Modern history shews the causes, when experience presents the effects alone: and ancient history enables us to guess at the effects, when experience presents the causes alone. Let me explain my meaning by two examples of these kinds; one past, the other actually present.

Of the STUDY of HISTORY. 27

WHEN the revolution of one thousand six hundred and eighty-eight happened, few men then alive, I suppose, went farther in their search after the causes of it, than the extravagant attempt of king JAMES against the religion and liberty of his people. His former conduct, and the passages of king CHARLES the second's reign might rankle still at the hearts of some men, but could not be set to account among the causes of his deposition; since he had succeeded, notwithstanding them, peaceably to the throne: and the nation in general, even many of those who would have excluded him from it, were desirous, or at least, willing, that he should continue in it. Now this example, thus stated, affords, no doubt, much good instruction to the kings, and people of Britain. But this instruction is not entire, because the example thus stated, and confined to the experience of that age, is imperfect. King JAMES's mal-administration rendered a revolution necessary and practicable; but his mal-administration, as well as all his preceding conduct, was caused by his bigot-attachment to popery, and to the principles of arbitrary government, from which no warning could divert him. His bigot-attachment to these was caused, by the exile of the royal family, this exile was caused by the usurpation of CROMWEL: and CROMWEL's usurpation was the effect of a former rebellion, begun not without reason on account of liberty, but without any valid pretence on account of religion. During this exile, our princes caught the taint of popery and foreign politics. We made them unfit to govern us, and after that were forced to recal them that they might rescue us out of anarchy. It was necessary therefore, your lordship sees, at the revolution, and it is more so now, to go back in history, at least as far as I have mentioned, and perhaps farther, even to the beginning of King JAMES the first's reign, to render this event a complete example, and to develop all the wise, honest, and salutary precepts, with which it is pregnant, both to king and subject.

THE other example shall be taken from what has succeeded the revolution. Few men at that time looked forward enough, to foresee the necessary consequences of the new constitution of the revenue, that was soon afterwards formed; nor of the method of funding that immediately took place; which, absurd as they are, have continued ever since, till it is become scarce possible to alter them. Few people, I say, foresaw how the creation of funds, and the multiplication of taxes, would encrease yearly the power of the crown, and bring our liberties, by a natural and necessary progression, into more real, though less apparent danger, than they were in before the revolution. The excessive ill husbandry practised form the very beginning of king WILLIAM's reign, and which laid the foundations of all we feel and all we fear, was not the effect of ignorance, mistake, or what we call chance, but of design and scheme in those who had the sway at that time. I am not so uncharitable, however, as to believe that they intended to bring upon their country all the mischiefs that we, who came after them, experience, and apprehend. No, they saw the measures they took singly, and unrelatively, or relatively alone to some immediate object. The notion of attaching men to the new government, by tempting them to embark their fortunes on the same bottom, was a reason of state to some: the notion of creating a new, that is, a moneyed interest, in opposition to the landed interest, or as a balance to it, and of acquiring a superior influence in the city of London at least by the establishment of great corporations, was a reason of party to others: and I make no doubt that the opportunity of amassing immense estates by the management of funds, by trafficking in paper, and by all the arts of jobbing, was a reason of private interest to those who supported and improved this scheme of iniquity, if not to those who devised it. They looked no farther. Nay, we who came after them, and have long tasted the bitter fruits of the corruption they planted, were far from taking such an alarm at our distress, and our danger, as they deserved; till the most remote and fatal effect of causes, laid by the last generation, was very near becoming an object of experience in this. Your lordship, I am sure, sees at once how much a due reflection on the passages of former times, as they stand recorded in the history of our own, and of other countries, would have deterred a free people from trusting the sole management of so great a revenue, and the sole nomination of those legions of officers employed in it, to their chief magistrate. There remained indeed no pretence for doing so, when once a salary was settled on the prince, and the public revenue was no longer in any sense his revenue, nor the public expence his expence. Give me leave to add, that it would have been, and would be still, more decent with regard to the prince, and less repugnant if not more conformable to the principles and practice too of our government, to take this power and influence from the prince, or to share it with him; than to exclude men from the privilege of representing their fellow-subjects who would chuse them in parliament, purely because they are employed and trusted by the prince.

YOUR lordship sees not only, how much a due reflection upon the experience of other ages and countries would have pointed out national corruption, as the natural and necessary consequence of investing the crown with the management of so great a revenue; but also the loss of liberty, as the natural and necessary consequence of national corruption.

THESE two examples explain sufficiently what they are intended to explain. It only remains therefore upon this head, to observe the difference between the two manners in which history supplies the defects of our own experience. It shews us causes as in fact they were laid, with their immediate effects; and it enables us to guess at future events. It can do no more, in the nature of things. My lord BACON, in his second book of the Advancement of learning, having in his mind, I suppose, what PHILO and JOSEPHUS asserted of MOSES, affirms divine history to have this prerogative, that the narration may be before the fact as well as after. But since the ages of prophecy, as well as miracles, are past, we must content ourselves to guess at what will be, by what has been: we have no other means in our power, and history furnishes us with these. How we are to improve, and apply these means, as well as how we are to acquire them, shall be deduced more particularly in another letter.

OF THE
STUDY OF HISTORY.

LETTER III.

1. *An objection against the utility of history removed.* 2. *The false and true aims of those who study it.* 3. *Of the history of the first ages, with reflections on the state of ancient history, prophane and sacred.*

WERE these letters to fall into the hands of some ingenious persons who adorn the age we live in, your lordship's correspondent would be joked upon for his project of improving men in virtue and wisdom by the study of history. The general characters of men it would be said, are determined by their natural constitutions, as their particular actions are by immediate objects. Many very conversant in history would be cited, who have proved ill men, or bad politicians; and a long roll would be produced of others, who have arrived at a great pitch of private, and public virtue, without any assistance of this kind. Something has been said already to anticipate this objection; but, since I have heard several persons affirm such propositions with great confidence, a loud laugh, or a silent sneer at the pedants who presumed to think otherwise; I will spend a few paragraphs, with your lordship's leave, to shew that such affirmations, for to affirm amongst these

fine

fine men is to reason, either prove too much, or prove nothing.

IF our general characters were determined absolutely, as they are certainly influenced, by our constitutions, and if our particular actions were so by immediate objects; all instruction by precept, as well as example, and all endeavours to form the moral character by education, would be unnecessary. Even the little care that is taken, and surely it is impossible to take less, in the training up our youth, would be too much. But the truth is widely different from this representation of it; for, what is vice, and what is virtue? I speak of them in a large and philosophical sense. The former, is, I think, no more than the excess, abuse, and misapplication of appetites, desires, and passions, natural and innocent, nay useful and necessary. The latter consists in the moderation and government, in the use and application of these appetites, desires, and passions, according to the rules of reason, and therefore, often in opposition to their own blind impulse.

WHAT now is education? that part; that principal and most neglected part of it, I mean, which tends to form the moral character? It is, I think, an institution designed to lead men from their tender years, by precept and example, by argument and authority, to the practice, and to the habit of practising these rules. The stronger our appetites, desires, and passions are, the harder indeed is the task of education: but when the efforts of education are proportioned to this strength, although our keenest appetites and desires, and our ruling passions cannot be reduced to a quiet and uniform submission, yet, are not their excesses assuaged? are not their abuses and misapplications, in some degree, diverted or checked? Though the pilot cannot lay the storm, cannot he carry the ship, by his art, better through it, and often prevent the wreck that would always happen, without him? If ALEXANDER, who loved wine, and was naturally choleric, had been bred under the severity of Roman discipline, it is probable he would neither have made a bonfire of Persepolis for his whore, nor have killed his friend. If SCIPIO, who was naturally given to women, for which anecdote we have, if I mistake not, the authority of POLYBIUS, as well as some verses of NAEVIUS preserved by A. GELLIUS, had been educated by OLYMPIAS at the court of PHILIP, it is improbable that he would have restored the beautiful Spaniard. In short, if the renowned SOCRATES had not corrected nature by art, this first apostle of the gentiles had been a very profligate fellow, by his own confession; for he was inclined to all the vices ZOPYRUS imputed to him, as they say, on the observation of his physiognomy.

WITH him therefore, who denies the effects of education, it would be in vain to dispute; and with him who admits them, there can be no dispute, concerning that share which I ascribe to the study of history, in forming our moral characters, and making us better men. The very persons who pretend that inclinations cannot be restrained, nor habits corrected, against our natural bent, would be the first perhaps to prove, in certain cases, the contrary. A fortune at court, or the favour of a lady, have prevailed on many to conceal, and they could not conceal without restraining, which is one step towards correcting, the vices they were by nature addicted to the most. Shall we imagine now, that the beauty of virtue and the deformity of vice, the charms of a bright and lasting reputation, the terror of being delivered over as criminals to all posterity, the real benefit arising from a conscientious discharge of the duty we owe to others, which benefit fortune can neither hinder nor take away, and the reasonableness of conforming ourselves to the designs of GOD manifested in the constitution of the human nature; shall we imagine, I say, that all these are not able to acquire the same power over those who are continually called upon to a contemplation of them, and they who apply themselves to the study of history are so called upon, as other motives, mean and sordid in comparison of these, can usurp on other men?

2. That the study of history, far from making us wiser, and more useful citizens, as well as better men, may be of no advantage whatsoever; that it may serve to render us mere antiquaries and scholars; or that it may help to make us forward coxcombs, and prating pedants, I have already allowed. But this is not the fault of history: and to convince us that it is not, we need only contrast the true use of history with the use that is made of it by such men as these. We

ought always to keep in mind, that history is philosophy teaching by examples how to conduct ourselves in all the situations of private and public life; that therefore we must apply ourselves to it in a philosophical spirit and manner; that we must rise from particular to general knowledge, and that we must fit ourselves for the society and business of mankind by accustoming our minds to reflect and meditate on the characters we find described, and the course of events we find related there. Particular examples may be of use sometimes in particular cases; but the application of them is dangerous. It must be done with the utmost circumspection, or it will be seldom done with success. And yet one would think that this was the principal use of the study of history, by what has been written on the subject. I know not whether MACHIAVEL himself is quite free from defect on this account: he seems to carry the use and application of particular examples sometimes too far. MARIUS and CATULUS passed the Alps, met, and defeated the Cimbri beyond the frontiers of Italy. Is it safe to conclude from hence, that whenever one people is invaded by another, the invaded ought to meet and fight the invaders at a distance from their frontiers? MACHIAVEL's countryman, GUICCIARDIN, was aware of the danger that might arise from such an application of examples. PETER of Medicis had involved himself in great difficulties, when those wars and calamities began which LEWIS SFORZA first drew and entailed on Italy, by flattering the ambition of CHARLES the eighth in order to gratify his own, and calling the French into that country. PETER owed his diſtreſs to his folly in departing from the general tenor of conduct his father LAURENCE had held, and hoped to relieve himſelf by imitating his father's example in one particular inſtance. At a time when the wars with the pope and king of Naples had reduced LAURENCE to circumſtances of great danger, he took the reſolution of going to FERDINAND, and of treating in perſon with that prince. The reſolution appears in hiſtory imprudent and almoſt deſperate: were we informed of the ſecret reaſons on which this great man acted, it would appear very poſſibly a wiſe and ſafe meaſure. It ſucceeded, and LAURENCE brought back with him public peace, and private ſecurity. As ſoon as the French troops entered the dominions of Florence, PETER was ſtruck with a panic terror, went to CHARLES the eighth, put the port of Leghorn, the fortreſſes of Piſa, and all the keys of the country, into this prince's hands; whereby he diſarmed the Florentine commonwealth, and ruined himſelf. He was deprived of his authority, and driven out of the city, by the juſt indignation of the magiſtrates and people: and in the treaty which they made afterwards with the king of France, it was ſtipulated, that PETER should not remain within an hundred miles of the ſtate, nor his brothers within the ſame diſtance of the city of Florence. On this occaſion GUICCIARDIN obſerves how dangerous it is to govern ourſelves by particular examples; ſince, to have the ſame ſucceſs, we muſt have the

same prudence, and the same fortune; and since the example must not only answer the case before us in general, but in every minute circumstance. This is the sense of that admirable historian, and these are his words — "é senza dubbio molto
„ pericoloso il governarsi con gl' esempi, se non
„ concorrono, non solo in generale, ma in tutti li
„ particolari, le medesime ragioni; se le cose non
„ sono regolate colla medesima prudenza, e se
„ oltre a tutti gli altri fondamenti, non, v'ha la
„ parte sua la medesima fortuna." An observation that BOILEAU makes, and a rule he lays down in speaking of translations, will properly find their place here, and serve to explain still better what I would establish. " To translate servilely into mo-
„ dern language an ancient author phrase by phrase,
„ and word by word, is preposterous: nothing can
„ be more unlike the original than such a copy.
„ It is not to shew, it is to disguise the author,
„ and he who has known him only in this dress,
„ would not know him in his own. A good writer,
„ instead of taking this inglorious and unprofitable
„ task upon him, will jouster contre l'original,
„ rather imitate than translate, and rather emulate
„ than imitate: he will transfuse the sense and
„ spirit of the original into his own work, and
„ will endeavour to write as the ancient author
„ would have wrote, had he writ in the same
„ language." Now, to improve by examples is to improve by imitation. We must catch the spirit, if we can, and conform ourselves to the reason of them; but we must not affect to translate servilely into our conduct, if your lordship will allow me

the expreffion, the particular conduct of thofe good and great men, whofe images hiftory fets before us. CODRUS and the DECII devoted themfelves to death: one, becaufe an oracle had foretold that the army whofe general was killed would be victorious; the others in compliance with a fuperftition that bore great analogy to a ceremony practifed in the old Egyptian church, and added afterwards, as many others of the fame origin were, to the ritual of the Ifraelites. Thefe are examples of great magnanimity, to be fure, and of magnanimity employed in the moft worthy caufe. In the early days of the Athenian and Roman government, when the credit of oracles and all kinds of fuperftition prevailed, when heaven was pioufly thought to delight in blood and even human blood was shed under wild notions of atonement, propitiation, purgation, expiation, and fatisfaction; they who fee fuch examples as thefe, acted an heroical and a rational part too. But if a general should act the fame part now, and, in order to fecure his victory, get killed as faft as he could, he might pafs for an hero, but, I am fure, he would pafs for a madman. Even thefe examples, however, are of ufe: they excite us at leaft to venture our lives freely in the fervice of our country, by propofing to our imitation men who devoted themfelves to certain death in the fervice of theirs. They shew us what a turn of imagination can operate, and how the greateft trifle, nay the greateft abfurdity, dreffed up in the folemn airs of religion, can carry order and confidence, or the contrary sentiments, into the breasts of thousands.

THERE are certain general principles, and rules of life and conduct, which always must be true, because they are conformable to the invariable nature of things. He who studies history as he would study philosophy, will soon distinguish and collect them, and by doing so will soon form to himself a general system of ethics and politics on the surest foundations, on the trial of these principles and rules in all ages, and on the confirmation of them by universal experience. I said he will distinguish them; for once more I must say, that as to particular modes of actions, and measures of conduct, which the customs of different countries, the manners of different ages, and the circumstances of different conjunctures, have appropriated, as it were; it is always ridiculous, or imprudent and dangerous to employ them. But this is not all. By contemplating the vast variety of particular characters and events; by examining the strange combinations of causes, different, remote and seemingly opposite, that often concur in producing one effect; and the surprising fertility of one single and uniform cause in the producing of a multitude of effects as different, as remote, and seemingly as opposite; by tracing carefully, as carefully as if the subject he considers were of personal and immediate concern to him, all the minute and sometimes scarce perceivable circumstances, either in the characters of actors, or in the course of actions, that history enables him to trace, and according to which the success of affairs, even the greateſt, is moſtly determined; by theſe, and ſuch methods as theſe, for I might deſcend into a much greater detail, a man of parts may improve the ſtudy of hiſtory to it's proper and principal uſe; he may ſharpen the penetration, fix the attention of his mind, and ſtrengthen his judgment; he may acquire the faculty and the habit of diſcerning quicker, and looking farther; and of exerting that flexibility, and ſteadineſs, which are neceſſary to be joined in the conduct of all affairs that depend on the concurrence or oppoſition of other men.

Mr. LOCKE, I think, recommends the ſtudy of geometry even to thoſe who have no deſign of being geometricians: and he gives a reaſon for it, that may be applied to the preſent caſe. Such perſons may forget every problem that has been propoſed, and every ſolution that they or others have given; but the habit of purſuing long trains of ideas will remain with them, and they will appear through the mazes of ſophiſm, and diſcover a latent truth, where perſons who have not this habit will never find it.

IN this manner, the ſtudy of hiſtory will prepare us for action and obſervation. Hiſtory is the ancient author: experience is the modern language. We form our taſte on the firſt; we tranſlate the ſenſe and reaſon, we transfuſe the ſpirit and force; but we imitate only the particular graces of the original: we imitate them according to the idiom of our own tongue, that is, we ſubſtitute often equivalents in the lieu of them, and are far from affecting to copy them ſervilely. To conclude, as experience is conversant about the present, and the present enables us to guess at the future; so history is conversant about the past, and by knowing the things that have been, we become better able to judge of the things that are.

THIS use, my lord, which I make the proper and principal use of the study of history, is not insisted on by those who have writ concerning the method to be followed in this study: and since we propose different ends, we must of course take different ways. Few of their treatises have fallen into my hands: one, the method of BODIN, a man famous in his time, I remember to have read. I took it up with much expectation many years ago; I went through it, and remained extremely disappointed. He might have given almost any other title to his book as properly as that which stands before it. There are not many pages in it that relate any more to his subject than a tedious fifth chapter, wherein he accounts for the characters of nations according to their positions on the globe, and according to the influence of the stars; and assures his reader that nothing can be more necessary than such a disquisition, "ad universam historiarum cogni„ tionem, et incorruptum earum judicium." In his method, we are to take first a general view of universal history, and chronology, in short abstracts, and then to study all particular histories and systems. SENECA speaks of men who spend their whole lives in learning how to act in life, "dum vitae „ instrumenta conquirunt." I doubt that this method of BODIN would conduct us in the same, or as bad a way; would leave us no time for action, or would make us unfit for it. A huge common place book, wherein all the remarkable sayings and facts that we find in history are to be registered, may enable a man to talk or write like BODIN, but will never make him a better man, nor enable him to promote, like an useful citizen, the security, the peace, the welfare, or the grandeur of the community to which he belongs. I shall proceed therefore to speak of a method that leads to such purposes as these directly and certainly, without any regard to the methods that have been prescribed by others.

I THINK then we must be on our guard against this very affectation of learning, and this very wantonness of curiosity, which the examples and precepts we commonly meet with are calculated to flatter and indulge. We must neither dwell too long in the dark, nor wander about till we lose our way in the light. We are too apt to carry systems of philosophy beyond all our ideas, and systems of history beyond all our memorials. The philosopher begins with reason, and ends with imagination. The historian inverts this order: he begins without memorials and he sometimes ends with them. This silly custom is so prevalent among men of letters who apply themselves to the study of history, and has so much prejudice and so much authority on the side of it, that your lordship must give me leave to speak a little more particularly and plainly than I have done, in favor of common sense, against an absurdity which is almost sanctified.

LETTER III.

REFLECTIONS

On the state of ancient HISTORY.

THE nature of man, and the constant course of human affairs, render it impossible that the first ages of any new nation which forms itself, should afford authentic materials for history. We have none such concerning the originals of any of those nations that actually subsist. Shall we expect to find them concerning the originals of nations dispersed, or extinguished, two or three thousand years ago? If a thread of dark and uncertain traditions, therefore, is made, as it commonly is, the introduction to history, we should touch it lightly, and run swiftly over it, far from insisting on it, either as authors or readers. Such introductions are at best no more than fanciful preludes, that try the instruments, and precede the concert. He must be void of judgment, and taste, one would think, who can take the first for true history, or the last for true harmony. And yet so it has been, and so it is, not in Germany and Holland alone; but in Italy, in France, and in England, where genius has abounded, and taste has been long refined. Our great scholars have dealt and deal in fables at least as much as our poets, with this difference to the disadvantage of the former, to whom I may apply the remark as justly as SENECA applied it to the dialecticians — " tristius „ inepti sunt. Illi ex professo lasciviunt; hi agere „ seipsos aliquid existimant." Learned men, in learned and inquisitive ages, who possessed many advantages that we have not, and among others that of being placed so many centuries nearer the original truths that are the objects of so much laborious search, despaired of finding them, and gave fair warning to posterity, if posterity would have taken it. The ancient geographers, as PLU-TARCH says in the life of THESEUS, when they laid down in their maps the little extent of sea and land that was known to them, left great spaces void. In some of these spaces they wrote, Here are sandy deserts, in others, Here are impassable marshes, Here is a chain of inhospitable mountains, or Here is a frozen ocean. Just so, both he and other historians, when they related fabulous originals, were not wanting to set out the bounds beyond which there was neither history nor chronology. CENSORINUS has preserved the distinction of three aeras established by VARRO. This learned Roman antiquary did not determine whether the first period had any beginning, but fixed the end of it at the first, that is, according to him, the Ogygian, deluge; which he placed, I think, some centuries backwarder than JULIUS AFRICANUS thought fit to place it afterwards. To this aera of absolute darkness he supposed that a kind of twilight succeeded, from the Ogygian deluge to the Olympic aera, and this he called the fabulous age. From this vulgar aera when CORAEBUS was crowned victor, and long after the true aera when these games were instituted by IPHITUS, the Greeks pretend to be able to digest their history with some order, clearness, and certainty: VARRO therefore looked on it as the break of day, or the beginning of the historical age. He might do so the rather, perhaps, because he included by it the date he likewise fixed, or, upon recollection, that the elder CATO had fixed, of the foundation of Rome within the period from which he supposed that historical truth was to be found. But yet most certain it is, that the history and chronology of the ages that follow are as confused and uncertain, as the history and chronology of those which immediately precede this aera.

1. *The state of ancient profane history.*

THE Greeks did not begin to write in prose till PHERECIDES of SYROS introduced the custom: and CADMUS MILESIUS was their first historian. Now these men flourished long after the true, or even the vulgar Olympic aera; for JOSEPHUS affirms, and in this he has great probability on his side, that CADMUS MILESIUS, and ACUSILAUS ARGIVUS, in a word the oldest historians in Greece, were very little more ancient than the expedition of the Persians against the Greeks. As several centuries passed between the Olympic aera and these first historians, there passed likewise several more between these and the first Greek chronologers. TIMAEUS about the time of PTOLOMY PHILADELPHUS, and ERATOSTHENES about that of PTOLOMY EVERGETES, seem first to have digested the events recorded by them, according to the olympiads. Precedent writers mentioned

Of the STUDY of HISTORY.   47

sometimes the olympiads; but this rule of reckoning was not brought into established use sooner. The rule could not serve to render history more clear and certain till it was followed: it was not followed till about five hundred years after the Olympic aera. There remains therefore no pretence to place the beginning of the historical age so high as VARRO placed it, by five hundred years.

HELLANICUS indeed and others pretended to give the originals of cities and governments, and to deduce their narrations from great antiquity. Their works are lost, but we can judge how inconsiderable the loss is, by the writings of that age which remain, and by the report of those who had seen the others. For instance, HERODOTUS was cotemporary with HELLANICUS. HERODOTUS was inquisitive enough in all conscience, and proposed to publish all he could learn of the antiquities of the Ionians, Lydians, Phrygians, Egyptians, Babylonians, Medes, and Persians; that is, of almost all the nations who were known in his time to exist. If he wrote Assyriacs, we have them not; but we are sure that this word was used proverbially to signify fabulous legends, soon after his time, and when the mode of publishing such relations and histories prevailed among the Greeks.

IN the nine books we have, he goes back indeed almost to the Olympic aera, without taking notice of it however; but he goes back only to tell an old woman's tale, of a king who lost his crown for shewing his wife naked to his favourite; and from CANDAULES and GYGES he haftens, or rather he takes a great leap, down to CYRUS.

SOMETHING like a thread of hiftory of the Medes and then of the Perfians, to the flight of XERXES, which happened in his own time, is carried on. The events of his own time are related with an air of hiftory. But all accounts of the Greeks as well as the Perfians, which precede thefe, and all the accounts which he gives occafionally of other nations, were drawn up moft manifeftly on broken, perplexed, and doubtful fcraps of tradition. He had neither original records, nor any authentic memorials to guide him, and yet thefe are the fole foundations of true hiftory. HERODOTUS flourished, I think, little more than half a century, and XENOPHON little more than a whole century, after the death of CYRUS: and yet how various and repugnant are the relations made by thefe two hiftorians, of the birth, life, and death of this prince? If moft hiftories had come down from thefe ages to ours, the uncertainty and inutility of them all would be but the more manifeft. We should find that ACUSILAUS rejected the traditions of HESIOD, that HELLANICUS contradicted ACUSILAUS, that EPHORUS accufed HELLANICUS, that TIMAEUS accufed EPHORUS, and all pofterior writers TIMAEUS. This is the report of JOSEPHUS. But, in order to shew the ignorance and falshood of all thofe writers through whom the traditions of profane antiquity came to the Greeks, I will quote to your lordship a much

better

better authority than that of JOSEPHUS; the authority of one who had no prejudice to bias him, no particular cause to defend, nor system of ancient history to establish, and all the helps, as well as talents, necessary to make him a competent judge. The man I mean is STRABO.

SPEAKING of the Massagetae in his eleventh book, he writes to this effect: that no author had given a true account of them, though several had writ of the war that CYRUS waged against them; and that historians had found as little credit in what they had related concerning the affairs of the Persians, Medes, and Syrians: that this was due to their folly; for observing that those who wrote fables professedly were held in esteem, these men imagined they should render their writings more agreeable, if, under the appearance and pretence of true history, they related what they had neither seen nor heard from persons able to give them true information; and that accordingly their only aim had been to dress up pleasing and marvellous relations: that one may better give credit to HESIOD and HOMER, when they talk of their heroes, nay even to dramatic poets, than to CTESIAS, HERODOTUS, HELLANICUS, and their followers: that it is not safe to give credit even to the greatest part of the historians who writ concerning ALEXANDER; since they too, encouraged by the greater reputation of this conqueror, by the distance to which he carried his arms, and by the difficulty of disproving what they said of actions performed in regions so remote, were apt

D

LETTER III.

to deceive: that indeed when the Roman empire on one side, and the Parthian on the other, came to extend themselves, the truth of things grew to be better known.

You see, my lord, not only how late profane history began to be writ by the Greeks, but how much later it began to be writ with any regard to truth; and consequently what wretched materials the learned men, who arose after the age of ALEXANDER, had to employ, when they attempted to form systems of ancient history and chronology. We have some remains of that laborious compiler DIODORUS SICULUS, but do we find in him any thread of ancient history, I mean, that which passed for ancient in his time? What complaints, on the contrary, does he not make of former historians? how frankly does he confess the little and uncertain light he had to follow in his researches? Yet DIODORUS, as well as PLUTARCH, and others, had not only the older Greek historians, but the more modern antiquaries, who pretended to have searched into the records and registers of nations; even at that time renowned for their antiquity. BEROSUS, for instance, and MANETHO, one a Babylonian and the other an Egyptian priest, had published the antiquities of their countries in the time of the PTOLEMYS. BEROSUS pretended to give the history of four hundred and eighty years. PLINY, if I remember right, for I say this on memory, speaks to this effect in the sixth book of his Natural History: and if it was so, these years were probably years of NABONASSAR. MANETHO began his history, God knows when, from the progress of ISIS, or some other as well ascertained period. He followed the Egyptian traditions of dynasties of Gods and Demi-Gods; and derived his anecdotes from the first MERCURY, who had inscribed them in sacred characters, on antediluvian pillars, antediluvian at least according to our received chronology, from which the second MERCURY, had transcribed them, and inserted them into his works. We have not these antiquities; for the monk of VITERBO was soon detected: and if we had them, they would either add to our uncertainty, and encrease the chaos of learning, or tell us nothing worth our knowledge. For thus I reason. Had they given particular and historical accounts conformable to the scriptures of the Jews, JOSEPHUS, JULIUS AFRICANUS, and EUSEBIUS would have made quite other extracts from their writings, and would have altered and contradicted them less. The accounts they gave, therefore, were repugnant to sacred writ, or they were defective: they would have established pyrrhonism, or have baulked our curiosity.

2. Of sacred history.

WHAT memorials therefore remain to give us light into the originals of ancient nations, and the history of those ages, we commonly call the first ages? The Bible, it will be said; that is, the historical part of it in the Old Testament. But, my lord, even these divine books must be reputed insufficient to the purpose, by every candid and impartial man who considers either their authority as histories, or the matter they contain. For what are they? and how came they to us? At the time when ALEXANDER carried his arms into Asia, a people of Syria, till then unknown, became known to the Greeks: this people had been slaves to the Egyptians, Assyrians, Medes, and Persians, as these several empires prevailed: ten parts in twelve of them had been transplanted by ancient conquerors, and melted down and lost in the east, several ages before the establishment of the empire that ALEXANDER destroyed: the other two parts had been carried captive to Babylon a little before the same aera. This captivity was not indeed, perpetual, like the other; but it lasted so long, and such circumstances, whatever they were, accompanied it, that the captives forgot their country, and even their language, the Hebrew dialect at least and character: and a few of them only could be wrought upon, by the zeal of some particular men, to return home, when the indulgence of the Persian monarchs gave them leave to rebuild their city and to repeople their ancient patrimony. Even this remnant of the nation did not continue long entire. Another great transmigration followed; and the Jews, that settled under the protection of the PTOLEMYS, forgot their language in Egypt, as the forefathers of these Jews had forgot theirs in Chaldea. More attached however to their religion in Egypt, for reasons easy to be deduced from the new institutions that prevailed after the captivity among them, than their ancestors had been in Chaldea, a version of their sacred writings was made into Greek at Alexandria, not long after the canon of these scriptures had been finished at Jerusalem; for many years could not intervene between the death of SIMON the just, by whom this canon was finished, if he died during the reign of PTOLEMY SOTER, and the beginning of this famous translation under PTOLEMY PHILADELPHUS. The Hellenist Jews reported as many marvellous things to authorize, and even to sanctify this translation, as the other Jews had reported about ESDRAS who began, and SIMON the just who finished, the canon of their scriptures. These holy romances slid into tradition, and tradition became history: the fathers of our christian church did not disdain to employ them. St. JEROME, for instance, laughed at the story of the seventy-two elders, whose translations were found to be, upon comparison, word for word the same, though made separately, and by men who had no communication with one another. But the same St. JEROME, in the same place, quotes ARISTEAS, one of the guard of PTOLEMY PHILADELPHUS, as a real personage.

THE account pretended to be writ by this ARISTEAS, of all that passed relating to the translation, was enough for his purpose. This he retained, and he rejected only the more improbable circumstances, which had been added to the tale, and which laid it open to most suspicion. In this he shewed great prudence, and better judgment, than that zealous, but weak apologist JUSTIN, who believed the whole story himself, and endeavoured to impose it on mankind.

THUS you see, my lord, that when we consider these books barely as histories, delivered to us on the faith of a superstitious people among whom the custom and art of pious lying prevailed remarkably, we may be allowed to doubt whether greater credit is to be given to what they tell us concerning the original, compiled in their own country and as it were out of the sight of the rest of the world, than we know, with such a certainty as no scholar presumes to deny, that we ought to give to what they tell us concerning the copy?

THE Hellenist Jews were extremely pleased, no doubt, to have their scriptures in a language they understood, and that might spread the fame of their antiquity, and do honor to their nation, among their masters the Greeks. But yet we do not find that the authority of these books prevailed, or that even they were much known among the Pagan world. The reason of this cannot be, that the Greeks admired nothing that was not of their own growth, "sua tantum mirantur:" for, on the contrary, they were inquisitive and credulous in the highest degree, and they collected and published at least as many idle traditions of other nations, as they propagated of their own. JOSEPHUS pretended that THEOPOMPUS, a disciple of ISOCRATES, being about to insert in his history some things he had taken out of holy writ, the poor man became troubled in mind for several days; and that having prayed to GOD, during an intermission of his illness, to reveal to him the cause of it, he learned in his sleep that this attempt was the cause; upon which he quitted the design and was cured. If JOSEPHUS had been a little more consistent than he is very often, such a story as this would not have been told by one, who was fond, as Jews and Christians in general have been, to create an opinion that the Gentiles took not their history alone, but their philosophy and all their valuable knowledge, from the Jews. Notwithstanding this story therefore, which is told in the fifteenth book of the Jewish Antiquities, and means nothing, or means to shew that the divine Providence would not suffer anecdotes of sacred to be mingled with profane history; the practice of JOSEPHUS himself, and of all those who have had the same design in view, has been to confirm the former by the latter, and at any rate to suppose an appearance at least of conformity between them. We are told HECATAEUS ABDERITA, for there were two of that name, writ a history favorable to the Jews: and, not to multiply instances, though I might easily do it, even ALEXANDER POLYHISTOR is called in. He is quoted by JOSEPHUS, and praised by EUSEBIUS as a man of parts and great variety of learning. His testimony, about the deluge and tower of Babel, is produced by St. CYRIL in his first book against JULIAN: and JUSTIN the apologist and martyr, in his exhortation to the Greeks, makes use of the same

56 LETTER III.

authority, among those that mention MOSES as a leader and prince of the Jews. Though this POLYHISTOR, if I remember right what I think I have met with in SUIDAS, spoke only of a woman he called Moso, " cujus scriptum est lex hebraeo-
„ rum *." Had the Greek historians been conformable to the sacred, I cannot see that their authority, which was not cotemporary, would have been of any weight. They might have copied MOSES, and so they did CTESIAS. But even this was not the case: whatever use a particular writer here and there might make occasionally of the scriptures, certain it is that the Jews continued to be as much despised, and their history to be as generally neglected, nay almost as generally unknown, for a long time at least after the version was made at Alexandria, as they had been before. APION, an Egyptian, a man of much erudition, appeared in the world some centuries afterwards. He wrote, among other antiquities, those of his own country: and as he was obliged to speak very often of the Jews, he spoke of them in a manner neither much to their honor, nor to that of their histories. He wrote purposely against them: and JOSEPHUS attempted afterwards, but APION was then dead, to refute him. APION passed, I

---

* Μωσώ, γυνὴ Ἑβραία· ἧς ἐςι σύγγραμμα ὁ παρ' Ἑβραίοις νόμ@ ἅς φησιν Ἀλέξανδρ@ ὁ Μιλήσι@ ὁ Πολυίσωρ. Sui. Lex. tom. ii. p. 552.

Ἀλέξανδρ@ . . . ὁ Πολυίςωρ . . . συν'γραψε βιβλία ἀριθμῷ κρείσω, ᾧ περὶ Ῥωμης βιβλία πέντε. ἐν τούτοις λέγει, ὡς γυνὴ γέγονεν Ἑβραία Μωσώ, ἧς ἐςι σύγγραμμα ὁ παρ' Ἑβραίοις νόμος. Id. tom. i. p. 105. Edit. Cantab. 1725.

know, for a vain and noify pedant; but he paffed likewife for a curious, a laborious, and a learned antiquary. If he was cabaliftical or fuperftitious, JOSEPHUS was at leaft as much fo as he: and if he flattered CALIGULA, JOSEPHUS introduced himfelf to the court of NERO and the favour of POPPAEA, by no very honorable means, under the protection of ALITURUS, a player, and a Jew; to fay nothing of his applying to VESPASIAN the prophecies concerning the Meffiah, nor of his accompanying TITUS to the fiege of Jerufalem.

IN fhort, my lord, the Jewish hiftory never obtained any credit in the world, till chriftianity was eftablished. The foundations of this fyftem being laid partly in thefe hiftories, and in the prophecies joined to them or inferted in them, chriftianity has reflected back upon them an authority which they had not before, and this authority has prevailed wherever chriftianity has fpread. Both Jews and Chriftians hold the fame books in great veneration, whilft each condemns the other for not underftanding, or for abufing them. But I apprehend that the zeal of both has done much hurt, by endeavouring to extend their authority much farther than is neceffary for the fupport perhaps of Judaifm, but to be fure of chriftianity. I explain myfelf that I may offend no pious ear.

SIMON, in the preface to his Critical hiftory of the Old teftament, cites a divine of the faculty of Paris, who held that the infpirations of the authors of thofe books, which the church receives as the word of God, should be extended no farther

LETTER III.

than to matters purely of doctrine, or to such as have a near and necessary relation to these; and that whenever these authors writ on other subjects, such as Egyptian, Assyrian, or other history, they had no more of the divine assistance than any other persons of piety. This notion of inspirations that came occasionally, that illuminated the minds and guided the hands of the sacred penmen while they were writing one page, and restrained their influence while the same authors were writing another, may be cavilled against: and what is there that may not? But surely it deserves to be treated with respect, since it tends to establish a distinction between the legal, doctrinal, or prophetical parts of the Bible, and the historical: without which distinction it is impossible to establish the first, as evidently and as solidly as the interests of religion require: at least it appears impossible to me, after having examined and considered, as well as I am able, all the trials of this kind that have been made by subtile as well as learned men. The Old is said to be the foundation of the New, and so it is in one sense: the system of religion contained in the latter refers to the system of religion contained in the former, and supposes the truth of it. But the authority on which we receive the books of the New testament, is so far from being founded on the authority of the Old testament, that it is quite independent on it; the New being proved, gives authority to the Old, but borrows none from it; and gives this authority to the particular parts only. CHRIST came to fulfill the prophecies; but not to confecrate all the written, any more than the oral, traditions of the Jews. We must believe these traditions as far as they relate to christianity, as far as christianity refers to them, or supposes them necessary; but we can be under no obligation to believe them any farther, since without christianity we should be under no obligation to believe them at all.

It has been said by ABBADIE, and others, "That the accidents which have happened to alter the texts of the Bible, and to disfigure, if I may say so, the scriptures in many respects, could not have been prevented without a perpetual standing miracle, and that a perpetual standing miracle is not in the order of providence." Now I can by no means subscribe to this opinion. It seems evident to my reason that the very contrary must be true, if we suppose that GOD acts towards men according to the moral fitness of things: and if we suppose that he acts arbitrarily, we can form no opinion at all. I think that these accidents would not have happened, or that the scriptures would have been preserved entirely in their genuine purity notwithstanding these accidents, if they had been entirely dictated by the HOLY GHOST; and the proof of this probable proposition, according to our clearest and most distinct ideas of wisdom and moral fitness, is obvious and easy. But these scriptures are not so come down to us: they are come down broken and confused, full of additions, interpolations, and transpositions, made we neither know when, nor by whom; and such, in short, as never appeared on the face of any other book, on whose authority men have agreed to rely.

This being so, my lord, what hypothesis shall we follow? Shall we adhere to some such distinction as I have mentioned? Shall we say, for instance, that the scriptures were written originally by the authors to whom they are vulgarly ascribed, but that these authors writ nothing by inspiration, except the legal, the doctrinal, and the prophetical parts, and that in every other respect their authority is purely human, and therefore fallible? Or shall we say that these histories are nothing more than compilations of old traditions, and abridgments of old records, made in later times, as they appear to every one who reads them without prepossession, and with attention? Shall we add, that which ever of these probabilities be true, we may believe, consistently with either, notwithstanding the decision of any divines, who know no more than you or I, or any other man, of the order of providence, that all those parts and passages of the Old testament, which contain prophecies, or matters of law or doctrine, and which were from the first of such importance in the designs of providence to all future generations, and even to the whole race of mankind, have been from the first the peculiar care of providence? Shall we insist that such particular parts and passages, which are plainly marked out and sufficiently confirmed by the system of the Christian revelation, and by the completion of the prophecies, have been preserved from corruption by ways impenetrable to us, amidst all the changes and chances to which the books wherein they are recorded have been exposed; and that neither original writers, nor later compilers, have been suffered to make any essential alterations, such as would have falsified the law of GOD and the principles of the Jewish and Christian religions, in any of these divine fundamental truths? Upon such hypotheses, we may assert without scruple, that the genealogies and histories of the Old testament are in no respect sufficient foundations for a chronology from the beginning of time, nor for universal history. But then the same hypotheses will secure the infallibility of scripture authority as far as religion is concerned. Faith and reason may be reconciled a little better than they commonly are; I may deny that the Old testament is transmitted to us under all the conditions of an authentic history, and yet be at liberty to maintain that the passages in it which establish original sin, which seem favorable to the doctrine of the Trinity, which foretell the coming of the Messiah, and all others of similar kind, are come down to us as they were originally dictated by the HOLY GHOST.

In attributing the whole credibility of the Old testament to the authority of the New, and in limiting the authenticity of the Jewish scriptures to those parts alone that concern law, doctrine, and prophecy, by which their chronology and the far greatest part of their history are excluded, I will venture to assure your lordship that I do not assume so much, as is assumed in every hypothesis that affixes the divine seal of inspiration to the whole canon; that rests the whole proof on Jewish veracity; and that pretends to account particularly and positively for the descent of these ancient writings in their present state.

ANOTHER reason, for which I have insisted the rather on the distinction so often mentioned, is this. I think we may find very good foundation for it even in the Bible: and though this be a point very little attended to, and much disguised, it would not be hard to shew, upon great inducements of probability, that the law and the history were far from being blended together as they now stand in the Pentateuch, even from the time of MOSES down to that of ESDRAS. But the principal and decisive reason for separating in such manner the legal, doctrinal, and prophetical parts, from the historical, is the necessity of having some rule to go by: and, I protest, I know of none that is yet agreed upon. I content myself therefore to fix my opinion concerning the authority of the Old testament in this manner, and carry it thus far only. We must do so, or we must enter into that labyrinth of dispute and contradiction, wherein even the most orthodox Jews and Christians have wandered so many ages, and still wander. It is strange, but it is true; not only the Jews differ from the Christians, but Jews and Christians both differ among themselves, concerning almost every point that is necessary to be certainly known and agreed upon, in order to establish the authority of books which both have received already as authentic and sacred. So that whoever takes the pains to read what learned men have writ on this subject, will find that they leave the matter as doubtful as they took it up. Who were the authors of these scriptures, when they were published, how they were composed and preserved, or renewed, to use a remarkable expression of the famous HUET in his Demonstration; in fine, how they were lost during the captivity, and how they were retrieved after it, are all matters of controversy to this day.

IT would be easy for me to descend into a greater detail, and to convince your lordship of what I have been saying in general by an induction of particulars, even without any other help than that of a few notes which I took when I applied myself to this examination, and which now lie before me. But such a digression would carry me too far: and I fear that you will think I have said already more than enough upon this part of my subject. I go on therefore to observe to your lordship, that if the history of the Old testament was as exact and authentic, as the ignorance and impudence of some Rabbies have made them assert that it is: if we could believe with them that MOSES wrote every syllable in the Pentateuch as it now stands, or that all the psalms were written by DAVID: nay, if we could believe, with PHILO and JOSEPHUS, that MOSES wrote the account of his own death and sepulture, and made a sort of a funeral panegyric on himself, as we find them in the last chapter of Deuteronomy; yet still would I venture to assert, that he who expects to find a system of chronology, or a thread of history, or sufficient materials for either, in the books of the Old testament, expects to find what the authors of these books, whoever they were, never intended. They are extracts of genealogies, not genealogies; extracts of histories, not histories. The Jews themselves allow their genealogies to be very imperfect, and produce examples of omissions and errors in them, which denote sufficiently that these genealogies are extracts, wherein every generation in the course of descent is not mentioned. I have read somewhere, perhaps in the works of St. JEROME, that this father justifies the opinion of those who think it impossible to fix any certain chronology on that of the Bible: and this opinion will be justified still better, to the understanding of every man that considers how grosly the Jews blunder whenever they meddle with chronology; for this plain reason, because their scriptures are imperfect in this respect, and because they rely on their oral, to rectify and supply their written, traditions: that is, they rely on traditions compiled long after the canon of their scriptures, but deemed by them of equal antiquity and authority. Thus, for instance, DANIEL and SIMON the just, according to them, were members at the same time of the great synagogue which began and finished the canon of the Old testament, under the presidency of ESDRAS. This ESDRAS was the prophet MALACHI. DARIUS the son of HYSTASPES was ARTAXERXES LONGIMANUS; he was AHASUERUS, and he was the same DARIUS whom ALEXANDER conquered.

This

This may serve as a sample of Jewish chronology, formed on their scriptures which afford insufficient lights, and on their traditions which afford false lights. We are indeed more correct, and come nearer to the truth in these instances, perhaps in some others, because we make use of profane chronology to help us. But profane chronology is itself so modern, so precarious, that this help does not reach to the greatest part of that time to which sacred chronology extends; that when it begins to help, it begins to perplex us too; and finally, that even with this help we should not have had so much as the appearance of a complete chronological system, and the same may be said of universal history, if learned men had not proceeded very wisely, on one uniform maxim, from the first ages of christianity, when a custom of sanctifying profane learning, as well as prophane rites, which the Jews had imprudently laid aside, was taken up by the Christians. The maxim I mean is this, that prophane authority be admitted without scruple or doubt, whenever it says, or whenever it can be made to say, if not " totidem verbis, " yet " totidem syllabis," or " totidem literis." at least, or whenever it can be made by any interpretation to mean, what confirms, or supplies in a consistent manner, the holy writ; and that the same authority be rejected, when nothing of this kind can be done, but the contradiction or inconsistency remains irreconcileable. Such a liberty as this would not be allowed in any other case; because it supposes the very thing that is to be proved. But we see it taken, very properly to be sure, in favor of sacred and infallible writings, when they are compared with others.

In order to perceive with the utmost evidence, that the scope and design of the author or authors of the Pentateuch, and of the other books of the Old testament, answer as little the purpose of antiquaries, in history, as in chronology, it will be sufficient briefly to call to mind the sum of what they relate, from the creation of the world to the establishment of the Persian empire. If the antediluvian world continued one thousand six hundred and fifty-six years, and if the vocation of ABRAHAM is to be placed four hundred and twenty-six years below the deluge, these twenty centuries make almost two thirds of the period mentioned: and the whole history of them is comprized in eleven short chapters of Genesis; which is certainly the most compendious extract that ever was made. If we examine the contents of these chapters, do we find any thing like an universal history, or so much as an abridgment of it? ADAM and EVE were created, they broke the commandment of GOD, they were driven out of the garden of Eden, one of their sons killed his brother, but their race soon multiplied and peopled the earth. What geography now have we, what history of this antediluvian world? Why, none. The sons of GOD, it is said, lay with the daughters of men, and begot giants, and GOD drowned all the inhabitants of the earth, except one family. After this we read that the earth was repeopled; but these children of one family were divided into several languages, even whilst they lived together, spoke the same language, and were employed in the same work. Out of one of the countries into which they dispersed themselves, Chaldea, God called ABRAHAM some time afterwards, with magnificent promises, and conducted him to a country called Chanaan. Did this author, my lord, intend an universal history? Certainly not. The tenth chapter of Genesis names indeed some of the generations descending from the sons of NOAH, some of the cities founded, and some of the countries planted by them. But what are bare names, naked of circumstances, without descriptions of countries, or relations of events? They furnish matter only for guess and dispute; and even the similitude of them, which is often used as a clue to lead us to the discovery of historical truth, has notoriously contributed to propagate error, and to encrease the perplexity of ancient tradition. These imperfect and dark accounts have not furnished matter for guess and dispute alone; but a much worse use has been made of them by Jewish rabbies, Christian fathers, and Mahometan doctors, in their prophane extensions of this part of the Mosaic history. The creation of the first man is described by some, as if, Preadamites, they had assisted at it. They talk of his beauty as if they had seen him, of his gigantic size as if they had measured him, and of his prodigious knowledge as if they had conversed with him. They point out the very spot where EVE laid her head the first time he enjoyed her.

They have minutes of the whole conversation between this mother of mankind, who damned her children before she bore them, and the serpent. Some are positive that CAIN quarrelled with ABEL about a point of doctrine, and others affirm that the dispute arose about a girl. A great deal of such stuff may be easily collected about ENOCH, about NOAH, and about the sons of NOAH; but I wave any farther mention of such impertinencies as BONZES or TALAPOINS would almost blush to relate. Upon the whole matter, if we may guess at the design of an author, by the contents of his book, the design of MOSES, or of the author of the history ascribed to him, in this part of it, was to inform the people of Israel of their descent from NOAH by SEM, and of NOAH's from ADAM by SETH; to illustrate their original; to establish their claim to the land of Chanaan, and to justify all the cruelties committed by JOSHUA in the conquest of the Chanaanites, in whom, says BOCHART, " the prophecy of NOAH was completed, „ when they were subdued by the Israelites, who „ had been so long slaves to the Egyptians. "

ALLOW me to make, as I go along, a short reflection or two on this prophecy, and the completion of it, as they stand recorded in the Pentateuch, out of many that might be made. The terms of the prophecy then are not very clear: and the curse pronounced in it contradicts all our notions of order and of justice. One is tempted to think, that the patriarch was still drunk; and that no man in his senses could hold such language, or pass such a sentence. Certain it is, that no writer but a Jew could impute to the oeconomy of divine providence the accomplishment of such a prediction, nor make the Supreme Being the executor of such a curse.

HAM alone offended, CHANAAN was innocent; for the Hebrew and other doctors who would make the son an accomplice with his father, affirm not only without, but against, the express authority of the text. CHANAAN was however alone cursed: and he became, according to his grandfather's prophecy, "a servant of servants," that is, the vilest and worst of slaves (for I take these words in a sense, if not the most natural, the most favorable to the prophecy, and the least absurd) to SEM, though not to JAPHET, when the Israelites conquered Palestine; to one of his uncles, not to his brethren. Will it be said — it has been said — that where we read CHANAAN, we are to understand HAM, whose brethren SEM and JAPHET were. At this rate, we shall never know what we read: as these critics never care what they say. Will it be said — this has been said too — that HAM was punished in his posterity, when CHANAAN was cursed, and his descendants were exterminated. But who does not see that the curse, and the punishment, in this case, fell on CHANAAN and his posterity, exclusively of the rest of the posterity of HAM; and were therefore the curse and punishment of the son, not of the father, properly? The descendants of MESRAIM, another of his sons, were the Egyptians: and they were so far from being servants of servants to their cousins the Semites, that these were servants of servants to them, during more than fourscore years. Why the posterity of CHANAAN was to be deemed an accursed race, it is easy to account; and I have mentioned it just now. But it is not so easy to account, why the posterity of the righteous SEM, that great example of filial reverence, became slaves to another branch of the family of HAM.

It would not be worth while to lengthen this tedious letter, by setting down any more of the contents of the history of the bible. Your lordship may please to call the substance of it to your mind; and your native candor and love of truth will oblige you then to confess, that these sacred books do not aim, in any part of them, at any thing like universal chronology and history. They contain a very imperfect account of the Israelites themselves; of their settlement in the land of promise, of which, by the way, they never had entire, and scarce ever peaceable possession; of their divisions, apostasies, repentances, relapses, triumphs, and defeats under the occasional government of their judges, and under that of their kings; of the Galilean and Samaritan captivities, into which they were carried by the kings of Assyria, and of that which was brought on the remnant of this people when the kingdom of Judah was destroyed by those princes who governed the empire founded on the union of Niniveh and Babylon. These things are all related, your lordship knows, in a very summary and confused manner: and we learn so little of other nations by thefe accounts, that if we did not borrow fome light from the traditions of other nations, we should fcarce underftand them. One particular obfervation, and but one, I will make, to shew what knowledge in the hiftory of mankind, and in the computation of time, may be expected from thefe books. The Affyrians were their neighbours, powerful neighbours, with whom they had much and long to do. Of this empire therefore, if of any thing, we might hope to find fome fatisfactory account. What do we find? The fcripture takes no notice of any Affyrian kingdom, till juft before the time when prophane hiftory makes that empire to end. Then we hear of PHUL, of TEGLATH-PHALASSER, who was perhaps the fame perfon, and of SALMANASSER, who took Samaria in the twelfth of the aera of NABONASSER, that is, twelve years after the Affyrian empire was no more. SENACHERIB fucceeds to him, and ASSERHADDON to SENACHERIB. What shall we fay to this apparent contrariety? If the filence of the bible creates a ftrong prefumption againft the firft, may not the filence of prophane authority create fome againft the fecond Affyrian Monarchs? The pains that are taken to perfuade, that there is room enough between SARDANAPALUS and CYRUS for the fecond, will not refolve the difficulty. Something much more plaufible may be faid, but even this will be hypothetical, and liable to great contradiction. So that upon the whole matter, the scriptures are so far from giving us light into general history, that they encrease the obscurity even of those parts to which they have the nearest relation. We have therefore neither in prophane nor in sacred authors such authentic, clear, distinct, and full accounts of the originals of ancient nations, and of the great events of those ages that are commonly called the first ages, as deserve to go by the name of history, or as afford sufficient materials for chronology and history.

I MIGHT now proceed to observe to your lordship how this has happened, not only by the necessary consequences of human nature, and the ordinary course of human affairs, but by the policy, artifice, corruption, and folly of mankind. But this would be to heap digression upon digression, and to presume too much on your patience. I shall therefore content myself to apply these reflections on the state of ancient history to the study of history, and to the method to be observed in it; as soon as your lordship has rested yourself a little after reading, and I after writing so long a letter.

OF THE

STUDY OF HISTORY.

LETTER IV.

I. That there is in hiftory fufficient authenticity to render it ufeful, notwithftanding all objections to the contrary.

II. Of the method and due reftrictions to be obferved in the ftudy of it.

WHETHER the letter I now begin to write will be long or fhort, I know not: but I find my memory is refreshed, my imagination warmed, and matter flows in fo faft upon me, that I have not time to prefs it clofe. Since therefore you have provoked me to write, you muft be content to take what follows.

I HAVE obferved already that we are apt naturally to apply to ourfelves what has happened to other men, and that examples take their force from hence; as well thofe which hiftory, as thofe which experience, offers to our reflection. What we do not believe to have happened therefore, we shall not thus apply: and for want of the fame application, fuch examples will not have the fame effect. Ancient hiftory, fuch ancient hiftory as I have defcribed, is quite unfit therefore in this refpect to anfwer the ends that every reafonable man should propofe to himfelf in this ftudy; because such ancient history will never gain sufficient credit with any reasonable man. A tale well told, or a comedy or a tragedy well wrought up, may have a momentary effect upon the mind, by heating the imagination, surprizing the judgment, and affecting strongly the passions. The Athenians are said to have been transported into a kind of martial phrenzy by the representation of a tragedy of AESCHYLUS, and to have marched under this influence from the theatre to the plains of MARATHON. These momentary impressions might be managed, for aught I know, in such manner as to contribute a little, by frequent repetitions of them, towards maintaining a kind of habitual contempt of folly, detestation of vice, and admiration of virtue in well-policed common-wealths. But then these impressions cannot be made, nor this little effect be wrought, unless the fables bear an appearance of truth. When they bear this appearance, reason connives at the innocent fraud of imagination; reason dispenses, in favor of probability, with those strict rules of criticism that she has established to try the truth of fact: but, after all, she receives these fables as fables; and as such only she permits imagination to make the most of them. If they pretended to be history, they would be soon subjected to another and more severe examination. What may have happened, is the matter of an ingenious fable: what has happened, is that of an authentic history: the impressions which one or the other makes are in proportion. When imagination grows lawless and wild, rambles out of the precincts of nature, and tells of heroes and giants, fairies and enchanters, of events and of phaenomena repugnant to universal experience, to our clearest and most distinct ideas, and to all the known laws of nature, reason does not connive a moment; but, far from receiving such narrations as historical, she rejects them as unworthy to be placed even among the fabulous. Such narrations therefore cannot make the slightest momentary impressions on a mind fraught with knowledge, and void of superstition. Imposed by authority, and assisted by artifice, the delusion hardly prevails over common sense; blind ignorance almost sees, and rash superstition hesitates: nothing less than enthusiasm and phrenzy can give credit to such histories, or apply such examples. Don QUIXOTE believed; but even SANCHO doubted.

WHAT I have said will not be much controverted by any man who has read AMADIS of Gaul, or has examined our ancient traditions without prepossession. The truth is, the principal difference between them seems to be this. In AMADIS of Gaul, we have a thread of absurdities that are invented without any regard to probability, and that lay no claim to belief: ancient traditions are an heap of fables, under which some particular truths, inscrutable, and therefore useless to mankind, may lie concealed; which have a just pretence to nothing more, and yet impose themselves upon us, and become, under the venerable name of ancient history, the foundations of modern fables,

LETTER IV.

the materials with which so many systems of fancy have been erected.

BUT now, as men are apt to carry their judgments into extremes, there are some that will be ready to insist that all history is fabulous, and that the very best is nothing better than a probable tale, artfully contrived, and plausibly told, wherein truth and falshood are indistinguishably blended together. All the instances, and all the common-place arguments, that BAYLE and others have employed to establish this sort of Pyrrhonism, will be quoted: and from thence it will be concluded, that if the pretended histories of the first ages, and of the originals of nations, be too improbable and too ill-vouched to procure any degree of belief, those histories that have been writ later, that carry a greater air of probability, and that boast even cotemporary authority, are at least insufficient to gain that degree of firm belief, which is necessary to render the study of them useful to mankind. But here that happens which often happens: the premises are true, and the conclusion is false; because a general axiom is established precariously on a certain number of partial observations. This matter is of consequence; for it tends to ascertain the degrees of assent that we may give to history.

I AGREE then that history has been purposely and systematically falsified in all ages, and that partiality and prejudice have occasioned both voluntary and involuntary errors even in the best. Let me say without offence, my lord, since I may say it with truth and am able to prove it, that ecclesiastical authority has led the way to this corruption in all ages, and all religions. How monstrous were the absurdities that the priesthood imposed on the ignorance and superstition of mankind in the Pagan world, concerning the originals of religions and governments, their institutions and rites, their laws and customs? What opportunities had they for such impositions, whilst the keeping the records and collecting the traditions was in so many nations the peculiar office of this order of men? A custom highly extolled by JOSEPHUS, but plainly liable to the grossest frauds, and even a temptation to them. If the foundations of Judaism and Christianity have been laid in truth, yet what numberless fables have been invented to raise, to embellish, and to support these structures, according to the interest and taste of the several architects? That the Jews have been guilty of this will be allowed: and, to the shame of Christians, if not of Christianity, the fathers of one church have no right to throw the first stone at the fathers of the other. Deliberate systematical lying has been practised and encouraged from age to age; and among all the pious frauds that have been employed to maintain a reverence and zeal for their religion in the minds of men, this abuse of history has been one of the principal and most successful: an evident and experimental proof, by the way, of what I have insisted upon so much, the aptitude and natural tendency of history to form our opinions, and to settle our habits. This righteous expedient was in so much use and repute in the Greek church, that one METAPHRASTUS wrote a treatise on the art of composing holy romances: the fact, if I remember right, is cited by BAILLET in his book of the lives of the saints. He and other learned men of the Roman church have thought it of service to their cause, since the resurrection of letters; to detect some impostures, and to depose, or to unniche, according to the French expression, now and then a reputed saint; but they seem in doing this to mean no more than a sort of composition: they give up some fables that they may defend others with greater advantage, and they make truth serve as a stalking-horse to error. The same spirit, that prevailed in the Eastern church, prevailed in the Western, and prevails still. A strong proof of it appeared lately in the country where I am. A sudden fury of devotion seized the people of Paris for a little priest*, undistinguished during his life, and dubbed a saint by the Jansenists after his death. Had the first minister been a Jansenist, the saint had been a saint still. All France had kept his festival: and, since there are thousands of eye-witnesses ready to attest the truth of all the miracles supposed to have been wrought at his tomb, notwithstanding the discouragement which these zealots have met with from the government; we may assure ourselves, that these silly impostures would have been transmitted in all the solemn

* The abbé Paris.

pomp of history, from the knaves of this age to the fools of the next.

This lying spirit has gone forth from ecclesiastical to other historians: and I might fill many pages with instances of extravagant fables that have been invented in several nations, to celebrate their antiquity, to ennoble their originals, and to make them appear illustrious in the arts of peace and the triumphs of war. When the brain is well heated, and devotion or vanity, the semblance of virtue or real vice, and, above all, disputes and contests, have inspired that complication of passions we term zeal, the effects are much the same, and history becomes very often a lying panegyric or a lying satire; for different nations, or different parties in the same nation, belie one another without any respect for truth, as they murder one another without any regard to right or sense of humanity. Religious zeal may boast this horrid advantage over civil zeal, that the effects of it have been more sanguinary, and the malice more unrelenting. In another respect they are more alike, and keep a nearer proportion: different religions have not been quite so barbarous to one another as sects of the same religion; and, in like manner, nation has had better quarter from nation, than party from party. But, in all these controversies, men have pushed their rage beyond their own and their adversaries lives: they have endeavoured to interest posterity in their quarrels, and by rendering history subservient to this wicked purpose, they have done their utmost to perpetuate scandal, and to immortalise their animosity. The Heathen taxed the Jews even with idolatry; the Jews joined with the Heathen to render Christianity odious: but the church, who beat them at their own weapons during these contests, has had this further triumph over them, as well as over the several sects that have arisen within her own pale: the works of those who have writ against her have been destroyed; and whatever she advanced, to justify herself and to defame her adversaries, is preserved in her annals, and the writings of her doctors.

THE charge of corrupting history, in the cause of religion, has been always committed to the most famous champions, and greatest saints of each church; and, if I was not more afraid of tiring, than of scandalising your lordship, I could quote to you examples of modern churchmen who have endeavoured to justify foul language by the New testament; and cruelty by the Old: nay, what is execrable beyond imagination, and what strikes horror into every mind that entertains due sentiments of the Supreme Being, GOD himself has been cited for rallying and insulting ADAM after his fall. In other cases, this charge belongs to the pedants of every nation, and the tools of every party. What accusations of idolatry and superstition have not been brought, and aggravated against the Mahometans? Those wretched Christians who returned from those wars, so improperly called the holy wars, rumoured these stories about the West: and you may find, in
some

some of the old chroniclers and romance-writers, as well as poets, the Saracens called Paynims; though surely they were much further off from any suspicion of Polytheism, than those who called them by that name. When Mahomet the second took Constantinople in the fifteenth century, the Mahometans began to be a little better, and but a little better known, than they had been before, to these parts of the world. But their religion, as well as their customs and manners, was strangely misrepresented by the Greek refugees that fled from the Turks: and the terror and hatred which this people had inspired by the rapidity of their conquests, and by their ferocity, made all these misrepresentations universally pass for truths. Many such instances may be collected from Maraccio's refutation of the koran, and Relandus has published a very valuable treatise on purpose to refute these calumnies, and to justify the Mahometans. Does not this example incline your lordship to think, that the Heathens, and the Arians, and other heretics, would not appear quite so absurd in their opinions, nor so abominable in their practice, as the orthodox Christians have represented them; if some Relandus could arise, with the materials necessary to their justification in his hands?

He who reflects on the circumstances that attended letters, from the time when Constantine, instead of uniting the characters of emperor and sovereign pontiff in himself when he became Christian, as they were united in him and all the other emperors in the Pagan system of government, gave so much independent wealth and power to the clergy, and the means of acquiring so much more: he who carries these reflections on through all the latter empire, and through those ages of ignorance and superstition, wherein it was hard to say which was greatest, the tyranny of the clergy, or the servility of the laity: he who considers the extreme severity, for instance, of the laws made by THEODOSIUS in order to stifle every writing that the orthodox clergy, that is, the clergy then in fashion, disliked; or the character and influence of such a priest as GREGORY called the great, who proclaimed war to all heathen learning in order to promote Christian verity; and flattered BRUNEHAULT, and abetted PHOCAS: he who considers all these things, I say, will not be at a loss to find the reasons, why history, both that which was writ before, and a great part of that which has been writ since the Christian aera, is come to us so imperfect and so corrupt.

WHEN the imperfection is due to a total want of memorials, either because none were originally written, or because they have been lost by devastations of countries, extirpations of people, and other accidents in a long course of time; or because zeal, malice, and policy have joined their endeavours to destroy them purposely; we must be content to remain in our ignorance, and there is no great harm in that. Secure from being deceived, I can submit to be uninformed. But when there is not a total want of memorials, when some have been lost or destroyed, and others have been preserved and propagated; then we are in danger of being deceived: and therefore he must be very implicit indeed who receives for true the history of any religion or nation, and much more that of any sect or party; without having the means of confronting it with some other history. A reasonable man will not be thus implicit. He will not establish the truth of history on single, but on concurrent testimony. If there be none such, he will doubt absolutely: if there be a little such, he will proportion his assent or dissent accordingly. A small gleam of light, borrowed from foreign anecdotes, serves often to discover a whole system of falshood: and even they who corrupt history frequently betray themselves by their ignorance or inadvertency. Examples whereof I could easily produce. Upon the whole matter, in all these cases we cannot be deceived essentially, unless we please: and therefore there is no reason to establish Pyrrhonism, that we may avoid the ridicule of credulity.

In all other cases, there is less reason still to do so; for when histories and historical memorials abound, even those that are false serve to the discovery of the truth. Inspired by different passions, and contrived for opposite purposes, they contradict; and, contradicting, they convict one another. Criticism separates the ore from the dross, and extracts from various authors a series of true history, which could not have been found entire in any one of them, and will command our assent, when it is formed with judgment, and represented with candor. If this may be done, as it has been done sometimes,

with the help of authors who writ on purpose to deceive; how much more easily, and more effectually may it be done, with the help of those who paid a greater regard to truth? In a multitude of writers there will be always some, either incapable of gross prevarication from the fear of being discovered, and of acquiring infamy whilst they seek for fame; or else attached to truth upon a nobler and surer principle. It is certain that these, even the last of them, are fallible. Bribed by some passion or other, the former may venture now and then to propagate a falshood, or to disguise a truth; like the painter that drew in profile, as LUCIAN says, the picture of a prince that had but one eye. MONTAGNE objects to the memorials of DU BELLAY, that though the gross of the facts be truly related, yet these authors turned every thing they mentioned to the advantage of their master, and mentioned nothing which could not be so turned. The old fellow's words are worth quoting. — " De contourner le jugement des evene-
„ mens souvent contre raison à notre avantage,
„ et d'obmettre tout ce qu'il y a de chatouilleux
„ en la vie de leur maistre, ils en font mestier."
These, and such as these, deviate occasionally and voluntarily from truth; but even they who are attached to it the most religiously may slide sometimes into involuntary error. In matters of history we prefer very justly cotemporary authority; and yet cotemporary authors are the most liable to be warped from the straight rule of truth, in writing on subjects which have affected them strongly,

Of the STUDY of HISTORY.

" et quorum pars magna fuerunt." I am so persuaded of this from what I have felt in myself, and observed in others, that if life and health enough fall to my share, and I am able to finish what I meditate, a kind of history, from the late queen's accession to the throne, to the peace of Utrecht, there will be no materials that I shall examine more scrupulously and severely, than those of the time when the events to be spoken of were in transaction. But though the writers of these two sorts, both of whom pay as much regard to truth as the various infirmities of our nature admit, are fallible; yet this fallibility will not be sufficient to give colour to Pyrrhonism. Where their sincerity as to fact is doubtful, we strike out truth by the confrontation of different accounts: as we strike out sparks of fire by the collision of flints and steel. Where their judgments are suspicious of partiality, we may judge for ourselves; or adopt their judgments, after weighing them with certain grains of allowance. A little natural sagacity will proportion these grains according to the particular circumstances of the authors, or their general characters; for even these influence. Thus MONTAGNE pretends, but he exaggerates a little that GUICCIARDIN no where ascribes any one action to a virtuous, but every one to a vicious principle. Something like this has been reproached to TACITUS; and, notwithstanding all the sprightly loose observations of MONTAGNE in one of his essays, where he labours to prove the contrary, read PLUTARCH's comparisons in what language, you please, I am of BODIN's mind, you will perceive that they were made by a Greek. In short, my lord, the favorable opportunities of corrupting history have been often interrupted, and are now over in so many countries, that truth penetrates even into those where lying continues still to be part of the policy ecclesiastical and civil; or where, to say the best we can say, truth is never suffered to appear, till she has passed through hands, out of which she seldom returns entire and undefiled.

But it is time I should conclude this head, under which I have touched some of those reasons that shew the folly of endeavouring to establish universal Pyrrhonism in matters of history, because there are few histories without some lies, and none without some mistakes; and that prove the body of history which we possess, since ancient memorials have been so critically examined, and modern memorials have been so multiplied, to contain in it such a probable series of events, easily distinguishable from the improbable, as force the assent of every man who is in his senses, and are therefore sufficient to answer all the purposes of the study of history. I might have appealed perhaps, without entering into the argument at all, to any man of candor whether his doubts concerning the truth of history have hindered him from applying the examples he has met with in it, and from judging of the present, and sometimes of the future, by the past? whether he has not been touched with reverence and admiration, at the virtue and wisdom of some men, and of some ages; and whether he has not felt indignation and contempt for others? whether EPAMINONDAS, or PHOCION, for inftance, the DECII, or the SCIPIOS, have not raifed in his mind a flame of public fpirit, and private virtue? and whether he has not shuddered with horror at the profcriptions of MARIUS and SYLLA, at the treachery of THEO-DOTUS and ACHILLAS, and at the confummate cruelty of an infant king? " Quis non contra Marii „ arma, et contra Syllae profcriptionem concitatur? „ Quis non THEODOTO, et ACHILLAE, et ipfi „ puero, non puerile aufo facinus, infeftus eft?" If all this be a digreffion therefore, your lordship will be fo good as to excufe it.

II. WHAT has been faid concerning the multiplicity of hiftories, and of hiftorical memorials wherewith our libraries abound fince the refurrection of letters happened, and the art of printing began, puts me in mind of another general rule, that ought to be obferved by every man who intends to make a real improvement, and to become wifer as well as better, by the ftudy of hiftory. I hinted at this rule in a former letter, where I faid that we should neither grope in the dark, nor wander in the light. Hiftory muft have a certain degree of probability, and authenticity, or the examples we find in it will not carry a force fufficient to make due impreffions on our minds, nor to illuftrate nor to ftrenghten the precepts of philofophy and the rules of good policy. But befides, when hiftories have this neceffary authenticity and probability, there is

much discernment to be employed in the choice
and the use we make of them. Some are to be
read, some are to be studied; and some may be
neglected entirely, not only without detriment,
but with advantage. Some are the proper objects
of one man's curiosity, some of another's, and
some of all men's, but all history is not an object
of curiosity for any man. He who improperly,
wantonly, and absurdly makes it so, indulges a
sort of canine appetite: the curiosity of one, like
the hunger of the other, devours ravenously and
without distinction whatever falls in it's way, but
neither of them digests. They heap crudity upon
crudity, and nourish and improve nothing but
their distemper. Some such characters I have
known, though it is not the most common extreme
into which men are apt to fall. One of them I
knew in this country. He joined, to a more than
athletic strength of body, a prodigious memory;
and to both a prodigious industry. He had read
almost constantly twelve or fourteen hours a day,
for five and twenty or thirty years; and had
heaped together as much learning as could be
crowded into an head. In the course of my
acquaintance with him, I consulted him once or
twice, not oftener; for I found this mass of learning of as little use to me as to the owner. The
man was communicative enough; but nothing was
distinct in his mind. How could it be otherwise?
he had never spared time to think, all was
employed in reading. His reason had not the merit
of common mechanism. When you press a watch

Of the STUDY of HISTORY.

or pull a clock, they anſwer your queſtion with preciſion; for they repeat exactly the hour of the day, and tell you neither more nor leſs than you deſire to know. But when you asked this man a queſtion, he overwhelmed you by pouring forth all that the ſeveral terms or words of your queſtion recalled to his memory: and if he omitted any thing, it was that very thing to which the ſenſe of the whole queſtion ſhould have led him and confined him. To ask him a queſtion, was to wind up a ſpring in his memory, that rattled on with vaſt rapidity, and confuſed noiſe, till the force of it was ſpent: and you went away with all the noiſe in your ears, ſtunned and un-informed. I never left him that I was not ready to ſay to him, " Dieu vous faſſe la grace de devenir moins ſa- „ vant!" a wish that LA MOTHE LE VAYER mentions upon ſome occaſion or other, and that he would have done well to have applied to himſelf upon many.

HE who reads with diſcernment and choice, will acquire leſs learning, but more knowledge: and as this knowledge is collected with deſign, and cultivated with art and method, it will be at all times of immediate and ready uſe to himſelf and others,

> Thus uſeful arms in magazines we place,
> All rang'd in order, and diſpos'd with grace:
> Nor thus alone the curious eye to pleaſe;
> But to be found, when need requires, with eaſe:

You remember the verses, my lord, in our friend's Essay on criticism, which was the work of his childhood almost; but is such a monument of good sense and poetry as no other, that I know, has raised in his riper years.

He who reads without this discernment and choice, and, like Bodin's pupil, resolves to read all, will not have time, no, nor capacity neither, to do any thing else. He will not be able to think, without which it is impertinent to read; nor to act, without which it is impertinent to think. He will assemble materials with much pains, and purchase them at much expence, and have neither leisure nor skill to frame them into proper scantlings, or to prepare them for use. To what purpose should he husband his time, or learn architecture? he has no design to build. But then to what purpose all these quarries of stone, all these mountains of sand and lime, all these forests of oak and deal? "Magno impendio temporum, magna ,, alienarum aurium molestia, laudatio haec constat, ,, O hominem literatum! Simus hoc titulo rusticiore ,, contenti, O virum bonum!" We may add, ,, and SENECA might have added in his own style, and according to the manners and characters of his own age, another title as rustic, and as little in fashion, " O virum sapientia sua simplicem, et ,, simplicitate sua sapientem! O virum utilem sibi, ,, suis, reipublicae, et humano generi!" I have said perhaps already, but no matter, it cannot be repeated too often, that the drift of all philosophy, and of all political speculations, ought to be the making us better men, and better citizens. Those studies, which have no intention towards improving our moral characters, have no pretence to be styled philosophical. "Quis est enim," says TULLY in his Offices, " qui nullis officii praeceptis tradendis, philosophum se audeat dicere?" Whatever political speculations, instead of preparing us to be useful to society and to promote the happiness of mankind, are only systems for gratifying private ambition, and promoting private interests at the public expence; all such, I say, deserve to be burnt, and the authors of them to starve, like MACHIAVEL, in a jail.

LETTER V.

I. The great ufe of hiftory, properly fo called, as diftinguifhed from the writings of mere annalifts and antiquaries.

II. Greek and Roman hiftorians.

III. Some idea of a complete hiftory.

IV. Further cautions to be obferved in this ftudy, and the regulation of it according to the different profeffions, and fituations of men: above all, the ufe to be made of it (1) by divines, and (2) by thofe who are called to the fervice of their country.

I REMEMBER my laft letter ended abruptly, and a long interval has fince paffed: fo that the thread I had then fpun has flipt from me. I will try to recover it, and to purfue the task your lordship has obliged me to continue. Befides the pleafure of obeying your orders, it is likewife of fome advantage to myfelf, to recollect my thoughts, and refume a ftudy in which I was converfant formerly. For nothing can be more true than that faying of SOLON reported by PLATO, though cenfured by him, impertinently enough in one of his wild books of laws — "Affidue addifcens, ad fenium venio." The truth is, the moft knowing man in the courſe of the longeſt life, will have always much to learn, and the wiſeſt and beſt much to improve. This rule will hold in the knowledge and improvement to be acquired by the ſtudy of hiſtory: and therefore even he who has gone to this ſchool in his youth, should not neglect it in his age. "I read in LIVY," ſays MONTAGNE, "what another man does not, and PLUTARCH read there what I do not." Juſt ſo the ſame man may read at fifty what he did not read in the ſame book at five-and-twenty: at leaſt I have found it ſo, by my own experience, on many occaſions.

BY comparing, in this ſtudy, the experience of other men and other ages with our own, we improve both: we analyſe, as it were, philoſophy. We reduce all the abſtract ſpeculations of ethics, and all the general rules of human policy, to their firſt principles. With theſe advantages every man may, though few men do, advance daily towards thoſe ideas, thoſe increated eſſences a Platoniſt would ſay, which no human creature can reach in practice, but in the neareſt approaches to which the perfection of our nature conſiſts; becauſe every approach of this kind renders a man better, and wiſer for himſelf, for his family, for the little community of his own country, and for the great community of the world. Be not ſurpriſed, my lord, at the order in which I place theſe objects. Whatever order divines and moraliſts, who contemplate the duties belonging to theſe objects, may place them in, this is the order they hold in nature: and I have always thought that we might

LETTER V.

lead ourselves and others to private virtue, more effectually by a due observation of this order, than by any of those sublime refinements that pervert it.

> Self-Love but serves the virtuous mind to wake;
> As the small pebble stirs the peaceful lake.
> The centre mov'd, a circle strait succeeds;
> Another still, and still another spreads:
> Friend, parent, neighbour, first it will embrace,
> His country next, and next all human race.

So sings our friend POPE, my lord, and so I believe. So I shall prove too, if I mistake not, in an epistle I am about to write to him, in order to complete a set that were writ some years ago.

A MAN of my age, who returns to the study of history, has no time to lose, because he has little to live: a man of your lordship's age has no time to lose, because he has much to do. For different reasons therefore the same rules will suit us. Neither of us must grope in the dark, neither of us must wander in the light. I have done the first formerly a good deal; " ne verba mihi daren-
„ tur; ne aliquid esse, in hac recondita antiquitatis
„ scientia, magni ac secreti boni judicaremus." If you take my word, you will throw none of your time away in the same manner: and I shall have the less regret for that which I have misspent, if I persuade you to hasten down from the broken traditions of antiquity, to the more entire as well as more authentic histories of ages more modern. In the study of these we shall find many a

complete series of events, preceded by a deduction of their immediate and remote causes, related in their full extent, and accompanied with such a detail of circumstances, and characters, as may transport the attentive reader back to the very time, make him a party to the councils, and an actor in the whole scene of affairs. Such draughts as these, either found in history or extracted by our own application from it, and such alone, are truly useful. Thus history becomes what she ought to be, and what she has been sometimes called, " magistra vitae," the mistress, like philosophy of human life. If she is not this, she is at best " nuntia vetustatis," the gazette of antiquity, or a dry register of useless anecdotes. SUETONIUS says that TIBERIUS used to enquire of the grammarians, " quae mater Hecubae? quod Achillis „ nomen inter virgines fuisset? quid Syrenes „ cantare sint solitae?" SENECA mentions certain Greek authors, who examined very accurately, whether ANACREON loved wine or women best, whether SAPPHO was a common whore, with other points of equal importance: and I make no doubt but that a man, better acquainted than I have the honor to be with the learned persons of our own country, might find some who have discovered several anecdotes concerning the giant ALBION, concerning SAMOTHES the son of BRITO the grand-son of JAPHET, and concerning BRUTUS who led a colony into our island after the siege of Troy, as the others re-peopled it after the deluge. But ten millions of such anecdotes as these, though they were true; and complete authentic volumes of Egyptian or Chaldean, of Greek or Latin, of Gallic or British, of French or Saxon records, would be of no value in my sense, because of no use towards our improvement in wisdom and virtue; if they contained nothing more than dynasties and genealogies, and a bare mention of remarkable events in the order of time, like journals, chronological tables; or dry and meagre annals.

I SAY the same of all those modern compositions in which we find rather the heads of history, than any thing that deserves to be called history. Their authors are either abridgers or compilers. The first do neither honor to themselves nor good to mankind: for surely the abridger is in a form below the translator: and the book, at least the history, that wants to be abridged, does not deserve to be read. They have done anciently a great deal of hurt by substituting many a bad book in the place of a good one; and by giving occasion to men, who contented themselves with extracts and abridgments, to neglect and, through their neglect, to lose the invaluable originals: for which reason I curse CONSTANTINE PORPHYROGENETES as heartily as I do GREGORY. The second are of some use, as far as they contribute to preserve public acts, and dates, and the memory of great events. But they who are thus employed have seldom the means of knowing those private passages on which all public transactions depend, and as seldom the skill and the talents necessary to

put

put what they do know well together: they cannot see the working of the mine, but their industry collects the matter that is thrown out. It is the business, or it should be so, of others to separate the pure ore from the dross, to stamp it into coin, and to enrich not encumber mankind. When there are none sufficient to this task, there may be antiquaries, and there may be journalists or annalists, but there are no historians.

It is worth while to observe the progress that the Romans and the Greeks made towards history. The Romans had journalists or annalists from the very beginning of their state. In the sixth century, or very near it at soonest, they began to have antiquaries, and some attempts were made towards writing of history. I call these first historical productions attempts only or essays: and they were no more, neither among the Romans nor among the Greeks. " Graeci ipsi sic initio scripti-
„ tarunt ut noster CATO, ut PICTOR, ut PISO." It is ANTONY, not the triumvir, my lord, but his grandfather the famous orator, who says this in the second book of TULLY De oratore: he adds afterwards, " Itaque qualis apud Graecos
„ PHERECYDES, HELLANICUS, ACUSILAUS, alii-
„ que permulti, talis noster CATO, et PICTOR,
„ et PISO." I know that ANTONY speaks here strictly of defect of style and want of oratory. They were " tantummodo narratores, non exor-
„ natores," as he expresses himself: but as they wanted style and skill to write in such a manner as might answer all the ends of history, so they

G

wanted materials. PHERECYDES writ something about IPHIGENIA, and the festivals of BACCHUS. HELLANICUS was a poetical historian, and ACUSILAUS graved genealogies on plates of brass. PICTOR, who is called by LIVY "scriptorum „ antiquissimus," published, I think, some short annals of his own time. Neither he nor PISO could have sufficient materials for the history of Rome; nor CATO, I presume, even for the antiquities of Italy. The Romans, with the other people of that country, were then just rising out of barbarity, and growing acquainted with letters; for those that the Grecian colonies might bring into Sicily, and the southern parts of Italy, spread little, or lasted little, and made in the whole no figure. And whatever learning might have flourished among the ancient Etrurians, which was perhaps at most nothing better than augury, and divination, and superstitious rites, which were admired and cultivated in ignorant ages, even that was almost entirely worn out of memory. Pedants, who would impose all the traditions of the four first ages of Rome, for authentic history, have insisted much on certain annals, of which mention is made in the very place I have just now quoted. " Ab initio rerum Romanarum," says the same interlocutor, " usque ad P. MUCIUM pontificem
„ maximum, res omnes singulorum annorum
„ mandabat literis pontifex maximus, efferebatque
„ in album, et proponebat tabulam domi, potestas
„ ut esset populo cognoscendi; iidemque etiam
„ nunc annales maximi nominantur." But, my

lord, be pleased to take notice, that the very distinction I make is made here between a bare annalist and an historian: "erat historia nihil aliud," in these early days, "nisi annalium confectio." Take notice likewise, by the way, that LIVY, whose particular application it had been to search into this matter, affirms positively that the greatest part of all public and private monuments, among which he specifies these very annals, had been destroyed in the sack of Rome by the Gauls: and PLUTARCH cites CLODIUS for the same assertion, in the life of NUMA POMPILIUS. Take notice, in the last place, of that which is more immediately to our present purpose. These annals could contain nothing more than short minutes or memorandums hung up in a table at the pontiff's house, like the rules of the game in a billiard-room, and much such history as we have in the epitomes prefixed to the books of LIVY or of any other historian, in lapidary inscriptions, or in some modern almanacks. Materials for history they were no doubt, but scanty and insufficient; such as those ages could produce when writing and reading were accomplishments so uncommon, that the praetor was directed by law, clavum pangere, to drive a nail into the door of a temple, that the number of years might be reckoned by the number of nails. Such in short as we have in monkish annalists, and other ancient chroniclers of nations now in being; but not such as can entitle the authors of them to be called historians, nor can enable others to write history in that fulness in which it must be written to become a lesson of ethics and politics. The truth is, nations, like men, have their infancy: and the few passages of that time, which they retain, are not such as deserved most to be remembered; but such as, being most proportioned to that age, made the strongest impressions on their minds. In those nations that preserve their dominion long and grow up to manhood, the elegant as well as the necessary arts and sciences are improved to some degree of perfection: and history, that was at first intended only to record the names, or perhaps the general characters of some famous men, and to transmit in gross the remarkable events of every age to posterity, is raised to answer another, and a nobler end.

II. Thus it happened among the Greeks, but much more among the Romans, notwithstanding the prejudices in favor of the former even among the latter. I have sometimes thought that Virgil might have justly ascribed to his countrymen the praise of writing history better, as well as that of affording the noblest subjects for it, in those famous verses, * where the different excellencies of the two nations are so finely touched: but he would have weakened perhaps by lengthening, and have flattened the climax. Open Herodotus,

---

* Excudent alii spirantia mollius aera,
Credo equidem: vivos ducent de marmore vultus;
Orabunt causas melius: coelique meatus
Describent radio, et surgentia sidera dicent:
Tu regere imperio populos, Romane, memento:
Hae tibi erunt artes; pacisque imponere morem,
Parcere subjectis, et debellare superbos.

you are entertained by an agreeable story-teller, who meant to entertain, and nothing more. Read THUCYDIDES or XENOPHON, you are taught indeed as well as entertained: and the statesman or the general, the philosopher or the orator, speaks to you in every page. They wrote on subjects on which they were well informed, and they treated them fully: they maintained the dignity of history, and thought it beneath them to vamp up old traditions, like the writers of their age and country, and to be the trumpeters of a lying antiquity. The Cyropaedia of XENOPHON may be objected perhaps; but if he gave it for a romance, not an history, as he might for aught we can tell, it is out of the case: and if he gave it for an history, not a romance, I should prefer his authority to that of HERODOTUS or any other of his countrymen. But however this might be, and whatever merit we may justly ascribe to these two writers, who were almost single in their kind, and who treated but small portions of history; certain it is in general, that the levity as well as loquacity of the Greeks made them incapable of keeping up to the true standard of history: and even POLYBIUS and DIONYSIUS of Halicarnassus must bow to the great Roman authors. Many principal men of that commonwealth wrote memorials of their own actions and their own times: SYLLA, CAESAR, LABIENUS, POLLIO, AUGUSTUS, and others. What writers of memorials, what compilers of the materia historica were these? What genius was necessary to finish up the pictures that such masters had sketched? Rome afforded men that were equal to the task. Let the remains, the precious remains of Sallust, of Livy, and of Tacitus, witness this truth. When Tacitus wrote, even the appearances of virtue had been long proscribed, and taste was grown corrupt as well as manners. Yet history preserved her integrity, and her lustre. She preserved them in the writings of some whom Tacitus mentions, in none perhaps more than his own; every line of which out-weighs whole pages of such a rhetor as Famianus Strada I single him out among the moderns, because he had the foolish presumption to censure Tacitus, and to write history himself: and your lordship will forgive this short excursion in honor of a favorite author.

What a school of private and public virtue had been opened to us at the resurrection of learning, if the latter historians of the Roman commonwealth, and the first of the succeeding monarchy, had come down to us entire? The few that are come down, though broken and imperfect, compose the best body of history that we have, nay the only body of ancient history that deserves to be an object of study. It fails us indeed most at that remarkable and fatal period, where our reasonable curiosity is raised the highest. Livy employed five-and-forty books to bring his history down to the end of the sixth century, and the breaking out of the third Punic war: but he employed ninety-five to bring it down from thence to the death of Drusus; that is, through the course of one hundred and twenty or thirty years. APIAN, DION CASSIUS and others, nay even PLUTARCH included, make us but poor amends for what is loſt of LIVY. Among all the adventitious helps by which we endeavour to ſupply this loſs in ſome degree, the beſt are thoſe that we find ſcattered up and down in the works of TULLY. His Orations particularly, and his Letters, contain many curious anecdotes and inſtructive reflections, concerning the intrigues and machinations that were carried on againſt liberty, from CATILINE's conſpiracy to CAESAR's. The ſtate of the government, the conſtitution and temper of the ſeveral parties, and the characters of the principal perſons who figured at that time on the public ſtage, are to be ſeen there in a ſtronger and truer light than they would have appeared perhaps if he had writ purpoſely on this ſubject, and even in thoſe memorials which he ſomewhere promiſes ATTICUS to write. "Excudam aliquod Heraclidium opus, ,, quod lateat in theſauris tuis." He would hardly have unmasked in ſuch a work, as freely as in familiar occaſional letters, POMPEY, CATO, BRUTUS, nay himſelf; the four men of Rome, on whoſe praiſes he dwelt with the greateſt complacency. The age in which LIVY flouriſhed abounded with ſuch materials as theſe: they were freſh; they were authentic; it was eaſy to procure them, it was ſafe to employ them. How he did employ them in executing the ſecond part of his deſign, we may judge by his execution of the firſt: and, I own to your lordſhip, I ſhould be glad to exchange, if it were poffible, what we have of this hiftory for what we have not. Would you not be glad, my lord, to fee, in one ftupendous draught, the whole progrefs of that government from liberty to fervitude? the whole feries of caufes and effects, apparent and real, public and private? thofe which all men faw, and all good men lamented and oppofed at the time; and thofe which were fo difguifed to the prejudices, to the partialities of a divided people, and even to the corruption of mankind, that many did not, and that many could pretend they did not, difcern them, till it was too late to refift them? I am forry to fay it, this part of the Roman hiftory would be not only more curious and more authentic than the former, but of more immediate and more important application to the prefent ftate of Britain. But it is loft: the lofs is irreparable, and your lordfhip will not blame me for deploring it.

III. They who fet up for fcepticifm may not regret the lofs of fuch an hiftory: but this I will be bold to affert to them, that an hiftory muft be writ on this plan, and muft aim at leaft at thefe perfections, or it will anfwer fufficiently none of the intentions of hiftory. That it will not anfwer fufficiently the intention I have infifted upon in thefe letters, that of inftructing pofterity by the example of former ages, is manifeft: and I think it is as manifeft, that an hiftory cannot be faid even to relate faithfully, and inform us truly, that does not relate fully, and inform us of all that is neceffary to make a true judgment concerning the matters contained in it. Naked facts, without the causes that produced them and the circumstances that accompanied them, are not sufficient to characterise actions or counsels. The nice degrees of wisdom and of folly, of virtue and of vice, will not only be undiscoverable in them; but we must be very often unable to determine under which of these characters they fall in general. The sceptics I am speaking of are therefore guilty of this absurdity: the nearer an history comes to the true idea of history, the better it informs and the more it instructs us, the more worthy to be rejected it appears to them. I have said and allowed enough to content any reasonable man about the uncertainty of history. I have owned that the best are defective, and I will add in this place an observation which did not, I think, occur to me before. Conjecture is not always distinguished perhaps as it ought to be; so that an ingenious writer may sometimes do very innocently, what a malicious writer does very criminally as often as he dares, and as his malice requires it; he may account for events after they have happened, by a system of causes and conduct that did not really produce them, though it might possibly or even probably have produced them. But this observation, like several others, becomes a reason for examining and comparing authorities, and for preferring some, not for rejecting all. DAVILA, a noble historian surely, and one whom I should not scruple to confess equal in many respects to LIVY, as I should not scruple to prefer his countryman GUICCIARDIN to THUCYDIDES in every respect: DAVILA, my lord, was accused, from the first publication of his history, or at least was suspected, of too much refinement and subtilty, in developing the secret motives of actions, in laying the causes of events too deep, and deducing them often through a series of progressions too complicated, and too artiftly wrought. But yet the suspicious person who should reject this historian upon such general inducements as these, would have no grace to oppose his suspicions to the authority of the first duke of EPERNON, who had been an actor, and a principal actor too, in many of the scenes that DAVILA recites. GIRARD, secretary to this duke, and no contemptible biographer, relates, that this history came down to the place where the old man resided in Gascony, a little before his death; that he read it to him, that the duke confirmed the truth of the narrations in it, and seemed only surprised by what means the author could be so well informed of the most secret councils and measures of those times.

IV. I HAVE said enough on this head, and your lordship may be induced perhaps, by what I have said, to think with me, that such histories as these, whether ancient or modern, deserve alone to be studied. Let us leave the credulous learned to write history without materials, or to study those who do so; to wrangle about ancient traditions, and to ring different changes on the same set of bells. Let us leave the sceptics, in modern as well as ancient history, to triumph in the notable discovery of the ides of one month mistaken for the calends of another, or in the various dates and contradictory circumstances which they find in weekly gazettes and monthly mercuries. Whilst they are thus employed, your lordship and I will proceed, if you pleafe, to confider more clofely, than we have yet done, the rule mentioned above; that I mean of ufing difcernment and choice in the ftudy of the moft authentic hiftory, that of not wandering in the light, which is as neceffary as that of not groping in the dark.

MAN is the fubject of every hiftory; and to know him well, we muft fee him and confider him, as hiftory alone can prefent him to us, in every age, in every country, in every ftate, in life and in death. Hiftory therefore of all kinds, of civilized and uncivilized, of ancient and modern nations, in short of all hiftory, that defcends to a fufficient detail of human actions and characters, is ufeful to bring us acquainted with our fpecies, nay with ourfelves. To teach and to inculcate the general principles of virtue, and the general rules of wifdom and good policy, which refult from fuch details of actions and characters, comes for the moft part, and always fhould come, exprefsly and directly into the defign of thofe who are capable of giving fuch details: and therefore whilft they narrate as hiftorians, they hint often as philofophers; they put into our hands, as it were, on every proper occafion, the end of a clue, that ferves to remind us of fearching, and to guide us in the fearch of that truth which the example before us either eftablishes or illuftrates. If a writer neglects this part, we are able however to fupply his neglect by our own attention and industry: and when he gives us a good history of Peruvians or Mexicans, of Chinese or Tartars, of Muscovites or Negroes, we may blame him, but we must blame ourselves much more, if we do not make it a good lesson of philosophy. This being the general use of history, it is not to be neglected. Every one may make it, who is able to read and to reflect on what he reads: and every one who makes it will find, in his degree, the benefit that arises from an early acquaintance contracted in this manner with mankind. We are not only passengers or sojourners in this world, but we are absolute strangers at the first steps we make in it. Our guides are often ignorant, often unfaithful. By this map of the country, which history spreads before us, we may learn, if we please, to guide ourselves. In our journey through it, we are beset on every side. We are besieged sometimes even in our strongest holds. Terrors and temptations, conducted by the passions of other men, assault us: and our own passions, that correspond with these, betray us. History is a collection of the journals of those who have travelled through the same country, and been exposed to the same accidents: and their good and their ill success are equally instructive. In this pursuit of knowledge an immense field is opened to us: general histories, sacred and prophane; the histories of particular countries, particular events, particular orders, particular men; memorials, anecdotes, travels. But we must not ramble in this field without discernment or choice, nor even with these must we ramble too long.

As to the choice of authors, who have writ on all thefe various fubjects, fo much has been faid by learned men concerning all thofe that deferve attention, and their feveral characters are fo well eftablished, that it would be a fort of pedantic affectation to lead your lordfhip through fo voluminous, and at the fame time fo eafy, a detail. I pafs it over therefore in order to obferve, that as foon as we have taken this general view of mankind, and of the courfe of human affairs in different ages and different parts of the world, we ought to apply, and, the fhortnefs of human life confidered, to confine ourfelves almoft entirely, in our ftudy of hiftory, to fuch hiftories as have an immediate relation to our profeffions, or to our rank and fituation in the fociety to which we belong. Let me inftance in the profeffion of divinity, as the nobleft and the moft important.

(1) I HAVE faid fo much concerning the share which divines of all religions have taken in the corruption of hiftory, that I should have anathemas pronounced againft me, no doubt, in the eaft and the weft, by the dairo, the mufti, and the pope, if thefe letters were fubmitted to ecclefiaftical cenfure; for furely, my lord, the clergy have a better title, than the fons of Apollo, to be called "genus irritabile vatum." What would it be, if I went about to shew, how many of the chriftian clergy abufe, by mifreprefentation and falfe quotation, the hiftory they can no longer corrupt? And yet this task would not be even to me, an hard one. But as I mean to fpeak in this place of

LETTER V.

christian divines alone, so I mean to speak of such of them particularly as may be called divines without any sneer; of such of them, for some such I think there are, as believe themselves, and would have mankind believe; not for temporal but spiritual interest, not for the sake of the clergy, but for the sake of mankind. Now it has been long matter of astonishment to me, how such persons as these could take so much silly pains to establish mystery on metaphysics, revelation on philosophy, and matters of fact on abstract reasoning? A religion founded on the authority of a divine mission, confirmed by prophesies and miracles, appeals to facts: and the facts must be proved as all other facts that pass for authentic are proved; for faith, so reasonable after this, proof is absurd before it. If they are thus proved, the religion will prevail without the assistance of so much profound reasoning: if they are not thus proved, the authority of it will sink in the world even with this assistance. The divines object in their disputes with atheists, and they object very justly, that these men require improper proofs; proofs that are not suited to the nature of the subject, and then cavil that such proofs are not furnished. But what then do they mean, to fall into the same absurdity themselves in their disputes with theists, and to din improper proofs in ears that are open to proper proofs? The matter is of great moment, my lord, and I make no excuse for the zeal which obliges me to dwell a little on it. A serious and honest application to the study of ecclesiastical history, and every part of prophane history and chronology relative to it, is incumbent on such reverend persons as are here spoken of, on a double account: because history alone can furnish the proper proofs, that the religion they teach is of God; and because the unfair manner, in which these proofs have been and are daily furnished, creates prejudices, and gives advantages against christianity that require to be removed. No scholar will dare to deny, that false history, as well as sham miracles, has been employed to propagate christianity formerly: and whoever examines the writers of our own age will find the same abuse of history continued. Many and many instances of this abuse might be produced. It is grown into custom, writers copy one another, and the mistake that was committed, or the falshood that was invented by one, is adopted by hundreds.

ABBADIE says in his famous book, that the gospel of St. MATTHEW is cited by CLEMENS bishop of Rome, a disciple of the Apostles; that BARNABAS cites it in his epistle; that IGNATIUS and POLYCARPE receive it; and that the same fathers, that give testimony for MATTHEW, give it likewise for MARK. Nay your lordship will find, I believe, that the present bishop of London, in his third pastoral letter, speaks to the same effect. I will not trouble you nor myself with any more instances of the same kind. Let this, which occurred to me as I was writing, suffice. It may well suffice; for I presume the fact advanced by the minister and the bishop is a mistake. If the fathers of the first century do mention some passages that are agreeable to what we read in our evangelists, will it follow that these fathers had the same gospels before them? To say so is a manifest abuse of history, and quite inexcusable in writers that knew, or should have known, that these fathers made use of other gospels, wherein such passages might be contained, or they might be preserved in unwritten tradition. Besides which I could almost venture to affirm that these fathers of the first century do not expressly name the gospels we have of MATTHEW, MARK, LUKE, and JOHN. To the two reasons that have been given why those who make divinity their profession should study history, particularly ecclesiastical history, with an honest and serious application; in order to support christianity against the attacks of unbelievers, and to remove the doubts and prejudices that the unfair proceedings of men of their own order have raised in minds candid but not implicit, willing to be informed but curious to examine; to these, I say, we may add another consideration that seems to me of no small importance. Writers of the Roman religion have attempted to shew, that the text of the holy writ is on many accounts insufficient to be the sole criterion of orthodoxy: I apprehend too that they have shewn it. Sure I am that experience, from the first promulgation of christianity to this hour, shews abundantly with how much ease and success the most opposite, the most extravagant, nay the most impious opinions, and the most contradictory faiths, may be founded on the same

text,

text, and plausibly defended by the same authority. Writers of the reformed religion have erected their batteries against tradition; and the only difficulty they had to encounter in this enterprise lay in levelling and pointing their cannon so as to avoid demolishing in one common ruin, the traditions they retain, and those they reject. Each side has been employed to weaken the cause and explode the system of his adversary: and, whilst they have been so employed, they have jointly laid their axes to the root of christianity; for thus men will be apt to reason upon what they have advanced. " If the text has not that authenticity, clearness, and precision which are necessary to establish it as a divine and a certain rule of faith and practice; and if the tradition of the church, from the first ages of it till the days of LUTHER and CALVIN, has been corrupted itself, and has served to corrupt the faith and practice of christians; there remains at this time no standard at all of christianity. By consequence either this religion was not originally of divine institution, or else God has not provided effectually for preserving the genuine purity of it, and the gates of hell have actually prevailed, in contradiction to his promise, against the church." The best effect of this reasoning that can be hoped for, is, that men should fall into theism, and subscribe to the first proposition: he must be worse than an atheist who can affirm the last. The dilemma is terrible, my lord. Party-zeal and private interest have formed it: the common interest of christianity

LETTER V.

is deeply concerned to solve it. Now, I presume, it can never be solved without a more accurate examination, not only of the christian but of the jewish system, than learned men have been hitherto impartial enough and sagacious enough to take, or honest enough to communicate. Whilst the authenticity and sense of the text of the Bible remain as disputable, and whilst the tradition of the church remains as problematical, to say no worse, as the immense labors of the christian divines in several communions have made them appear to be; christianity may lean on the civil and ecclesiastical power, and be supported by the forcible influence of education: but the proper force of religion, that force which subdues the mind and awes the conscience by conviction, will be wanting.

I HAD reason therefore to produce divinity, as one instance of those professions that require a particular application to the study of some particular parts of history: and since I have said so much on the subject in my zeal for christianity, I will add this further. The resurrection of letters was a fatal period; the christian system has been attacked, and wounded too, very severely since that time. The defence has been better made indeed by modern divines, than it had been by ancient fathers and apologists. The moderns have invented new methods of defence, and have abandoned some posts that were not tenable: but still there are others, in defending which they lie under great disadvantages. Such are various facts, piously believed in former times, but on which the truth

Of the STUDY of HISTORY.   115

of christianity has been rested very imprudently in more enlightened ages; because the falsity of some, and the gross improbability of others are so evident, that, instead of answering the purpose for which they were invented, they have rendered the whole tenor of ecclesiastical history and tradition precarious, ever since a strict but just application of the rules of criticism has been made to them. I touch these things lightly; but if your lordship reflects upon them, you will find reason perhaps to think as I do, that it is high time the clergy in all christian communions should join their forces, and establish those historical facts, which are the foundations of the whole system, on clear and unquestionable historical authority, such as they require in all cases of moment from others; reject candidly what cannot be thus established; and pursue their enquiries in the same spirit of truth through all the ages of the church; without any regard to historians, fathers, or councils, more than they are strictly entitled to on the face of what they have transmitted to us, on their own consistency, and on the concurrence of other authority. Our pastors would be thus, I presume, much better employed than they generally are. Those of the clergy who make religion merely a trade, who regard nothing more than the subsistence it affords them, or in higher life the wealth and power they enjoy by the means of it, may say to themselves, that it will last their time, or that policy and reason of state will preserve the form of a church when the spirit of religion is

H 2

extinct. But those whom I mentioned above, those who act for spiritual not temporal ends, and are desirous that men should believe and practise the doctrines of christianity, as well as go to church and pay tithes, will feel and own the weight of such considerations as these; and agree, that however the people have been, and may be still amused, yet christianity has been in decay ever since the resurrection of letters; and that it cannot be supported as it was supported before that aera, nor by any other way than that which I propose, and which a due application to the study of history, chronology, and criticism, would enable our divines to pursue, no doubt, with success.

I MIGHT instance, in other professions, the obligation men lie under of applying themselves to certain parts of history, and I can hardly forbear doing it in that of the law; in it's nature the noblest and most beneficial to mankind, in it's abuse and debasement the most sordid and the most pernicious. A lawyer now is nothing more, I speak of ninety-nine in an hundred at least, to use some of TULLY's words, "nisi leguleius quidam „ cautus, et acutus praeco actionum, cantor for- „ mularum, auceps syllabarum." But there have been lawyers that were orators, philosophers, historians; there have been BACONS and CLARENDONS, my lord. There will be none such any more, till, in some better age, true ambition or the love of fame prevails over avarice; and till men find leisure and encouragement to prepare themselves for the exercise of this profession, by climbing up to the "vantage ground," so my lord BACON calls it, of science: instead of groveling all their lives below, in a mean but gainful application to all the little arts of chicane. Till this happen, the profession of the law will scarce deserve to be ranked among the learned professions: and whenever it happens, one of the vantage grounds, to which men must climb, is metaphysical, and the other, historical knowledge. They must pry into the secret recesses of the human heart, and become well acquainted with the whole moral world, that they may discover the abstract reason of all laws: and they must trace the laws of particular states, especially of their own, from the first rough sketches to the more perfect draughts; from the first causes or occasions that produced them, through all the effects, good and bad, that they produced. But I am running insensibly into a subject, which would detain me too long from one that relates more immediately to your lordship, and with which I intend to conclude this long letter.

(2) I PASS from the consideration of those professions to which particular parts or kinds of history seem to belong: and I come to speak of the study of history, as a necessary mean to prepare men for the discharge of that duty which they owe to their country, and which is common to all the members of every society that is constituted according to the rules of right reason, and with a due regard to the common good. I have met,

in St. Real's works, or some other French book, with a ridicule cast on private men who make history a political study, or who apply themselves in any manner to affairs of state. But the reflection is too general. In governments so arbitrary by their constitution, that the will of the prince is not only the supreme but the sole law, it is so far from being a duty that it may be dangerous, and must be impertinent in men, who are not called by the prince to the administration of public affairs, to concern themselves about it, or to fit themselves for it. The sole vocation there is the favor of the court; and whatever designation God makes by the talents he bestows, though it may serve, which it seldom ever does, to direct the choice of the prince, yet I presume that it cannot become a reason to particular men, or create a duty on them, to devote themselves to the public service. Look on the Turkish government. See a fellow taken, from rowing in a common passage-boat, by the caprice of the prince: see him invested next day with all the power the soldans took under the caliphs, or the mayors of the palace under the successors of Clovis: see a whole empire governed by the ignorance, inexperience, and arbitrary will of this tyrant, and a few other subordinate tyrants, as ignorant and unexperienced as himself. In France indeed, though an absolute government, things go a little better. Arts and sciences are encouraged, and here and there an example may be found of a man who has risen by some extraordinary talents, amidst

Of the STUDY of HISTORY. 119

innumerable examples of men who have arrived at the greatest honors and highest posts by no other merit than that of assiduous fawning, attendances, or of skill in some despicable puerile amusement; in training wasps, for instance, to take regular flights like hawks, and stoop at flies. The nobility of France, like the children of tribute among the ancient Saracens and modern Turks, are set apart for wars. They are bred to make love, to hunt, and to fight: and, if any of them should acquire knowledge superior to this, they would acquire that which might be prejudicial to themselves, but could not become beneficial to their country. The affairs of state are trusted to other hands. Some have risen to them by drudging long in business: some have been made ministers almost in the cradle: and the whole power of the government has been abandoned to others in the dotage of life. There is a monarchy, an absolute monarchy too, I mean that of China, wherein the administration of the government is carried on, under the direction of the prince, ever since the dominion of the Tartars has been established, by several classes of Mandarins, and according to the deliberation and advice of several orders of councils: the admission to which classes and orders depends on the abilities of the candidates, as their rise in them depends on the behaviour they hold, and the improvements they make afterwards. Under such a government, it is neither impertinent nor ridiculous, in any of the subjects who are invited by their circumstances, or pushed to it by their talents, to make the history of their own and of other countries a political study, and to fit themselves by this and all other ways for the service of the public. It is not dangerous neither; or an honor, that outweighs the danger, attends it: since private men have a right by the ancient constitution of this government, as well as councils of state, to represent to the prince the abuses of his administration. But still men have not there the same occasion to concern themselves in the affairs of the state, as the nature of a free government gives to the members of it. In our own country, for in our own the forms of a free government at least are hitherto preserved, men are not only designed for the public service by the circumstances of their situation, and their talents, all which may happen, in others: but they are designed to it by their birth in many cases, and in all cases they may dedicate themselves to this service, and take, in different degrees, some share in it, whether they are called to it by the prince or no. In absolute governments, all public service is to the prince, and he nominates all those that serve the public. In free governments, there is a distinct and a principal service due to the state. Even the king, of such a limited monarchy as ours, is but the first servant of the people. Among his subjects, some are appointed by the constitution, and others are elected by the people, to carry on the exercice of the legislative power jointly with him, and to controul the executive power independently on him. Thus your lordship is born a member of that order of men, in whom a third part of the supreme power of the government resides: and your right to the exercise of the power belonging to this order not being yet opened, you are chosen into another body of men, who have a different power and a different constitution, but who possess another third part of the supreme legislative authority, for as long a time as the commission or trust delegated to them by the people lasts. Free-men, who are neither born to the first, nor elected to the last, have a right however to complain, to represent, to petition, and, I add, even to do more in cases of the utmost extremity. For sure there cannot be a greater absurdity, than to affirm, that the people have a remedy in resistance, when their prince attempts to enslave them; but that they have none, when their representatives sell themselves and them.

THE sum of what I have been saying is, that, in free governments, the public service is not confined to those whom the prince appoints to different posts in the administration under him; that there the care of the state is the care of multitudes; that many are called to it in a particular manner by their rank, and by other circumstances of their situation; and that even those whom the prince appoints are not only answerable to him, but like him, and before him, to the nation, for their behaviour in their several posts. It can never be impertinent nor ridiculous therefore in such a country, whatever it might be in the

LETTER V.

abbot of St. Real's, which was Savoy I think; or in Peru, under the Incas, where, Garcilasso de la Vega says, it was lawful for none but the nobility to study — for men of all degrees to instruct themselves in those affairs wherein they may be actors, or judges of those that act, or controulers of those that judge. On the contrary, it is incumbent on every man to instruct himself, as well as the means and opportunities he has permit, concerning the nature and interests of the governments, and those rights and duties that belong to him, or to his superiors, or to his inferiors. This in general; but in particular, it is certain that the obligations under which we lie to serve our country increase, in proportion to the ranks we hold, and the other circumstances of birth, fortune, and situation that call us to this service; and, above all, to the talents which God has given us to perform it.

It is in this view, that I shall address to your lordship whatever I have further to say on the study of history.

LETTER VI.

From what period modern history is peculiarly useful to the service of our country, viz.

From the end of the fifteenth century to the present.

The division of this into three particular periods:

In order to a sketch of the history and state of Europe from that time.

Since then you are, my lord, by your birth, by the nature of our government, and by the talents God has given you, attached for life to the service of your country; since genius alone cannot enable you to go through this service with honor to yourself and advantage to your country, whether you support or whether you oppose the administrations that arise; since a great stock of knowledge, acquired betimes and continually improved, is necessary to this end; and since one part of this stock must be collected from the study of history, as the other part is to be gained by observation and experience; I come now to speak to your lordship of such history as has an immediate relation to the great duty and business of your life, and of the method to be observed in this study. The notes I have by me, which were

LETTER VI.

of some little use thus far, serve me no farther, and I have no books to consult. No matter; I shall be able to explain my thoughts without their assistance, and less liable to be tedious. I hope to be as full and as exact on memory alone, as the manner in which I shall treat the subject requires me to be.

I SAY then, that however closely affairs are linked together in the progression of governments, and how much soever events that follow are dependent on those that precede, the whole connexion diminishes to sight as the chain lengthens; till at last it seems to be broken, and the links that are continued from that point bear no proportion nor any similitude to the former. I would not be understood to speak only of those great changes, that are wrought by a concurrence of extraordinary events; for instance the expulsion of one nation, the destruction of one government, and the establishment of another: but even of those that are wrought in the same governments and among the same people, slowly and almost imperceptibly, by the necessary effects of time, and flux condition of human affairs. When such changes as these happen in several states about the same time, and consequently affect other states by their vicinity, and by many different relations which they frequently bear to one another; then is one of those periods formed, at which the chain spoken of is so broken as to have little or no real or visible connexion with that which we see continue. A new situation, different from the former, begets new interests in the same proportion of difference; not in this or that particular state alone, but in all those that are concerned by vicinity or other relations, as I said just now, in one general system of policy. New interests beget new maxims of government, and new methods of conduct. These, in their turns, beget new manners, new habits, new customs. The longer this new constitution of affairs continues, the more will this difference increase: and although some analogy may remain long between what preceded and what succeeded such a period, yet will this analogy soon become an object of mere curiosity, not of profitable enquiry. Such a period therefore is, in the true sense of the words, an epocha or an aera, a point of time at which you stop, or from which you reckon forward. I say forward; because we are not to study in the present case, as chronologers compute, backward. Should we persist to carry our researches much higher, and to push them even to some other period of the same kind, we should misemploy our time; the causes then laid having spent themselves, the series of effects derived from them being over, and our concern in both consequently at an end. But a new system of causes and effects, that subsists in our time, and whereof our conduct is to be a part, arising at the last period, and all that passes in our time being dependent on what has passed since that period, or being immediately relative to it, we are extremely concerned to be well informed about all those passages. To be entirely ignorant: about the ages that precede this aera would be shameful. Nay some indulgence may be had to a temperate curiosity in the review of them. But to be learned about them is a ridiculous affectation in any man who means to be useful to the present age. Down to this aera let us read history: from this aera, and down to our own time, let us study it.

THE end of the fifteenth century seems to be just such a period as I have been describing, for those who live in the eighteenth, and who inhabit the western parts of Europe. A little before, or a little after this point of time, all those events happened, and all those revolutions began, that have produced so vast a change in the manners, customs, and interests of particular nations, and in the whole policy, ecclesiastical and civil, of these parts of the world. I must descend here into some detail, not of histories, collections, or memorials; for all these are well enough known: and though the contents are in the heads of few, the books are in the hands of many. But instead of shewing your lordship where to look, I shall contribute more to your entertainment and instruction, by marking out, as well as my memory will serve me to do it, what you are to look for, and by furnishing a kind of clue to your studies. I shall give, according to custom, the first place to religion.

A view of the ecclesiastical government of Europe from the beginning of the sixteenth century.

OBSERVE then, my lord, that the demolition of the papal throne was not attempted with success till the beginning of the sixteenth century. If you are curious to cast your eyes back, you will find BERENGER in the eleventh, who was soon silenced; ARNOLDUS in the same, who was soon hanged; VALDO in the twelfth, and our WICKLIFF in the fourteenth, as well as others perhaps whom I do not recollect. Sometimes the doctrines of the church were alone attacked; and sometimes the doctrine, the discipline, and the usurpations of the pope. But little fires, kindled in corners of a dark world, were soon stifled by that great abettor of christian unity, the hangman. When they spread and blazed out, as in the case of the Albigeois and of the Hussites, armies were raised to extinguish them by torrents of blood; and such saints as DOMINIC, with the crucifix in their hands, instigated the troops to the utmost barbarity. Your lordship will find that the church of Rome was maintained by such charitable and salutary means, among others, till the period spoken of: and you will be curious, I am sure, to enquire how this period came to be more fatal to her than any former conjuncture. A multitude of circumstances, which you will easily trace in the histories of the fifteenth and sixteenth centuries, to go no further back, concurred to bring about this great event: and a multitude of others

as eafy to be traced, concurred to hinder the demolition from becoming total, and to prop the tottering fabric. Among thefe circumftances, there is one lefs complicated and more obvious than others, which was of principal and univerfal influence. The art of printing had been invented about forty or fifty years before the period we fix: from that time, the refurrection of letters haftened on a-pace; and at this period they had made great progrefs, and were cultivated with great application. MAHOMET the fecond drove them out of the eaft into the weft; and the popes proved worfe politicians than the mufties in this refpect. NICHOLAS the fifth encouraged learning and learned men. SIXTUS the fourth was, if I miftake not, a great collector of books at leaft: and LEO the tenth was the patron of every art and fcience. The magicians themfelves broke the charm by which they had bound mankind for fo many ages: and the adventure of that knight-errant, who, thinking himfelf happy in the arms of a celeftial nymph, found that he was the miferable flave of an infernal hag, was in fome fort renewed. As foon as the means of acquiring and fpreading information grew common, it is no wonder that a fyftem was unravelled, which could not have been woven with fuccefs in any ages, but thofe of grofs ignorance, and credulous fuperftition. I might point out to your lordship many other immediate caufes, fome general like this that I have mentioned, and fome particular. The great fchifm, for inftance, that ended in the
beginning

beginning of the fifteenth century, and in the council of Constance, had occasioned prodigious scandal. Two or three vicars of CHRIST, two or three infallible heads of the church, roaming about the world at a time, furnished matter of ridicule as well as scandal: and whilst they appealed, for so they did in effect, to the laity, and reproached and excommunicated one another, they taught the world what to think of the institution, as well as exercise of the papal authority. The same lesson was taught by the council of Pisa, that preceded, and by that of Basle, that followed the Council of Constance. The horrid crimes of ALEXANDER the sixth, the sawcy ambition of JULIUS the second, the immense profusion and scandalous exactions of LEO the tenth; all these events and characters, following in a continued series from the beginning of one century, prepared the way for the revolution that happened in the beginning of the next. The state of Germany, the state of England, and that of the North, were particular causes, in these several countries, of this revolution. Such were many remarkable events that happened about the same time, and a little before it, in these and in other nations; and such were likewise the characters of many of the princes of that age, some of whom favored the reformation, like the elector of Saxony, on a principle of conscience; and most of whom favored it, just as others opposed it, on a principle of interest. This your lordship will discover manifestly to have been the case; and

LETTER VI.

the sole difference you will find between HENRY the eighth and FRANCIS the first, one of whom separated from the pope, as the other adhered to him, is this: HENRY the eighth divided, with the secular clergy and his people, the spoil of the pope, and his satellites, the monks: FRANCIS the first divided, with the pope, the spoil of his clergy, secular and regular, and of his people. With the same impartial eye that your lordship surveys the abuses of religion, and the corruptions of the church as well as court of Rome, which brought on the reformation at this period; you will observe the characters and conduct of those who began, who propagated, and who favored the reformation: and from your observation of these, as well as of the unsystematical manner in which it was carried on at the same time in various places, and of the want of concert, nay even of charity, among the reformers, you will learn what to think of the several religions that unite in their opposition to the Roman, and yet hate one another most heartily; what to think of the several sects that have sprouted, like suckers, from the same great roots; and what the true principles are of protestant ecclesiastical policy. This policy had no being till LUTHER made his establishment in Germany; till ZWINGLIUS began another in Swisserland, which CALVIN carried on, and, like AMERICUS VESPUCIUS who followed CHRISTOPHER COLUMBUS, robbed the first adventurer of his honor; and till the reformation in our country was perfected under EDWARD the sixth and ELIZABETH. Even popish ecclefiaftical policy is no longer the fame fince that aera. His holinefs is no longer at the head of the whole weftern church: and to keep the part that adheres to him, he is obliged to loofen their chains, and to lighten his yoke. The fpirit and pretenfions of his court are the fame, but not the power. He governs by expedient and management more, and by authority lefs. His decrees and his briefs are in danger of being refufed, explained away, or evaded, unlefs he negociates their acceptance before he gives them, governs in concert with his flock, and feeds his sheep according to their humor and intereft. In short, his excommunications, that made the greateft emperors tremble, are defpifed by the loweft members of his own communion; and the remaining attachment to him has been, from this aera, rather a political expedient to preferve an appearance of unity, than a principle of confcience; whatever fome bigotted princes may have thought, whatever ambitious prelates and hireling fcribblers may have taught, and whatever a people, worked up to enthufiafm by fanatical preachers, may have acted. Proofs of this would be eafy to draw, not only from the conduct of fuch princes as FERDINAND the firft and MAXIMILIAN the fecond, who could fcarce be efteemed papifts though they continued in the pope's communion: but even from that of princes who perfecuted their proteftant fubjects with great violence. Enough has been faid, I think to shew your lordship how little need there is of going up higher than the beginning of the sixteenth century in the study of history, to acquire all the knowledge necessary at this time in ecclesiastical policy, or in civil policy as far as it is relative to this. Historical monuments of this sort are in every man's hand, the facts are sufficiently verified, and the entire scenes lie open to our observation: even that scene of solemn refined banter exhibited in the council of Trent, imposes on no man who reads PAOLO, as well as PALLAVICINI, and the letters of VARGAS.

A view of the civil government of Europe in the beginning of the sixteenth century.

I. In FRANCE.

A VERY little higher need we go, to observe those great changes in the civil constitutions of the principal nations of Europe, in the partition of power among them, and by consequence in the whole system of European policy, which have operated so strongly for more than two centuries, and which operate still. I will not affront the memory of our HENRY the seventh so much as to compare him to LEWIS the eleventh: and yet I perceive some resemblance between them; which would perhaps appear greater, if PHILIP of Commines had wrote the History of HENRY as well as that of LEWIS; or if my lord BACON had wrote that of LEWIS as well as that of HENRY. This prince came to the crown of England a little before the close of the fifteenth century: and LEWIS began his reign in France about twenty years sooner. These reigns make remarkable periods in the histories of both nations. To reduce the power, privileges, and possessions of the nobility, and to increase the wealth and authority of the crown, was the principal object of both. In this their success was so great, that the constitutions of the two governments have had, since that time, more resemblance, in name and in form than in reality, to the constitutions that prevailed before. LEWIS the eleventh was the first, say the French, " qui „ mit les rois hors de page." The independency of the nobility had rendered the state of his predecessors very dependent, and their power precarious. They were the sovereigns of great vassals; but these vassals were so powerful, that one of them was sometimes able, and two or three of them always, to give law to the sovereign. Before LEWIS came to the crown, the English had been driven out of their possessions in France, by the poor character of HENRY the sixth, the domestic troubles of his reign, and the defection of the house of Burgundy from his alliance, much more than by the ability of CHARLES the seventh, who seems to have been neither a greater hero nor a greater politician than HENRY the sixth; and even than by the vigor and union of the French nobility in his service. After LEWIS came to the crown, EDWARD the fourth made a shew of carrying the war again into France; but he soon returned home, and your lordship will not be at a loss to find much better reasons for his doing so, in the situation of his affairs and the characters of his allies, than those which PHILIP of Commines draws from the artifice of LEWIS, from his good cheer, and his pensions. Now from this time our pretensions on France were in effect given up: and CHARLES the bold, the last prince of the house of Burgundy, being killed, LEWIS had no vassal able to molest him. He re-united the dutchy of Burgundy and Artois to his crown, he acquired Provence by gift, and his son Britany by marriage: and thus France grew, in the course of a few years, into that great and compact body which we behold at this time. The History of France before this period, is like that of Germany, a complicated history of several states and several interests; sometimes concurring like members of the same monarchy, and sometimes warring on one another. Since this period, the history of France is the history of one state under a more uniform and orderly government; the history of a monarchy wherein the prince is possessor of some, as well as lord of all the great fiefs: and, the authority of many tyrants centering in one, though the people are not become more free, yet the whole system of domestic policy is entirely changed. Peace at home is better secured, and the nation grown fitter to carry war abroad. The governors of great provinces and of strong fortresses have opposed their king, and taken arms against his authority and commission since that time: but yet there is no more ressemblance between the authority and pretensions of these governors, or the nature and occasions of these disputes, and the authority and pretensions of the vassals of the crown in former days, or the nature and occasions of their disputes with the prince and with one another, than there is between the ancient and the present peers of France. In a word, the constitution is so altered, that any knowledge we can acquire about it, in the history that precedes this period, will serve to little purpose in our study of the history that follows it, and to less purpose still in assisting us to judge of what passes in the present age. The kings of France since that time, more masters at home, have been able to exert themselves more abroad: and they began to do so immediately; for CHARLES the eighth, son and successor of LEWIS the eleventh, formed great designs of foreign conquests, though they were disappointed by his inability, by the levity of the nation, and by other causes. LEWIS the twelfth and FRANCIS the first, but especially FRANCIS, meddled deep in the affairs of Europe: and though the superior genius of FERDINAND called the catholic, and the star of CHARLES the fifth prevailed against them, yet the efforts they made shew sufficiently how the strength and importance of this monarchy were increased in their time. From whence we may date likewise the rivalship of the house of France, for we may reckon that of Valois and that of Bourbon as one upon this occasion, and the house of Austria; that continues at this day, and that has cost so much blood and so much treasure in the course of it.

LETTER VI.

II. In ENGLAND.

THOUGH the power and influence of the nobility funk in the great change that began under HENRY the feventh in England, as they did in that which began under LEWIS the eleventh in France; yet the new conflitutions that thefe changes produced were very different. In France the lords alone loft, the king alone gained; the clergy held their poffeffions and their immunities, and the people remained in a ftate of mitigated flavery. But in England the people gained as well as the crown. The commons had already a fhare in the legiflature; fo that the power and influence of the lords being broken by HENRY the feventh, and the property of the commons increafing by the fale that his fon made of churchlands, the power of the latter increafed of courfe by this change in a conflitution, the forms whereof were favorable to them. The union of the rofes put an end to the civil wars of York and Lancafter, that had fucceeded thofe we commonly call the barons wars, and the humor of warring in France, that had lafted near four hundred years under the Normans and Plantagenets for plunder as well as conqueft, was fpent. Our temple of JANUS was fhut by HENRY the feventh. We neither laid wafte our own nor other countries any longer: and wife laws and a wife government changed infenfibly the manners, and gave a new turn to the fpirit of our people. We were no longer the free-booters we had been. Our nation maintained her reputation in arms whenever the public interest or the public authority required it; but war ceased to be; what it had been, our principal and almost our sole profession. The arts of peace prevailed among us. We became husbandmen, manufacturers, and merchants, and we emulated neighbouring nations in literature. It is from this time that we ought to study the history of our country, my lord, with the utmost application. We are not much concerned to know with critical accuracy what were the ancient forms of our parliaments, concerning which, however, there is little room for dispute from the reign of HENRY the third at least; nor in short the whole system of our civil constitution before HENRY the seventh, and of our ecclesiastical constitution before HENRY the eighth. But he who has not studied and acquired a thorough knowledge of them both, from these periods down to the present time, in all the variety of events by which they have been affected, will be very unfit to judge or to take care of either. Just as little are we concerned to know, in any nice detail, what the conduct of our princes, relatively to their neighbours on the continent, was before this period, and at a time when the partition of power and a multitude of other circumstances rendered the whole political system of Europe so vastly different from that which has existed since. But he who has not traced this conduct from the period we fix, down to the present age, wants a principal part of the knowledge that every English minister of state should have. Ignorance in the respects here spoken of is the less pardonable, because we have more, and more authentic, means of information concerning this, than concerning any other period. Anecdotes enow to glut the curiosity of some persons, and to silence all the captious cavils of others, will never be furnished by any portion of history; nor indeed can they according to the nature and course of human affairs: but he who is content to read and observe, like a senator and a statesman, will find in our own and in foreign historians as much information as he wants, concerning the affairs of our island, her fortune at home and her conduct abroad, from the fifteenth century to the eighteenth. I refer to foreign historians, as well as to our own, for this series of our own history; not only because it is reasonable to see in what manner the historians of other countries have related the transactions wherein we have been concerned, and what judgment they have made of our conduct, domestic and foreign, but for another reason likewise. Our nation has furnished as ample and as important matter, good and bad, for history, as any nation under the sun: and yet we must yield the palm in writing history most certainly to the Italians and to the French, and, I fear, even to the Germans. The only two pieces of history we have, in any respect to be compared with the ancient, are, the reign of HENRY the seventh by my lord BACON, and the History of our civil war in the laſt century by your noble anceſtor my lord chancellor CLARENDON. But we have no general hiſtory to be compared with ſome of other countries: neither have we, which I lament much more, particular hiſtories, except the two I have mentioned, nor writers of memorials, nor collectors of monuments and anecdotes, to vie in number or in merit with thoſe that foreign nations can boaſt; from COMMINES, GUICCIARDIN, DU BELLAY, PAOLO, DAVILA, THUANUS, and a multitude of others, down through the whole period that I propoſe to your lordſhip. But although this be true to our ſhame; yet it is true likewiſe that we want no neceſſary means of information. They lie open to our induſtry and our diſcernment. Foreign writers are for the moſt part ſcarce worth reading when they ſpeak of our domeſtic affairs: nor are our Engliſh writers for the moſt part of greater value when they ſpeak of foreign affairs. In this mutual defect, the writers of other countries are, I think, more excuſable than ours: for the nature of our government, the political principles in which we are bred, our diſtinct intereſt as iſlanders, and the complicated various intereſts and humors of our parties, all theſe are ſo peculiar to ourſelves, and ſo different from the notions, manners and habits of other nations, that it is not wonderful they ſhould be puzzled or ſhould fall into error, when they undertake to give relations of events that reſult from all theſe, or to paſs any judgment upon them. But all theſe hiſtorians are mutually

LETTER VI.

defective, so they mutually supply each other's defects. We must compare them therefore, make use of our discernment, and draw our conclusions from both. If we proceed in this manner, we have an ample fund of history in our power, from whence to collect sufficient authentic information; and we must proceed in this manner, even with our own historians of different religions, sects, and parties, or run the risque of being misled by domestic ignorance and prejudice in this case, as well as by foreign ignorance and prejudice in the other.

III. In SPAIN and the Empire.

SPAIN figured little in Europe till the latter part of the fifteenth century; till Castile and Arragon were united by the marriage of FERDINAND and ISABELLA; till the total expulsion of the Moors, and till the discovery of the West-Indies. After this, not only Spain took a new form, and grew into immense power; but, the heir of FERDINAND and ISABELLA being heir likewise of the houses of Burgundy and Austria, such an extent of dominion accrued to him by all these successions, and such an addition of rank and authority by his election to the empire, as no prince had been master of in Europe from the days of CHARLES the great. It is proper to observe here how the policy of the Germans altered in the choice of an emperor, because the effects of this alteration have been great. When RODOLPHUS of Hapsburg was chosen in the year one thousand two hundred and seventy, or about that time, the poverty and the low estate of this prince, who had been marshal of the court to a king of Bohemia, was an inducement to elect him. The disorderly and lawless state of the empire made the princes of it in those days unwilling to have a more powerful head. But a contrary maxim took place at this aera: CHARLES the fifth and FRANCIS the first, the two most powerful princes of Europe, were the sole candidates; for the elector of Saxony, who is said to have declined, was rather unable to stand in competition with them: and CHARLES was chosen by the unanimous suffrages of the electoral college if I mistake not. Another CHARLES, CHARLES the fourth, who was made emperor illegally enough on the deposition of LEWIS of Bavaria, and about one hundred and fifty years before, seems to me to have contributed doubly to establish this maxim; by the wise constitutions that he procured to pass, that united the empire in a more orderly form and better system of government; and by alienating the imperial revenues to such a degree, that they were no longer sufficient to support an emperor who had not great revenues of his own. The same maxim and other circumstances have concurred to keep the empire in this family ever since, as it had been often before; and this family having large dominions in the empire, and larger pretensions, as well as dominions, out of it, the other states of Europe, France, Spain and England particularly, have been more concerned since this

LETTER VI.

period in the affairs of Germany, than they were before it: and by consequence the history of Germany, from the beginning of the sixteenth century, is of importance, and a necessary part of that knowledge which your lordship desires to acquire.

The Dutch commonwealth was not formed till near a century later. But as soon as it was formed, nay even whilst it was forming, these provinces, that were lost to observation among the many that composed the dominions of Burgundy and Austria, became so considerable a part of the political system of Europe, that their history must be studied by every man who would inform himself of this system.

Soon after this state had taken being, others of a more ancient original began to mingle in those disputes and wars, those councils, negociations, and treaties, that are to be the principal objects of your lordship's application in the study of history. That of the northern crowns deserves your attention little, before the last century. Till the election of FREDERIC the first to the crown of Denmark, and till that wonderful revolution which the first GUSTAVUS brought about in Sweden, it is nothing more than a confused rhapsody of events, in which the great kingdoms and states of Europe neither had any concern, nor took any part. From the time I have mentioned, the northern crowns have turned their counsels and their arms often southwards, and Sweden particularly, with prodigious effect.

Of the STUDY of HISTORY.   143

To what purpose should I trouble your lordship with the mention of histories of other nations? they are either such as have no relation to the knowledge you would acquire, like that of the Poles, the Muscovites, or the Turks; or they are such as, having an occasional or a secondary relation to it, fall of course into your scheme; like the history of Italy for instance, which is sometimes a part of that of France, sometimes of that of Spain, and sometimes of that of Germany. The thread of history, that you are to keep, is that of the nations who are and must always be concerned in the same scenes of action with your own. These are the principal nations of the west. Things that have no immediate relation to your own country, or to them, are either too remote, or too minute, to employ much of your time: and their history and your own is, for all your purposes, the whole history of Europe.

THE two great powers, that of France and that of Austria, being formed, and a rivalship established by consequence between them; it began to be the interest of their neighbours to oppose the strongest and most enterprising of the two, and to be the ally and friend of the weakest. From hence arose the notion of a balance of power in Europe, on the equal poize of which the safety and tranquillity of all must depend. To destroy the equality of this balance has been the aim of each of these rivals in his turn: and to hinder it from being destroyed, by preventing too much power from falling into one scale, has been the principle of all the wise councils of Europe, relative to France and to the house of Austria, through the whole period that began at the aera we have fixed, and subsists at this hour. To make a careful and just observation, therefore, of the rise and decline of these powers, in the two last centuries and in the present; of the projects which their ambition formed; of the means they employed to carry these projects on with success; of the means employed by others to defeat them; of the issue of all these endeavours in war and in negociation; and particularly, to bring your observations home to your own country and your own use, of the conduct that England held, to her honor or dishonor, to her advantage or disadvantage, in every one of the numerous and important conjunctures that happened — ought to be the principal subject of your lordship's attention in reading and reflecting on this part of modern history.

Now to this purpose you will find it of great use, my lord, when you have a general plan of the history in your mind, to go over the whole again in another method; which I propose to be this. Divide the entire period into such particular periods as the general course of affairs will mark out to you sufficiently, by the rise of new conjunctures, of different schemes of conduct, and of different theatres of action. Examine this period of history as you would examine a tragedy or a comedy; that is, take first the idea or a general notion of the whole, and after that examine every act and every scene apart. Consider them in themselves, and consider them relatively to one another.

Read

Read this history as you would that of any ancient period; but study it afterwards, as it would not be worth your while to study the other; nay as you could not have in your power the means of studying the other, if the study was really worth your while. The former part of this period abounds in great historians: and the latter part is so modern, that even tradition is authentic enough to supply the want of good history, if we are curious to enquire, and if we hearken to the living with the same impartiality and freedom of judgment as we read the dead: and he that does one will do the other. The whole period abounds in memorials, in collections of public acts and monuments of private letters, and of treaties. All these must come into your plan of study, my lord: many not to be read through, but all to be consulted and compared. They must not lead you, I think, to your enquiries, but your enquiries must lead you to them. By joining history and that which we call the materia historica together in this manner, and by drawing your information from both, your lordship will acquire not only that knowledge, which many have in some degree, of the great transactions that have passed, and the great events that have happened in Europe during this period, and of their immediate and obvious causes and consequences; but your lordship will acquire a much superior knowledge, and such a one as very few men possess almost in any degree, a knowledge of the true political system of Europe during this time. You will see it in it's primitive principles, in the constitutions of governments, the situations of countries, their national and true interests, the characters and the religion of people, and other permanent circumstances. You will trace it through all its fluctuations, and observe how the objects vary seldom, but the means perpetually, according to the different characters of princes and of those who govern; the different abilities of those who serve; the course of accidents, and a multitude of other irregular and contingent circumstances.

THE particular periods into which the whole period should be divided, in my opinion, are these. 1. From the fifteenth to the end of the sixteenth century. 2. From thence to the Pyrenean treaty. 3. From thence down to the present time.

YOUR lordship will find this division as apt and as proper, relatively to the particular histories of England, France, Spain, and Germany, the principal nations concerned, as it is relatively to the general history of Europe.

THE death of queen ELIZABETH, and the accession of king JAMES the first, made a vast alteration in the government of our nation at home, and in her conduct abroad, about the end of the first of these periods. The wars that religion occasioned, and ambition fomented in France, through the reigns of FRANCIS the second, CHARLES the ninth, HENRY the third, and a part of HENRY the fourth, ended: and the furies of the league were crushed by this great prince, about the same time. PHILIP the second of Spain marks this period likewise by his death, and by the exhausted condition in which he left the monarchy he governed: which took the lead no longer in disturbing the peace of mankind, but acted a second part in abetting the bigotry and ambition of FERDINAND the second and the third. The thirty years war that devasted Germany did not begin till the eighteenth year of the seventeenth century, but the seeds of it were sowing some time before, and even at the end of the sixteenth. FERDINAND the first and MAXIMILIAN had shewn much lenity and moderation in the disputes and troubles that arose on account of religion. Under RODOLPHUS and MATTHIAS, as the succession of their cousin FERDINAND approached, the fires that were covered began to smoke and to sparkle: and if the war did not begin with this century, the preparation for it, and the expectation of it did.

THE second period ends in one thousand six hundred and sixty, the year of the restoration of CHARLES the second to the throne of England; when our civil wars, and all the disorders which CROMWELL's usurpation had produced, were over; and therefore a remarkable point of time, with respect to our country. It is no less remarkable with respect to Germany, Spain, and France.

As to Germany; the ambitious projects of the German branch of Austria had been entirely defeated, the peace of the empire had been restored, and almost a new constitution formed, or an old one revived, by the treaties of Westphalia; nay the imperial eagle was not only fallen, but her wings were clipped.

As to Spain; the Spanish branch was fallen as low twelve years afterwards, that is, in the year one thousand six hundred and sixty. PHILIP the second left his successors a ruined monarchy. He left them something worse; he left them his example and his principles of government, founded in ambition, in pride, in ignorance, in bigotry, and all the pedantry of state. I have read somewhere or other, that the war of the Low Countries alone cost him, by his own confession, five hundred and sixty-four millions, a prodigious sum in what species soever he reckoned. PHILIP the third and PHILIP the fourth followed his example and his principles of government, at home and abroad. At home, there was much form, but no good order, no œconomy, nor wisdom of policy in the state. The church continued to devour the state, and that monster the inquisition to dispeople the country, even more than perpetual war, and all the numerous colonies that Spain had sent to the West-Indies: for your lordship will find that PHILIP the third drove more than nine hundred thousand Moriscoes out of his dominions by one edict, with such circumstances of inhumanity in the execution of it, as Spaniards alone could exercise, and that tribunal who had provoked this unhappy race to revolt, could alone approve. Abroad, the conduct of these princes was directed by the same wild spirit of ambition: rash in undertaking though slow to execute, and obstinate in pursuing though unable to succeed, they opened a new sluice to let out the little life and vigor that remained in their monarchy. PHILIP the second is said to have been piqued against his uncle FERDINAND, for refusing to yield the empire to him on the abdication of CHARLES the fifth. Certain it is, that as much as he loved to disturb the peace of mankind, and to meddle in every quarrel that had the appearance of supporting the Roman and oppressing every other church, he meddled little in the affairs of Germany. But, FERDINAND and MAXIMILIAN, dead, and the offspring of MAXIMILIAN, extinct, the kings of Spain espoused the interests of the other branch of their family, entertained remote views of ambition in favor of their own branch, even on that side, and made all the enterprises of FERDINAND of Gratz, both before and after his elevation to the empire, the common cause of the house of Austria. What compleated their ruin was this: they knew not how to lose, nor when to yield. They acknowledged the independency of the Dutch commonwealth, and became the allies of their ancient subjects at the treaty of Munster: but they would not forego their usurped claim on Portugal, and they persisted to carry on singly the war against France. Thus they were reduced to such a lowness of power as can hardly be paralleled in any other case: and PHILIP the fourth was obliged at last to conclude a peace, on terms repugnant to his inclination, to that of his people, to the interest of Spain, and to that of all Europe, in the Pyrenean treaty.

LETTER VI

As to France; this aera of the entire fall of the Spanish power is likewise that from which we may reckon that France grew as formidable, as we have seen her, to her neighbours, in power and pretensions. HENRY the fourth meditated great designs, and prepared to act a great part in Europe in the very beginning of this period, when RAVAILLAC stabbed him. His designs died with him, and are rather guessed at than known; for surely those which his historian PEREFIXE and the compilers of SULLY's memorials ascribe to him, of a christian commonwealth, divided into fifteen states, and of a senate to decide all differences, and to maintain this new constitution of Europe, are too chimerical to have been really his: but his general design of abasing the house of Austria, and establishing the superior power in that of Bourbon, was taken up, about twenty years after his death, by RICHELIEU, and was pursued by him and by MAZARIN with so much ability and success, that it was effected entirely by the treaties of Westphalia and by the Pyrenean treaty: that is, at the end of the second of those periods I have presumed to propose to your lordship.

WHEN the third, in which we now are, will end, and what circumstances will mark the end of it, I know not: but this I know, that the great events and revolutions, which have happened in the course of it, interest us still more nearly than those of the two precedent periods. I intended to have drawn up an elenchus or summary of the three, but I doubted, on further reflection, whether my memory would enable me to do it with exactness enough: and I saw that, if I was able to do it, the deduction would be immeasurably long. Something of this kind however it may be reasonable to attempt, in speaking of the last period: which may hereafter occasion a further trouble to your lordship.

But to give you some breathing-time, I will postpone it at present, and am in the mean while,

My Lord,

Your, etc.

LETTER VII.

A sketch of the state and history of Europe from the Pyrenean treaty in one thousand six hundred and fifty nine, to the year one thousand six hundred and eighty eight.

THE first observation I shall make on this third period of modern history is, that as the ambition of CHARLES the fifth, who united the whole formidable power of Austria in himself, and the restless temper, the cruelty, and bigotry of PHILIP the second, were principally objects of the attention and solicitude of the councils of Europe, in the first of these periods; and as the ambition of FERDINAND the second, and the third, who aimed at nothing less than extirpating the protestant interest, and under that pretence subduing the liberties of Germany, were objects of the same kind in the second: so an opposition to the growing power of France, or to speak more properly, to the exorbitant ambition of the house of Bourbon, has been the principal affair of Europe, during the greatest part of the present period. The design of aspiring to universal monarchy was imputed to CHARLES the fifth, as soon as he began to give proofs of his ambition and capacity. The same design was imputed to LEWIS the fourteenth, as soon as he began to feel his own strength, and the weakness of his neighbours. Neither of these princes was induced, I believe, by the flattery of his courtiers, or the apprehensions of his adversaries, to entertain so chimerical a design as this would have been, even in that false sense wherein the word universal is so often understood: and I mistake very much if either of them was of a character, or in circumstances, to undertake it. Both of them had strong desires to raise their families higher, and to extend their dominions farther; but neither of them had that bold and adventurous ambition which makes a conqueror and an hero. These apprehensions however were given wisely, and taken usefully. They cannot be given nor taken too soon when such powers as these arise; because when such powers as these are besieged as it were early, by the common policy and watchfulness of their neighbours, each of them may in his turn of strength sally forth, and gain a little ground; but none of them will be able to push their conquests far, and much less to consummate the entire projects of their ambition. Besides the occasional opposition that was given to CHARLES the fifth by our HENRY the eighth, according to the different moods of humor he was in; by the popes, according to the several turns of their private interest; and by the princes of Germany according to the occasions or pretences that religion or civil liberty furnished, he had from his first setting out a rival and an enemy in FRANCIS the first, who did not maintain his cause "in forma pauperis," if I may use such an expression: as we have seen the house of Austria sue, in our days, for dominion at the gate of every palace in Europe. FRANCIS the first was the principal in his own quarrels, paid his own armies, fought his own battles; and though his valor alone did not hinder CHARLES the fifth from subduing all Europe, as BAYLE, a better philologer than politician, somewhere asserts, but a multitude of other circumstances easily to be traced in history; yet he contributed by his victories, and even by his defeats, to waste the strength and check the course of that growing power. LEWIS the fourteenth had no rival of this kind in the house of Austria, nor indeed any enemy of this importance to combat, till the prince of Orange became king of Great Britain: and he had great advantages in many other respects, which it is necessary to consider in order to make a true judgment on the affairs of Europe from the year one thousand six hundred and sixty. You will discover the first of these advantages, and such as were productive of all the rest, in the conduct of RICHELIEU and of MAZARIN. RICHELIEU formed the great design, and laid the foundations; MAZARIN pursued the design, and raised the superstructure. If I do not deceive myself extremely, there are few passages in history that deserve your lordship's attention more than the conduct that the first and greatest of these ministers held, in laying the foundations I speak of. You will observe how he helped to embroil affairs on every side, and to keep the house of Austria at bay as it were; how he entered into the quarrels of Italy against Spain, into that concerning the Valteline, and that concerning the succession of Mantua; without engaging so deep as to divert him from another great object of his policy, subduing Rochelle and disarming the Huguenots. You will observe how he turned himself, after this was done, to stop the progress of FERDINAND in Germany. Whilst Spain fomented discontents at the court and disorders in the kingdom of France, by all possible means, even by taking engagements with the duke of ROHAN, and for supporting the protestants; RICHELIEU abetted the same interest in Germany against FERDINAND; and in the Low Countries against Spain. The emperor was become almost the master in Germany. CHRISTIAN the fourth, king of Denmark, had been at the head of a league, wherein the United Provinces, Sweden, and Lower Saxony entered, to oppose his progress: but CHRISTIAN had been defeated by TILLY and VALSTEIN, and obliged to conclude a treaty at Lubec, where FERDINAND gave him the law. It was then that GUSTAVUS ADOLPHUS, with whom RICHELIEU made an alliance, entered into this war, and soon turned the fortune of it. The French minister had not yet engaged his master openly in the war; but when the Dutch grew impatient, and threatened to renew their truce with Spain, unless France declared; when the king of SWEDEN was killed, and the battle of Nordlingen lost; when Saxony had turned again to the side of the emperor, and Brandenburg and so many others had followed this example, that Hesse almost alone persisted in the Swedish alliance:

then RICHELIEU engaged his master, and profited of every circumstance which the conjuncture afforded, to engage him with advantage. For, first, he had a double advantage by engaging so late: that of coming fresh into the quarrel against a wearied and almost exhausted enemy; and that of yielding to the impatience of his friends, who, pressed by their necessities and by the want they had of France, gave this minister an opportunity of laying those claims and establishing those pretensions, in all his treaties with Holland, Sweden, and the princes and states of the empire, on which he had projected the future aggrandisement of France. The manner in which he engaged, and the air that he gave to his engagement, were advantages of the second sort, advantages of reputation and credit; yet were these of no small moment in the course of the war, and operated strongly in favor of France as he designed they should, even after his death, and at and after the treaties of Westphalia. He varnished ambition with the most plausible and popular pretences. The elector of TREVES had put himself under the protection of France: and, if I remember right, he made this step when the emperor could not protect him against the Swedes, whom he had reason to apprehend. No matter, the governor of Luxemburg was ordered to surprise Treves and to seize the elector. He executed his orders with success, and carried this prince prisoner into Brabant. RICHELIEU seized the lucky circumstance; he reclaimed the elector: and on the refusal of the cardinal infant, the war was declared. France, you see, appeared the common friend of liberty, the defender of it in the Low Countries against the king of SPAIN, and in Germany against the emperor, as well as the protector of the princes of the empire, many of whose estates had been illegally invaded, and whose persons were no longer safe from violence even in their own palaces. All these appearances were kept up in the negociations at Munster, where MAZARIN reaped what RICHELIEU had sowed. The demands that France made for herself were very great; but the conjuncture was favorable, and she improved it to the utmost. No figure could be more flattering than her's, at the head of these negociations; nor more mortifying than the emperor's through the whole course of the treaty. The princes and states of the empire had been treated as vassals by the emperor: France determined them to treat with him on this occasion as sovereigns, and supported them in this determination. Whilst Sweden seemed concerned for the protestant interest alone, and shewed no other regard, as she had no other alliance; France affected to be impartial alike to the protestant and to the papist, and to have no interest at heart but the common interest of the Germanic body. Her demands were excessive, but they were to be satisfied principally out of the emperor's patrimonial dominions. It had been the art of her ministers to establish this general maxim on many particular experiences, that the grandeur of France was a real, and would be a constant security to the rights and liberties of the empire againſt the emperor: and it is no wonder therefore, this maxim prevailing, injuries, refentments, and jealoufies being fresh on one fide, and fervices, obligations, and confidence on the other, that the Germans were not unwilling France should extend her empire on this fide of the Rhine, whilſt Sweden did the fame on this fide of the Baltic. Thefe treaties, and the immenfe credit and influence that France had acquired by them in the empire, put it out of the power of one branch of the houſe of Auſtria to return the obligations of affiſtance to the other, in the war that continued between France and Spain, till the Pyrenean treaty. By this treaty the fuperiority of the houfe of Bourbon over the houfe of Auſtria was not only completed and confirmed, but the great defign of uniting the Spanish and the French monarchies under the former was laid.

The third period therefore begins by a great change of the balance of power in Europe, and by the profpect of one much greater and more fatal. Before I defcend into the particulars I intend to mention, of the courfe of affairs, and of the political conduct of the great powers of Europe in this third period; give me leave to caſt my eyes once more back on the fecond. The reflection I am going to make feems to me important, and leads to all that is to follow.

The Dutch made their peace feparately at Munſter with Spain, who acknowledged then the fovereignty and independency of their commonwealth. The French, who had been, after our ELIZABETH, their principal support, reproached them severely for this breach of faith. They excused themselves in the best manner, and by the best reasons, they could. All this your lordship will find in the monuments of that time. But I think it not improbable that they had a motive you will not find there, and which it was not proper to give as a reason or excuse to the French. Might not the wise men amongst them consider even then, besides the immediate advantages that accrued by this treaty to their commonwealth, that the imperial power was fallen; that the power of Spain was vastly reduced; that the house of Austria was nothing more than the shadow of a great name, and that the house of Bourbon was advancing, by large strides, to a degree of power as exorbitant, and as formidable as that of the other family had been in the hands of CHARLES the fifth, of PHILIP the second, and lately of the two FERDINANDS? Might they not foresee, even then, what happened in the course of very few years, when they were obliged, for their own security, to assist their old enemies the Spaniards against their old friends the French? I think they might. Our CHARLES the first was no great politician, and yet he seemed to discern that the balance of power was turning in favor of France, some years before the treaties of Westphalia. He refused to be neuter, and threatened to take part with Spain, if the French pursued the design of besieging Dunkirk and Graveline, according to a concert taken between them and the Dutch, and in purfuance of a treaty for dividing the Spanish Low Countries, which RICHELIEU had negociated. CROMWELL either did not difcern this turn of the balance of power, long afterwards when it was much more vifible; or, difcerning it, he was induced by reafons of private intereft to act againft the general intereft of Europe. CROMWELL joined with France againft Spain, and though he got Jamaica and Dunkirk, he drove the Spaniards into a neceffity of making a peace with France, that has difturbed the peace of the world almoft fourfcore years, and the confequences of which have well-nigh beggared in our times the nation he enflaved in his. There is a tradition, I have heard it from perfons who lived in thofe days, and I believe it came from THURLOE, that CROMWELL was in treaty with Spain, and ready to turn his arms againft France when he died. If this fact was certain, as little as I honor his memory, I should have fome regret that he died fo foon. But whatever his intentions were, we muft charge the Pyrenean treaty, and the fatal confequences of it, in great meafure to his account. The Spaniards abhorred the thought of marrying their Infanta to LEWIS the fourteenth. It was on this point that they broke the negociation LIONNE had begun: and your lordship will perceive, that if they refumed it afterwards, and offered the marriage they had before rejected, CROMWELL's league with France was a principal inducement to this alteration of their refolutions.

THE

THE precise point at which the scales of power turn like that of the solstice in either tropic, is imperceptible to common observation: and, in one case as in the other, some progress must be made in the new direction, before the change is perceived. They who are in the sinking scale, for in the political balance of power, unlike to all others, the scale that is empty sinks, and that which is full rises; they who are in the sinking scale, do not easily come off from the habitual prejudices of superior wealth, or power, or skill, or courage, nor from the confidence that these prejudices inspire. They who are in the rising scale do not immediately feel their strength, nor assume that confidence in it which successful experience gives them afterwards. They who are the most concerned to watch the variations of this balance, misjudge often in the same manner, and from the same prejudices. They continue to dread a power no longer able to hurt them, or they continue to have no apprehensions of a power that grows daily more formidable. Spain verified the first observation at the end of the second period, when, proud and poor, and enterprising and feeble, she still thought herself a match for France. France verified the second observation at the beginning of the third period, when the triple alliance stopped the progress of her arms, which alliances much more considerable were not able to effect afterwards. The other principal powers of Europe, in their turns, have verified the third observation

L

in both it's parts, through the whole course of this period.

When Lewis the fourteenth took the administration of affairs into his own hands, about the year one thousand six hundred and sixty, he was in the prime of his age, and had, what princes seldom have, the advantages of youth and those of experience together. Their education is generally bad; for which reason royal birth, that gives a right to the throne among other people, gave an absolute exclusion from it among the Mammelukes. His was, in all respects, except one, as bad as that of other princes. He jested sometimes on his own ignorance; and there were other defects in his character, owing to his education, which he did not see. But Mazarin had initiated him betimes into the mysteries of his policy. He had seen a great part of those foundations laid, on which he was to raise the fabric of his future grandeur: and as Mazarin finished the work that Richelieu began, he had the lessons of one, and the examples of both, to instruct him. He had acquired habits of secrecy and method, in business; of reserve, discretion, decency, and dignity, in behaviour. If he was not the greatest king, he was the best actor of majesty at least, that ever filled a throne. He by no means wanted that courage which is commonly called bravery, though the want of it was imputed to him in the midst of his greatest triumphs: nor that other courage, less ostentatious and more rarely found, calm, steady, persevering resolution: which seems to arise less from the temper of the body, and is therefore called courage of the mind. He had them both most certainly, and I could produce unquestionable anecdotes in proof. He was, in one word, much superior to any prince with whom he had to do, when he began to govern. He was surrounded with great captains bred in former wars, and with great ministers bred in the same school as himself. They who had worked under MAZARIN, worked on the same plan under him; and as they had the advantage of genius and experience over most of the ministers of other countries, so they had another advantage over those who were equal or superior to them: the advantage of serving a master whose absolute power was established; and the advantage of a situation wherein they might exert their whole capacity without contradiction; over that, for instance, wherein your lordship's great grand-father was placed, at the same time, in England, and JOHN DE WIT in Holland. Among these ministers, COLBERT must be mentioned particularly upon this occasion; because it was he who improved the wealth, and consequently the power of France extremely, by the order he put into the finances, and by the encouragement he gave to trade and manufactures. The soil, the climate, the situation of France, the ingenuity, the industry, the vivacity of her inhabitants are such; she has so little want of the product of other countries, and other countries have so many real or imaginary wants to be supplied by her; that when she is not at war with all her neighbours, when her domestic quiet is preserved and any tolerable administration of government prevails, she must grow rich at the expence of those who trade, and even of those who do not open a trade, with her. Her bawbles, her modes, the follies and extravagancies of her luxury, cost England, about the time we are speaking of, little less than eight hundred thousand pounds sterling a year, and other nations in their proportions. COLBERT made the most of all these advantageous circumstances, and whilst he filled the national spunge, he taught his successors how to squeeze it; a secret that he repented having discovered, they say, when he saw the immense sums that were necessary to supply the growing magnificence of his master.

THIS was the character of LEWIS the fourteenth, and this was the state of his kingdom at the beginning of the present period. If his power was great, his pretensions were still greater He had renounced, and, the Infanta with his consent had renounced, all right to the succession of Spain, in the strongest terms that the precaution of the councils of Madrid could contrive. No matter; he consented to these renunciations, but your lordship will find by the letters of MAZARIN, and by other memorials, that he acted on the contrary principle, from the first, which he avowed soon afterwards. Such a power, and such pretensions, should have given, one would think, an immediate alarm to the rest of Europe. PHILIP the fourth was broken and decayed, like the monarchy he governed. One of his sons died, as I remember, during the negociations that preceded the year one thousand six hundred and sixty: and the survivor, who was CHARLES the second, rather languished, than lived, from the cradle to the grave. So dangerous a contingency, therefore, as the union of the two monarchies of France and Spain, being in view forty years together; one would imagine that the principal powers of Europe had the means of preventing it constantly in view during the same time. But it was otherwise. France acted very systematically from the year one thousand six hundred and sixty, to the death of king CHARLES the second of Spain. She never lost sight of her great object, the succession to the whole Spanish monarchy; and she accepted the will of the king of SPAIN in favor of the duke of ANJOU. As she never lost sight of her great object during this time, so she lost no opportunity of increasing her power, while she waited for that of succeeding in her pretensions. The two branches of Austria were in no condition of making a considerable opposition to her designs and attempts. Holland, who of all other powers was the most concerned to oppose them, was at that time under two influences that hindered her from pursuing her true Interest. Her true interest was to have used her utmost endeavours to unite closely and intimately with England on the restoration of king CHARLES. She did the very contrary. JOHN DE WIT, at the head of the Louvestein faction, governed. The interest of his party was to keep the house of Orange down; he courted therefore the friendship of

France, and neglected that of England. The alliance between our nation and the Dutch was renewed, I think, in one thousand six hundred and sixty two; but the latter had made a defensive league with France a little before, on the supposition principally of a war with England. The war became inevitable very soon. CROMWELL had chastised them for their usurpations in trade, and the outrages and cruelties they had committed; but he had not cured them. The same spirit continued in the Dutch, the same resentments in the English: and the pique of merchants became the pique of nations. France entered into the war on the side of Holland; but the little assistance she gave the Dutch shewed plainly enough that her intention was to make these two powers waste their strength against one another, whilst she extended her conquests in the Spanish Low Countries. Her invasion of these provinces obliged DE WIT to change his conduct. Hitherto he had been attached to France in the closest manner, had led his republic to serve all the purposes of France, and had renewed with the marshal D'ESTRADES a project of dividing the Spanish Netherlands between France and Holland, that had been taken up formerly, when RICHELIEU made use of it to flatter their ambition, and to engage them to prolong the war against Spain. A project not unlike to that which was held out to them by the famous preliminaries, and the extravagant barrier-treaty, in one thousand seven hundred and nine; and which engaged them to continue a war on the principle of ambition, into which they had entered with more reasonable and more moderate views.

As the private interests of the two DE WITS hindered that common-wealth from being on her guard, as early as she ought to have been, against France; so the mistaken policy of the court of England, and the short views, and the profuse temper of the prince who governed, gave great advantages to LEWIS the fourteenth in the pursuit of his designs. He bought Dunkirk: and your lordship knows how great a clamor was raised on that occasion against your noble ancestor; as if he alone had been answerable for the measure, and his interest had been concerned in it. I have heard our late friend Mr. GEORGE CLARK quote a witness, who was quite unexceptionable, but I cannot recal his name at present, who, many years after all these transactions, and the death of my lord CLARENDON, affirmed, that the earl of SANDWICH had owned to him, that he himself gave his opinion, among many others, officers, and ministers, for selling Dunkirk. Their reasons could not be good, I presume to say; but several, that might be plausible at that time, are easily guessed. A prince like king CHARLES, who would have made as many bad bargains as any young spendthrift, for money, finding himself thus backed, we may assure ourselves, was peremptorily determined to sell: and whatever your great grand father's opinion was, this I am able to pronounce upon my own experience, that his treaty for the sale is no proof he was of opinion to sell. When the resolution of selling was once taken, to whom could the sale be made? To the Dutch? No. This measure would have been at least as impolitic, and, in that moment, perhaps more odious than the other. To the Spaniards? They were unable to buy: and, as low as their power was sunk, the principle of opposing it still prevailed. I have sometimes thought that the Spaniards, who were forced to make peace with Portugal, and to renounce all claim to that crown, four or five years afterwards, might have been induced to take this resolution then, if the regaining Dunkirk without any expence had been a condition proposed to them; and that the Portuguese, who, notwithstanding their alliance with England and the indirect succours that France afforded them, were little able, after the treaty especially, to support a war against Spain, might have been induced to pay the price of Dunkirk, for so great an advantage as immediate peace with Spain, and the extinction of all foreign pretences on their crown. But this speculation concerning events so long ago passed is not much to the purpose here. I proceed therefore to observe, that notwithstanding the sale of Dunkirk, and the secret leanings of our court to that of France, yet England was first to take the alarm, when LEWIS the fourteenth invaded the Spanish Netherlands in one thousand six hundred and sixty seven: and the triple alliance was the work of an English minister. It was time to take this alarm; for from the moment that the king of FRANCE claimed a right to the county of Burgundy, the dutchy of Brabant, and other portions of the Low Countries as devolved on his queen by the death of her father PHILIP the fourth, he pulled off the mask entirely. Volumes were written to establish, and to refute this supposed right. Your lordship no doubt will look into a controversy that has employed so many pens and so many swords; and I believe you will think it was sufficiently bold in the French, to argue from customs, that regulated the course of private successions in certain provinces, to a right of succeeding to the sovereignty of those provinces; and to assert the divisibility of the Spanish monarchy, with the same breath with which they asserted the indivisibility of their own; although the proofs in one case were just as good as the proofs in the other, and the fundamental law of indivisibility was at least as good a law in Spain, as either this or the Salique law was in France. But however proper it might be for the French and Austrian pens to enter into long discussions, and to appeal, on this great occasion, to the rest of Europe; the rest of Europe had a short objection to make to the plea of France, which no sophisms, no quirks of law, could evade. Spain accepted the renunciations as a real security: France gave them as such to Spain, and in effect to the rest of Europe. If they had not been thus given, and thus taken, the Spaniards would not have married their Infanta to the king of FRANCE, whatever distress they might have endured by the prolongation of the war. These renunciations were renunciations of all rights whatsoever to the whole Spanish monarchy, and to every part of it. The provinces claimed by France at this time were parts of it. To claim them, was therefore to claim the whole; for if the renunciations were no bar to the rights accruing to MARY THERESA on the death of her father PHILIP the fourth, neither could they be any to the rights that would accrue to her and her children, on the death of her brother CHARLES the second: an unhealthful youth, and who at this inſtant was in immediate danger of dying; for to all the complicated diſtempers he brought into the world with him, the ſmall-pox was added. Your lordſhip ſees how the fatal contingency of uniting the two monarchies of France and Spain ſtared mankind in the face; and yet nothing, that I can remember, was done to prevent it: not ſo much as a guaranty given, or a declaration made to aſſert the validity of theſe renunciations, and for ſecuring the effect of them. The triple alliance indeed ſtopped the progreſs of the French arms, and produced the treaty of Aix la Chapelle. But England, Sweden, and Holland, the contracting powers in this alliance, ſeemed to look, and probably did look, no farther. France kept a great and important part of what ſhe had ſurprized or raviſhed, or purchaſed; for we cannot ſay with any propriety that ſhe conquered: and the Spaniards were obliged to ſet all they ſaved to the account of gain. The German branch of Auſtria had been reduced very low in power and in credit under FERDINAND the third, by the treaties of Weſtphalia, as I have ſaid already. LEWIS the fourteenth maintained, during many years, the influence these treaties had given him among the princes and states of the empire. The famous capitulation made at Frankfort on the election of LEOPOLD, who succeeded FERDINAND about the year one thousand six hundred and fifty seven, was encouraged by the intrigues of France: and the power of France was looked upon as the sole power that could ratify and secure effectually the observation of the conditions then made. The league of the Rhine was not renewed I believe after the year one thousand six hundred and sixty six; but though this league was not renewed, yet some of these princes and states continued in their old engagement with France: whilst others took new engagements on particular occasions, according as private and sometimes very paultry interests, and the emissaries of France in all their little courts, disposed them. In short the princes of Germany shewed no alarm at the growing ambition and power of LEWIS the fourteenth, but contributed to encourage one, and to confirm the other. In such a state of things the German branch was little able to assist the Spanish branch against France, either in the war that ended by the Pyrenean treaty, or in that we are speaking of here, the short war that began in one thousand six hundred and sixty seven, and was ended by the treaty of Aix la Chapelle, in one thousand six hundred and sixty eight. But it was not this alone that disabled the emperor from acting with vigor in the cause of his family then, nor that has rendered the house of Austria a dead weight upon all her allies ever since. Bigotry, and its inseparable companion, cruelty, as well as the tyranny and avarice of the court of Vienna, created in those days, and has maintained in ours, almost a perpetual diversion of the imperial arms from all effectual opposition to France. I mean to speak of the troubles in Hungary. Whatever they became in their progress, they were caused originally by the usurpations and persecutions of the emperor: and when the Hungarians were called rebels first, they were called so for no other reason than this, that they would not be slaves. The dominion of the emperor being less supportable than that of the Turks, this unhappy people opened a door to the latter to infest the empire, instead of making their country what it had been before, a barrier against the Ottoman power. France became a sure, though secret ally of the Turks, as well as the Hungarians, and has found her account in it, by keeping the emperor in perpetual alarms on that side, while she has ravaged the empire and the Low Countries on the other. Thus we saw, thirty two years ago, the arms of France and Bavaria in possession of Passau, and the malcontents of Hungary in the suburbs of Vienna. In a word, when LEWIS the fourteenth made the first essay of his power, by the war of one thousand six hundred and sixty seven, and founded, as it were, the councils of Europe concerning his pretensions on the Spanish succession, he found his power to be great beyond what his neighbours or even he perhaps thought it: great by the wealth, and greater by the united spirit of his people; greater still by the ill policy, and divided interests that governed those who had a superior common interest to oppose him. He found that the members of the triple alliance did not see, or seeing did not think proper to own that they saw, the injustice, and the consequence of his pretensions. They contented themselves to give to Spain an act of guaranty for securing the execution of the treaty of Aix la Chapelle. He knew even then how ill the guaranty would be observed by two of them at least, by England and by Sweden. The treaty itself was nothing more than a composition between the bully and the bullied. Tournay, and Lisle, and Douay, and other places that I have forgot, were yielded to him: and he restored the county of Burgundy, according to the option that Spain made, against the interest and expectation too of the Dutch, when an option was forced upon her. The king of SPAIN compounded for his possession: but the emperor compounded at the same time for his succession, by a private eventual treaty of partition, which the commander of GREMONVILLE and the count of AVERSBERG signed at Vienna. The same LEOPOLD, who exclaimed so loudly, in one thousand six hundred and ninety eight, against any partition of the Spanish monarchy, and refused to submit to that which England and Holland had then made, made one himself in one thousand six hundred and sixty eight, with so little regard to these two powers, that the whole ten provinces were thrown into the lot of France.

There is no room to wonder if such experience as Lewis the fourteenth had upon this occasion, and such a face of affairs in Europe, raising his hopes, raised his ambition: and if, in making peace at Aix la Chapelle, he meditated a new war, the war of one thousand six hundred and seventy two; the preparations he made for it, by negotiations in all parts, by alliances wherever he found ingression, and by the increase of his forces, were equally proofs of ability, industry, and power. I shall not descend into these particulars: your lordship will find them pretty well detailed in the memorials of that time. But one of the alliances he made I must mention, though I mention it with the utmost regret and indignation. England was fatally engaged to act a part in this conspiracy against the peace and the liberty of Europe, nay, against her own peace and her own liberty; for a bubble's part it was, equally wicked and impolitic. Forgive the terms I use, my lord, none can be too strong. The principles of the triple alliance, just and wise, and worthy of a king of England, were laid aside. Then, the progress of the French arms was to be checked, the ten provinces were to be saved, and by saving them the barrier of Holland was to be preserved. Now, we joined our counsels and our arms to those of France, in a project that could not be carried on at all, as it was easy to foresee, and as the event shewed, unless it was carried on against Spain, the emperor, and most of the princes of Germany, as well as the Dutch; and which could not be carried on succefsfully, without leaving the ten provinces entirely at the mercy of France and giving her pretence and opportunity of ravaging the empire, and extending her conquests on the Rhine. The medal of VAN BEUNINGHEN, and other pretences that France took for attacking the states of the Low Countries were ridiculous. They impofed on no one: and the true object of LEWIS the fourteenth was manifelt to all. But what could a king of England mean? CHARLES the fecond had reafons of refentment againft the Dutch, and juft ones too no doubt. Among the reft, it was not eafy for him to forget the affront he had fuffered, and the lofs he had fuftained, when, depending on the peace that was ready to be figned, and that was figned at Breda in July, he neglected to fit out his fleet; and when that of Holland, commanded by RUYTER, with CORNELIUS DE WIT on board as deputy or commiffioner of the ftates, burnt his ships at Chatham in June. The famous perpetual edict, as it was called but did not prove, in the event, againft the election of a ftate-holder, which JOHN DE WIT promoted, carried, and obliged the prince of ORANGE to fwear to maintain a very few days after the conclufion of the peace at Breda, might be another motive in the breaft of king CHARLES the fecond: as it was certainly a pretence of revenge on the Dutch, or at leaft on the DE WITS and the Louveftein faction, that ruled almoft defpotically in that commonwealth. But it is plain that neither thefe reafons, nor others of a more ancient date, determined him to this alliance with France; since he contracted the triple alliance within four or five months after the two events, I have mentioned, happened. What then did he mean? Did he mean to acquire one of the seven provinces, and divide them, as the Dutch had twice treated for the division of the ten, with France? I believe not; but this I believe, that his inclinations were favourable to the popish interest in general, and that he meant to make himself more absolute at home; that he thought it necessary to this end to humble the Dutch, to reduce their power, and perhaps to change the form of their government: to deprive his subjects of the correspondence with a neighbouring protestant and free state, and of all hope of succour and support from thence in their opposition to him; in a word to abet the designs of France on the continent, that France might abet his designs on his own kingdom. This, I say, I believe; and this I should venture to affirm, if I had in my hands to produce, and was at liberty to quote, the private relations I have read formerly, drawn up by those who were no enemies to such designs, and on the authority of those who were parties to them. But whatever king CHARLES the second meant, certain it is that his conduct established the superiority of France in Europe.

But this charge, however, must not be confined to him alone. Those who were nearer the danger, those who were exposed to the immediate attacks of France, and even those who were her rivals for the same succession, having either assisted her, or engaged to remain neuters, a strange fatality prevailed, and produced such a conjuncture as can hardly be paralleled in history. Your lordship will observe with astonishment even in the beginning of the year one thousand six hundred and seventy two, all the neighbours of France acting as if they had nothing to fear from her, and some as if they had much to hope, by helping her to oppress the Dutch and sharing with her the spoils of that commonwealth. " Delenda est „ Carthago," was the cry in England, and seemed too a maxim on the continent.

In the course of the same year, you will observe that all these powers took the alarm, and began to unite in opposition to France. Even England thought it time to interpose in favor of the Dutch. The consequences of this alarm, of this sudden turn in the policy of Europe, and of that which happened by the massacre of the De Wits, and the elevation of the prince of Orange, in the government of the seven provinces, saved these provinces, and stopped the rapid progress of the arms of France. Lewis the fourteenth indeed surprised the seven provinces in this war, as he had surprised the ten in that of one thousand six hundred and sixty seven, and ravaged defenceless countries with armies sufficient to conquer them, if they had been prepared to resist. In the war of one thousand six hundred and seventy two, he had little less than one hundred and fifty thousand men on foot, besides the bodies of English, Swifs, Italians, and Swedes, that amounted to thirty or forty thousand more. With this mighty force he took forty places in forty days, imposed extravagant conditions of peace, played the monarch a little while at Utrecht; and as soon as the Dutch recovered from their consternation, and, animated by the example of the prince of Orange and the hopes of succour, refused these conditions, he went back to Versailles, and left his generals to carry on his enterprize: which they did with so little success, that Grave and Maestricht alone remained to him of all the boasted conquests he had made; and even these he offered two years afterwards to restore, if by that concession he could have prevailed on the Dutch at that time to make peace with him. But they were not yet disposed to abandon their allies; for allies now they had. The emperor and the king of SPAIN had engaged in the quarrel against France, and many of the princes of the empire had done the same; not all. The Bavarian continued obstinate in his neutrality, and to mention no more, the Swedes made a great diversion in favor of France in the empire; where the duke of HANOVER abetted their designs as much as he could, for he was a zealous partisan of France, though the other princes of his house acted for the common cause. I descend into no more particulars. The war that LEWIS the fourteenth kindled by attacking in so violent a manner the Dutch commonwealth, and by making so arbitrary an use of his first success, became general, in the Low Countries, in Spain, in Sicily, on the upper and lower Rhine, in Denmark, in Sweden, and in the provinces of Germany belonging to thefe two crowns; on the Mediterranean, the Ocean, and the Baltic. France fupported this war with advantage on every fide: and when your lordſhip confiders in what manner it was carried on againſt her, you will not be furprifed that she did fo. Spain had fpirit, but too little ſtrength to maintain her power in Sicily, where Meſſina had revolted; to defend her frontier on that fide of the Pyrenees; and to refiſt the great efforts of the French in the Low Countries. The empire was divided; and, even among the princes who acted againſt France, there was neither union in their councils, nor concert in their projects, nor order in preparations, nor vigor in execution: and, to fay the truth, there was not, in the whole confederacy, a man whofe abilities could make him a match for the prince of CONDE or the marshal of TURENNE; nor many who were in any degree equal to LUXEMBURG, CREQUI, SCHOMBERG, and other generals of inferior note, who commanded the armies of France. The emperor took this very time to make new invafions on the liberties of Hungary, and to oppreſs his proteſtant fubjects. The prince of ORANGE alone acted with invincible firmnefs, like a patriot, and a hero. Neither the feductions of France nor thofe of England, neither the temptations of ambition nor thofe of private intereſt could make him fwerve from the true intereſt of his country, nor from the common intereſt of Europe. He had raifed more fieges, and loſt more battles, it was ſaid, than any general of his age had done. Be it ſo. But his defeats were manifeſtly due in great meaſure to circumſtances independent on him: and that ſpirit, which even theſe defeats could not depreſs, was all his own. He had difficulties in his own commonwealth; the governors of the Spaniſh Low Countries croſſed his meaſures ſometimes: the German allies diſappointed and broke them often: and it is not improbable that he was frequently betrayed. He was ſo perhaps even by SOUCHES, the imperial general: a Frenchman according to BAYLE, and a penſioner of Louvois according to common report, and very ſtrong appearances. He had not yet credit and authority ſufficient to make him a centre of union to a whole confederacy, the ſoul that animated and directed ſo great a body. He came to be ſuch afterwards; but at the time ſpoken of he could not take ſo great a part upon him. No other prince or general was equal to it: and the conſequences of this defect appeared almoſt in every operation. France was ſurrounded by a multitude of enemies, all intent to demoliſh her power. But, like the builders of Babel, they ſpoke different languages: and as thoſe could not build, theſe could not demoliſh, for want of underſtanding one another. France improved this advantage by her arms, and more by her negotiations. Nimeghen was, after Cologn, the ſcene of theſe. England was the mediating power, and I know not whether our CHARLES the ſecond did not ſerve her purpoſes more uſefully in the latter, and under the character of mediator, than he did or could have done by joining his arms to her's, and acting as her ally. The Dutch were induced to sign a treaty with him, that broke the confederacy, and gave great advantage to France: for the purport of it was to oblige France and Spain to make peace on a plan to be propofed to them, and no mention was made in it of the other allies that I remember. The Dutch were glad to get out of an expenfive war. France promifed to reftore Maeftricht to them, and Maeftricht was the only place that remained unrecovered of all they had loft. They dropped Spain at Nimeghen, as they had dropped France at Munfter, but many circumftances concurred to give a much worfe grace to their abandoning of Spain, than to their abandoning of France. I need not fpecify them. This only I would obferve: when they made a feparate peace at Munfter, they left an ally who was in condition to carry on the war alone with advantage, and they prefumed to impofe no terms upon him: when they made a feparate peace at Nimeghen, they abandoned an ally who was in no condition to carry on the war alone, and who was reduced to accept whatever terms the common enemy prefcribed. In their great diftrefs in one thoufand fix hundred and feventy three, they engaged to reftore Maeftricht to the Spaniards as foon as it should be retaken: it was not retaken, and they accepted it for themfelves as the price of the feparate peace they made with France. The Dutch had engaged farther, to make neither peace nor truce with the king of FRANCE, till that prince consented to restore to Spain all he had conquered since the Pyrenean treaty. But, far from keeping this promise in any tolerable degree, LEWIS the fourteenth acquired, by the plan imposed on Spain at Nimeghen, besides the county of Burgundy, so many other countries and towns on the side of the ten Spanish provinces, that these, added to the places he kept of those which had been yielded to him by the treaty of Aix la Chapelle (for some of little consequence he restored) put into his hands the principal strength of that barrier, against which we goaded ourselves almost to death in the last great war; and made good the saying of the marshal of SCHOMBERG, that to attack this barrier was to take the beast by his horns. I know very well what may be said to excuse the Dutch. The emperor was more intent to tyrannize his subjects on one side, than to defend them on the other. He attempted little against France, and the little he did attempt was ill ordered, and worse executed. The assistance of the princes of Germany was often uncertain, and always expensive. Spain was already indebted to Holland for great sums; greater still must be advanced to her if the war continued: and experience shewed that France was able, and would continue, to prevail against her present enemies. The triple league had stopped her progress, and obliged her to abandon the county of Burgundy; but Sweden was now engaged in the war on the side of France, as England had been in the beginning of it: and England was now privately favorable to her interests, as Sweden had been in the beginning of it. The whole ten provinces would have been subdued in the course of a few campaigns more: and it was better for Spain and the Dutch too, that part should be saved by accepting a sort of composition, than the whole be risqued by refusing it. This might be alledged to excuse the conduct of the States General, in imposing hard terms on Spain; in making none for their other allies, and in signing alone: by which steps they gave France an opportunity that she improved with great dexterity of management, the opportunity of treating with the confederates one by one, and of beating them by detail in the cabinet, if I may so say, as she had often done in the field. I shall not compare these reasons, which were but too well founded in fact, and must appear plausible at least, with other considerations that might be, and were at the time, insisted upon. I confine myself to a few observations, which every knowing and impartial man must admit. Your lordship will observe, first, that the fatal principle of compounding with LEWIS the fourteenth, from the time that his pretensions, his power, and the use he made of it, began to threaten Europe, prevailed still more at Nimeghen than it had prevailed at Aix: so that although he did not obtain to the full all he attempted, yet the dominions of France were by common consent, on every treaty, more and more extended; her barriers on all sides were more and more strengthened;

those of her neighbours were more and more weakened; and that power, which was to assert one day, against the rest of Europe, the pretended rights of the house of Bourbon to the Spanish monarchy, was more and more established, and rendered truly formidable in such hands at least, during the course of the first eighteen years of the period. Your lordship will please to observe, in the second place, that the extreme weakness of one branch of Austria, and the miserable conduct of both; the poverty of some of the princes of the empire, and the disunion, and, to speak plainly, the mercenary policy of all of them; in short, the confined views, the false notions, and, to speak as plainly of my own as of other nations, the iniquity of the councils of England, not only hindered the growth of this power from being stopped in time, but nursed it up into strength almost insuperable by any future confederacy. A third observation is this: If the excuses made for the conduct of the Dutch at Nimeghen are not sufficient, they too must come in for their share in this condemnation, even after the death of the De Wits; as they were to be condemned most justly, during that administration, for abetting and favoring France. If these excuses, grounded on their inability to pursue any longer a war, the principal profit of which was to accrue to their confederates, for that was the case after the year one thousand six hundred and seventy three, or one thousand six hundred and seventy four, and the principal burden of which was thrown on them by their confederates; if these are sufficient, they should not have acted for decency's sake as well as out of good policy, the part they did act in one thousand seven hundred and eleven and one thousand seven hundred and twelve, towards the late queen, who had complaints of the same kind, in a much higher degree and with circumstances much more aggravating, to make of them, of the emperor, and of all the princes of Germany; and who was far from treating them and their other allies, at that time, as they treated Spain and their other allies in one thousand six hundred and seventy eight. Immediately after the Dutch had made their peace, that of Spain was signed with France. The emperor's treaty with this crown and that of Sweden was concluded in the following year: and Lewis the fourteenth being now at liberty to assist his ally, whilst he had tied up the powers with whom he had treated from assisting theirs, he soon forced the king of Denmark and the elector of Brandenburg to restore all they had taken from the Swedes, and to conclude the peace of the north. In all these treaties he gave the law, and he was now at the highest point of his grandeur. He continued at this point for several years, and in this heighth of his power he prepared those alliances against it, under the weight of which he was at last well-nigh oppressed; and might have been reduced as low as the general interest of Europe required, if some of the causes, which worked now, had not continued to work in his favor, and if his enemies had not proved, in their turn of fortune, as infatiable as profperity had rendered him.

AFTER he had made peace with all the powers with whom he had been in war, he continued to vex both Spain and the empire, and to extend his conquefts in the Low Countries, and on the Rhine, both by the pen and the fword. He erected the chambers of Metz and of Brifach, where his own fubjects were profecutors, witneffes, and judges all at once. Upon the decifions of thefe tribunals, he feized into his own hands, under the notions of dependencies and the pretence of reunions, whatever towns or diftricts of country tempted his ambition, or fuited his conveniency: and added, by thefe and by other means, in the midft of peace, more territories to thofe the late treaties had yielded to him, than he could have got by continuing the war. He acted afterwards, in the fupport of all this, without any bounds or limits. His glory was a reafon for attacking Holland in one thoufand fix hundred and feventy two, and his conveniency a reafon for many of the attacks he made on others afterwards. He took Luxemburg by force: he ftole Strasburg; he bought Caffal: and, whilft he waited the opportunity of acquiring to his family the crown of Spain, he was not without thoughts, nor hopes perhaps, of bringing into it the imperial crown likewife. Some of the cruelties he exercifed in the empire may be afcribed to his difappointment in this view: I fay fome of them, becaufe in the war that ended by the treaty of Nimeghen, he had already exercised many. Though the French writers endeavour to slide over them, to palliate them, and to impute them particularly to the English that were in their service, for even this one of their writers has the front to advance: yet these cruelties unheard of among civilized nations, must be granted to have been ordered by the counsels, and executed by the arms of France, in the Palatinate, and in other parts.

IF LEWIS the fourteenth could have contented himself with the acquisitions that were confirmed to him by the treaties of one thousand six hundred and seventy eight, and one thousand six hundred and seventy nine, and with the authority and reputation which he then gained; it is plain that he would have prevented the alliances that were afterwards formed against him, and that he might have regained his credit amongst the princes of the empire, where he had one family-alliance by the marriage of his brother to the daughter of the elector Palatine, and another by that of his son to the sister of the elector of BAVARIA; where Sweden was closely attached to him, and where the same principles of private interest would have soon attached others as closely. He might have remained not only the principal, but the directing power of Europe, and have held this rank with all the glory imaginable, till the death of the king of SPAIN, or some other object of great ambition, had determined him to act another part. But, instead of this, he continued to vex and provoke all those who were, unhappily for them, his neighbours, and that, in many instances, for trifles. An example of this kind occurs to me. On the death of the duke of DEUX PONTS, he seized that little inconsiderable dutchy, without any regard to the indisputable right of the king of SWEDEN, to the services that crown had rendered him, or to the want he might have of that alliance hereafter. The consequence was, that Sweden entered, with the emperor, the king of SPAIN, the elector of Bavaria, and the States General, into the alliance of guaranty, as it was called, about the year one thousand six hundred and eighty three, and into the famous league of Augsburg, in one thousand six hundred and eighty six.

SINCE I have mentioned this league, and since we may date from it a more general and a more concerted opposition to France than there had been before; give me leave to recal some of the reflections that have presented themselves to my mind, in considering what I have read, and what I have heard related, concerning the passages of that time. They will be of use to form our judgment concerning later passages. If the king of FRANCE became an object of aversion on account of any invasions he made, any deviations from public faith, any barbarities exercised where his arms prevailed, or the persecution of his protestant subjects; the emperor deserved to be such an object, at least as much as he, on the same accounts. The emperor was so too, but with this difference relatively to the political system of the west: the Austrian ambition and bigotry exerted themselves in distant countries, whose interests were not considered as a part of this system; for, otherwise there would have been as much reason for assisting the people of Hungary and of Transylvania against the emperor, as there had been formerly for assisting the people of the seven united provinces against Spain, or as there have been lately for assisting them against France: but the ambition and bigotry of Lewis the fourteenth were exerted in the Low Countries, on the Rhine, in Italy, and in Spain, in the very midst of this system, if I may say so, and with success that could not fail to subvert it in time. The power of the house of Austria, that had been feared too long, was feared no longer: and that of the house of Bourbon, by having been feared too late, was now grown terrible. The emperor was so intent on the establishment of his absolute power in Hungary, that he exposed the empire doubly to desolation and ruin for the sake of it. He left the frontier almost quite defenceless on the side of the Rhine, against the inroads and ravages of France: and by shewing no mercy to the Hungarians, nor keeping any faith with them, he forced that miserable people into alliances with the Turk, who invaded the empire and besieged Vienna. Even this event had no effect upon him. Your lordship will find, that Sobieski king of Poland, who had forced the Turks to raise the siege, and had fixed the imperial crown that tottered on his head, could not prevail on him to take those measures by which alone it was possible to cover the empire, to secure the King of SPAIN, and to reduce that power which was probably one day to dispute with him this prince's succession. TEKELI and the malcontents made such demands as none but a tyrant could refuse, the preservation of their ancient privileges, liberty of conscience, the convocation of a free diet or parliament, and others of less importance. All was in vain. The war continued with them, and with the Turks, and France was left at liberty to push her enterprises almost without opposition, against Germany and the Low Countries. The distress in both was so great, that the States General saw no other expedient for stopping the progress of the French arms, than a cessation of hostilities, or a truce of twenty years; which they negotiated, and which was accepted by the emperor and the king of SPAIN, on the terms that LEWIS the fourteenth thought fit to offer. By these terms he was to remain in full and quiet possession of all he had acquired since the years one thousand six hundred and seventy eight, and one thousand six hundred and seventy nine; among which acquisitions that of Luxemburg and that of Strasburg were comprehended. The conditions of this truce were so advantageous to France, that all her intrigues were employed to obtain a definitive treaty of peace upon the same conditions. But this was neither the interest nor the intention of the other contracting powers. The imperial arms had been very succefsful againſt the Turks. This fuccefs, as well as the troubles that followed upon it in the Ottoman armies, and at the Porte, gave a reafonable expectation of concluding a peace on that fide: and, this peace concluded, the emperor, and the empire, and the king of SPAIN would have been in a much better poſture to treat with France. With thefe views, that were wife and juſt, the league of Augsburg was made between the emperor, the kings of SPAIN and SWEDEN as princes of the empire, and the other circles and princes. This league was purely defenfive. An exprefs article declared it to be fo: and as it had no other regard, it was not only conformable to the laws and conſtitutions of the empire, and to the practice of all nations, but even to the terms of the act of truce fo lately concluded. This pretence therefore for breaking the truce, feizing the electorate of Cologn, invading the Palatinate, befieging Philipsburg, and carrying unexpected and undeclared war into the empire, could not be fupported: nor is it poffible to read the reafons publiſhed by France at this time, and drawn from her fears of the imperial power, without laughter. As little pretence was there to complain, that the emperor refufed to convert at once the truce into a definitive treaty; fince, if he had done fo, he would have confirmed in a lump, and without any difcuffion, all the arbitrary decrees of thofe chambers, or courts, that France had erected to cover her ufurpations; and would have given up almoſt a fixth part of the provinces of the empire, that France one way or other had poſſeſſed herſelf of. The pretenſions of the Dutcheſs of ORLEANS on the ſucceſſion of her father, and her brother, which were diſputed by the then elector Palatine, and were to be determined by the laws and cuſtoms of the empire, afforded as little pretence for beginning this war, as any of the former allegations. The excluſion of the cardinal of FURSTENBERG, who had been elected to the archbiſhoprick of Cologn, was capable of being aggravated: but even in this caſe his moſt chriſtian majeſty oppoſed his judgment and his authority againſt the judgment and authority of that holy father, whoſe eldeſt ſon he was proud to be called. In ſhort, the true reaſon why LEWIS the fourteenth began that cruel war with the empire, two years after he had concluded a ceſſation of hoſtilities for twenty, was this: he reſolved to keep what he had got; and therefore he reſolved to encourage the Turks to continue the war. He did this effectually, by invading Germany at the very inſtant when the Sultan was ſuing for peace. Notwithſtanding this, the Turks were in treaty again the following year: and good policy ſhould have obliged the emperor, ſince he could not hope to carry on this war and that againſt France, at the ſame time, with vigor and effect, to conclude a peace with the leaſt dangerous enemy of the two. The deciſion of this diſpute with France could not be deferred, his deſigns againſt the Hungarians were in part accompliſhed, for his ſon was declared king, and the ſettlement of that crown in his family was

made;

made; and the reft of thefe, as well as thofe that he formed againſt the Turks, might be deferred. But the councils of Vienna judged differently, and infifted even at this critical moment on the moſt exorbitant terms; on fome of fuch a nature, that the Turks fhewed more humanity and a better fenfe of religion in refufing, than they in asking them. Thus the war went on in Hungary, and proved a conftant diverfion in favor of France, during the whole courfe of that which LEWIS the fourteenth began at this time: for the treaty of Carlowitz was pofterior to that of Ryfwic. The Empire, Spain, England, and Holland engaged in the war with France and on them the emperor left the burden of it. In the fhort war of one thoufand fix hundred and fixty feven, he was not fo much as a party, and inſtead of aſſiſting the king of SPAIN, which, it muſt be owned, he was in no good condition of doing, he bargained for dividing that prince's fucceſſion, as I have obferved above. In the war of one thoufand fix hundred and feventy two he made fome feeble efforts. In this of one thoufand fix hundred and eighty eight he did ſtill leſs: and in the war which broke out at the beginning of the prefent century he did nothing, at leaſt after the firſt campaign in Italy, and after the engagements that England and Holland took by the grand alliance. In a word, from the time that an oppofition to France became a common caufe in Europe, the houfe of Auſtria has been a clog upon it in many inſtances, and of confiderable aſſiſtance to it in none. The acceſſion of England to this cause, which was brought about by the revolution of one thousand six hundred and eighty eight, might have made amends, and more than amends, one would think, for this defect, and have thrown superiority of power and of success on the side of the confederates, with whom she took part against France. This, I say, might be imagined, without over-rating the power of England, or undervaluing that of France; and it was imagined at that time. How it proved otherwise in the event; how France came triumphant out of the war that ended by the treaty of Ryswic, and though she gave up a great deal, yet preserved the greatest and the best part of her conquests and acquisitions made since the treaties of Westphalia, and the Pyrenees; how she acquired, by the gift of Spain, that whole monarchy for one of her princes, though she had no reason to expect the least part of it without a war at one time, nor the great lot of it even by a war at any time; in short, how she wound up advantageously the ambitious system she had been fifty years in weaving; how she concluded a war, in which she was defeated on every side, and wholly exhausted, with little diminution of the provinces and barriers acquired to France, and with the quiet possession of Spain and the Indies to a prince of the house of Bourbon: all this, my lord, will be the subject of your researches, when you come down to the latter part of the last period of modern history.

LETTER VIII.

The same subject continued from the year one thousand six hundred and eighty-eight.

YOUR lordship will find, that the objects proposed by the alliance of one thousand six hundred and eighty nine between the emperor and the States, to which England acceded, and which was the foundation of the whole confederacy then formed, were no less than to restore all things to the terms of the Westphalian and Pyrenean treaties, by the war; and to preserve them in that state, after the war, by a defensive alliance and guaranty of the same confederate powers against France. The particular as well as general meaning of this engagement was plain enough: and if it had not been so, the sense of it would have been sufficiently determined, by that separate article, in which England and Holland obliged themselves to assist the " house of Austria, in taking and keeping „ possession of the Spanish monarchy, whenever „ the case should happen of the death of CHARLES „ the second, without lawful heirs. " This engagement was double, and thereby relative to the whole political system of Europe, alike affected by the power and pretensions of France. Hitherto the power of France had been alone regarded, and her pretenſions ſeemed to have been forgot: or to what purpoſe ſhould they have been remembered, whilſt Europe was ſo unhappily conſtituted, that the ſtates, at whoſe expence ſhe increaſed her power, and their friends and allies, thought that they did enough upon every occaſion if they made ſome tolerable compoſition with her? They who were not in circumſtances to refuſe confirming preſent, were little likely to take effectual meaſures againſt future uſurpations. But now, as the alarm was greater than ever, by the outrages that France had committed; and the intrigues ſhe had carried on; by the little regard ſhe had ſhewn to public faith, and by the airs of authority ſhe had aſſumed twenty years together: ſo was the ſpirit againſt her raiſed to an higher pitch, and the means of reducing her power, or at leaſt of checking it, were increaſed. The princes and ſtates who had neglected or favored the growth of this power, which all of them had done in their turns, ſaw their error; ſaw the neceſſity of repairing it, and ſaw that unleſs they could check the power of France, by uniting with a power ſuperior to her's, it would be impoſſible to hinder her from ſucceeding in her great deſigns on the Spaniſh ſucceſſion. The court of England had ſubmitted, not many years before, to abet her uſurpations, and the king of England had ſtooped to be her penſioner. But the crime was not national. On the contrary, the nation had cried out loudly againſt it, even whilſt it was committing: and as ſoon as ever the abdication of king JAMES, and the elevation of the prince of ORANGE to the throne of England happened, the nation engaged with all imaginable zeal in the common cause of Europe, to reduce the exorbitant power of France, to prevent her future and to revenge her past attempts; for even a spirit of revenge prevailed, and the war was a war of anger as well as of interest.

UNHAPPILY this zeal was neither well conducted, nor well seconded. It was zeal without success in the first of the two wars that followed the year one thousand six hundred and eighty-eight; and zeal without knowledge, in both of them. I enter into no detail concerning the events of these two wars. This only I observe on the first of them, that the treaties of Ryswic were far from answering the ends proposed and the engagements taken by the first grand alliance. The power of France, with respect to extent of dominions and strength of barrier, was not reduced to the terms of the Pyrenean treaty, no nor to those of the treaty of Nimeghen. Lorraine was restored indeed with very confiderable referves, and the places taken or usurped on the other side of the Rhine: but then Strasburg was yielded up absolutely to France by the emperor, and by the empire. The concessions to Spain were great, but so were the conquests and the encroachments made upon her by France, since the treaty of Nimeghen: and she got little at Ryswic, I believe nothing more than she had saved at Nimeghen before. All these concessions, however, as well as the acknowledgment of king

WILLIAM, and others made by LEWIS the fourteenth after he had taken Ath and Barcelona, even during the course of the negotiations, compared with the losses and repeated defeats of the allies and the ill state of the confederacy, surprised the generality of mankind, who had not been accustomed to so much moderation and generosity on the part of this prince. But the pretensions of the house of Bourbon on the Spanish succession remained the same. Nothing had been done to weaken them; nothing was prepared to oppose them: and the opening of this succession was visibly at hand: for CHARLES the second had been in immediate danger of dying about this time. His death could not be a remote event: and all the good queen's endeavours to be got with child had proved ineffectual. The league dissolved, all the forces of the confederates dispersed, and many disbanded; France continuing armed, her forces by sea and land increased and held in readiness to act on all sides, it was plain that the confederates had failed in the first object of the grand alliance, that of reducing the power of France; by succeeding in which alone they could have been able to keep the second engagement, that of securing the succession of Spain to the house of Austria.

AFTER this peace, what remained to be done? In the whole nature of things there remained but three. To abandon all care of the Spanish succession was one; to compound with France upon this succession was another; and to prepare, like her, during the interval of peace, to make an advantageous war whenever CHARLES the second should die, was a third. Now the first of these was to leave Spain, and, in leaving Spain, to leave all Europe in some sort at the mercy of France; since whatever disposition the Spaniards should make of their crown, they were quite unable to support it against France; since the emperor could do little without his alliance; and since Bavaria, the third pretender, could do still less, and might find, in such a case, his account perhaps better in treating with the house of Bourbon than with that of Austria. More needs not be said on this head; but on the other two, which I shall consider together, several facts are proper to be mentioned, and several reflections necessary to be made.

WE might have counter-worked, no doubt, in their own methods of policy,. the councils of France, who made peace to dissolve the confederacy, and great concessions, with very suspicious generosity, to gain the Spaniards: we might have waited, like them, that is in arms, the death of CHARLES the second, and have fortified in the mean time the dispositions of the king, the court, and people of Spain, against the pretensions of France: we might have made the peace, which was made some time after that, between the emperor and the Turks, and have obliged the former at any rate to have secured the peace of Hungary, and to have prepared, by these and other expedients, for the war that would inevitably break out on the death of the king of SPAIN.

But all such measures were rendered impracticable, by the emperor chiefly. Experience had shewn, that the powers who engaged in alliance with him must expect to take the whole burden of his cause upon themselves; and that Hungary would maintain a perpetual diversion in favor of France, since he could not resolve to lighten the tyrannical yoke he had established in that country and in Transilvania, nor his ministers to part with the immense confiscations they had appropriated to themselves. Past experience shewed this: and the experience that followed confirmed it very fatally. But further; there was not only little assistance to be expected from him by those who should engage in his quarrel: he did them hurt of another kind, and deprived them of many advantages by false measures of policy and unskilful negotiations. Whilst the death of CHARLES the second was expected almost daily, the court of Vienna seemed to have forgot the court of Madrid, and all the pretensions on that crown. When the count D'HARRACH was sent thither, the imperial councils did something worse. The king of SPAIN was ready to declare the archduke CHARLES his successor; he was desirous to have this young prince sent into Spain: the bent of the people was in favor of Austria, or it had been so, and might have been easily turned the same way again: at court no cabal was yet formed in favor of Bourbon, and a very weak intrigue was on foot in favor of the electoral prince of BAVARIA. Not only CHARLES might have been on the spot ready to reap the succession, but a German army might have been there to defend it; for the court of Madrid insisted on having twelve thousand of these troops, and, rather than not to have them offered to contribute to the payment of them privately: because it would have been too unpopular among the Spaniards, and too prejudicial to the Austrian interest, to have had it known that the emperor declined the payment of a body of his own troops that were demanded to secure that monarchy to his son. These proposals were half refused, and half evaded: and in return to the offer of the crown of Spain to the archduke, the imperial councils asked the government of Milan for him. They thought it a point of deep policy to secure the Italian provinces, and to leave to England and Holland the care of the Low countries, of Spain, and the Indies. By declining these proposals the house of Austria renounced in some sort the whole succession: at least she gave England and Holland reasons, whatever engagements these powers had taken, to refuse the harder task of putting her into possession by force; when she might, and would not, procure to the English and Dutch, and her other allies, the easier task of defending her in this possession.

I SAID that the measures mentioned above were rendered impracticable, by the emperor chiefly, because they were rendered so likewise by other circumstances at the same conjuncture. A principal one I shall mention, and it shall be drawn from the state of our own country, and the disposition of our people. Let us take this up from king WILLIAM's acceſſion to our crown. During the whole progreſs that LEWIS the fourteenth made towards ſuch exorbitant power, as gave him well grounded hopes of acquiring at laſt to his family the Spaniſh monarchy, England had been either an idle ſpectator of all that paſſed on the continent, or a faint and uncertain ally againſt France, or a warm and ſure ally on her ſide, or a partial mediator between her and the powers confederated in their common defence. The revolution produced as great a change in our foreign conduct, as in our domeſtic eſtabliſhment: and our nation engaged with great ſpirit in the war of one thouſand ſix hundred and eighty eight. But then this ſpirit was raſh, preſumptuous, and ignorant, ill conducted at home, and ill ſeconded abroad: all which has been touched already. We had waged no long wars on the continent, nor been very deeply concerned in foreign confederacies, ſince the fourteenth and fifteenth centuries. The hiſtory of EDWARD the third, however, and of the firſt twelve or fifteen years of HENRY the ſixth might have taught us ſome general but uſeful leſſons, drawn from remote times, but applicable to the preſent. So might the example of HENRY the eighth, who ſquandered away great ſums for the profit of taking a town or the honor of having an emperor in his pay; and who divided afterwards by treaty the kingdom of France between himſelf and CHARLES the fifth, with ſucceſs ſo little anſwerable to ſuch an undertaking, that it is hard to believe his imperial and English majesty were both in earnest. If they were so, they were both the bubbles of their presumption. But it seems more likely that HENRY the eighth was bubbled on this occasion by the great hopes that CHARLES held out to flatter his vanity: as he had been bubbled by his father-in-law FERDINAND, at the beginning of his reign, in the war of Navarre. But these reflections were not made, nor had we enough considered the example of ELIZABETH, the last of our princes who had made any considerable figure abroad, and from whom we might have learned to act with vigor, but to engage with caution, and always to proportion our assistance according to our abilities, and the real necessities of our allies. The frontiers of France were now so fortified, her commerce and her naval force were so encreased, her armies were grown so numerous, her troops were so disciplined, so inured to war, and so animated by a long course of succesful campaigns, that they who looked on the situation of Europe could not fail to see how difficult the enterprise of reducing her power was become. Difficult as it was, we were obliged, on every account and by reasons of all kinds, to engage in it: but then we should have engaged with more forecast, and have conducted ourselves in the management of it, not with less alacrity and spirit, but with more order, more oeconomy, and a better application of our efforts. But they who governed were glad to engage us at any rate: and we entered on this great scheme of action, as our nation is too apt to do, hurried on by the ruling paſſion of the day. I have been told by ſeveral, who were on the ſtage of the world at this time, that the generality of our people believed, and were encouraged to believe, the war could not be long, if the king was vigorouſly ſupported: and there is a humdrum ſpeech of a ſpeaker, of the houſe of commons, I think, who humbly deſired his majeſty to take this opportunity of reconquering his ancient dutchy of Aquitain. We were ſoon awakened from theſe gaudy dreams. In ſeven or eight years no impreſſion had been made on France, that was beſieged as it were on every ſide: and after repeated defeats in the Low Countries, where king WILLIAM laid the principal ſtreſs of the war, his ſole triumph was the retaking of Namur, that had been taken by the French a few years before. Unſuſtained by ſucceſs abroad, we are not to wonder that the ſpirit flagged at home; nor that the diſcontents of thoſe who were averſe to the eſtabliſhed government, uniting with the far greater number of thoſe who diſliked the adminiſtration, inflamed the general diſcontents of the nation, oppreſſed with taxes, pillaged by uſurers, plundered at ſea, and diſappointed at land. As we run into extremes always, ſome would have continued this war at any rate, even at the ſame rate: but it was not poſſible they ſhould prevail in ſuch a ſituation of affairs, and ſuch a diſpoſition of minds. They who got by the war, and made immenſe fortunes by the neceſſities of the public, were not ſo numerous nor so powerful, as they have been since. The moneyed interest was not yet a rival able to cope with the landed interest, either in the nation or in parliament. The great corporations that had been erected more to serve the turn of party, than for any real national use, aimed indeed even then at the strength and influence which they have since acquired in the legislature; but they had not made the same progress by promoting national corruption, as they and the court have made since. In short, the other extreme prevailed. The generality of people grew as fond of getting out of the war, as they had been of entering into it: and thus far perhaps, considering how it had been conducted, they were not much to be blamed. But this was not all; for when king WILLIAM had made the peace, our martial spirit became at once so pacific, that we seemed resolved to meddle no more in the affairs of the continent, at least to employ our arms no more in the quarrels that might arise there: and accordingly we reduced our troops in England to seven thousand men.

I HAVE sometimes considered, in reflecting on these passages, what I should have done, if I had sat in parliament at that time; and have been forced to own myself, that I should have voted for disbanding the army then; as I voted in the following parliament for censuring the partition-treaties. I am forced to own this, because I remember how imperfect my notions were of the situation of Europe in that extraordinary crisis, and how much I saw the true interest of my own country in an half light. But, my lord, I own it with some shame; because in truth nothing could be more absurd than the conduct we held. What! because we had not reduced the power of France by the war, nor excluded the house of Bourbon from the Spanish succession, nor compounded with her upon it by the peace; and because the house of Austria had not helped herself, nor put it into our power to help her with more advantage and better prospect of success — were we to leave that whole succession open to the invasions of France, and to suffer even the contingency to subsist, of seeing those monarchies united? What! because it was become extravagant, after the trials so lately made, to think ourselves any longer engaged by treaty, or obliged by good policy, to put the house of Austria in possession of the whole Spanish monarchy, and to defend her in this possession by force of arms, were we to leave the whole at the mercy of France? If we were not to do so, if we were not to do one of the three things that I said above remained to be done, and if the emperor put it out of our power to do another of them with advantage; were we to put it still more out of our power, and to wait unarmed for the death of the king of SPAIN? In fine, if we had not the prospect of disputing with France, so successfully as we might have had it, the Spanish succession, whenever it should be open; were we not only to shew by disarming, that we would not dispute it at all, but to censure likewise the second of the three things mentioned above, and which king

WILLIAM put in practice, the compounding with France, to prevent if possible a war, in which we were averse to engage?

ALLOW me to push these reflections a little further, and to observe to your lordship, that if the proposal of sending the archduke into Spain had been accepted in time by the imperial court, and taken effect and become a measure of the confederacy, that war indeed would have been protracted; but France could not have hindered the passage of this prince and his German forces: and our fleet would have been better employed in escorting them, and in covering the coasts of Spain and of the dominions of that crown both in Europe and in America, than it was in so many unmeaning expeditions from the battle of La Hogue to the end of the war. France indeed would have made her utmost efforts to have had satisfaction on her pretensions, as ill founded as they were. She would have ended that war, as we began the next, when we demanded a reasonable satisfaction for the emperor: and though I think that the allies would have had, in very many respects, more advantages in defending Spain, than in attacking France; yet, upon a supposition that the defence would have been as ill conducted as the attack was, and that by consequence, whether CHARLES the second had lived to the conclusion of this war, or had died before it, the war must have ended in some partition or other; this partition would have been made by the Spaniards themselves. They had been forced to compound with France on her former pretensions, and they must and they would have compounded on these, with an Austrian prince on the throne, just as they compounded, and probably much better than they compounded, on the pretensions we supported against them, when they had a prince of Bourbon on their throne. France could not have distressed the Spaniards, nor have over-run their monarchy, if they had been united; and they would have been united in this case, and supported by the whole confederacy: as we distressed both France and them, over-run their monarchy in one hemisphere, and might have done so in both, when they were disunited, and supported by France alone. France would not have acted, in such negotiations, the ridiculous part which the emperor acted in those that led to the peace of Utrecht, nor have made her bargain worse by neglecting to make it in time. But the war ending as it did, though I cannot see how king WILLIAM could avoid leaving the crown of Spain and that entire monarchy at the discretion of LEWIS the fourteenth, otherwise than by compounding to prevent a new war he was in no sort prepared to make; yet it is undeniable, that, by consenting to a partition of their monarchy, he threw the Spaniards into the arms of France. The first partition might have taken place, perhaps, if the electoral prince of BAVARIA had lived, whom the French and Spaniards too would have seen much more willingly than the archduke on the throne of Spain.

Spain. For among all the parties into which that court was divided in one thousand six hundred and ninety eight, when this treaty was made, that of Auſtria was grown the weakeſt, by the difguſt taken at a German queen, and at the rapacity and inſolence of her favorites. The French were looked upon with eſteem and kindneſs at Madrid; but the Germans were become, or growing to be, objects of contempt to the miniſters, and of averſion to the people. The electoral prince died in one thouſand ſix hundred and ninety nine. The ſtar of Auſtria, ſo fatal to all thoſe who were obſtacles to the ambition of that houſe, prevailed; as the elector expreſſed himſelf in the firſt pangs of his grief. The ſtate of things changed very much by his death. The archduke was to have Spain and the Indies, according to a ſecond partition: and the Spaniards, who had expreſſed great reſentment at the firſt, were puſhed beyond their bearing by this. They ſoon appeared to be ſo; for the ſecond treaty of partition was ſigned in March one thouſand ſeven hundred; and the will was made, to the beſt of my remembrance, in the October following. I ſhall not enter here into many particulars concerning theſe great events. They will be related faithfully, and I hope fully explained, in a work which your lordſhip may take the trouble very probably of peruſing ſome time or other, and which I ſhall rather leave, than give to the public. Something however muſt be ſaid more,

O

to continue and wind up this summary of the latter period of modern history.

FRANCE then saw her advantage, and improved it no doubt, though not in the manner, nor with the circumstances, that some lying scriblers of memorials and anecdotes have advanced. She had sent one of the ablest men of her court to that of Madrid, the marshal of HARCOURT, and she had stipulated in the second treaty of partition, that the archduke should go neither into Spain nor the dutchy of Milan, during the life of CHARLES the second. She was willing to have her option between a treaty and a will. By the acceptation of the will, all king WILLIAM's measures were broke. He was unprepared for war as much as when he made these treaties to prevent one; and if he meant in making them, what some wise, but refining men have suspected, and what I confess I see no reason to believe, only to gain time by the difficulty of executing them, and to prepare for making war, whenever the death of the king of SPAIN should alarm mankind, and rouse his own subjects out of their inactivity and neglect of foreign interests, if so, he was disappointed in that too; for France took possession of the whole monarchy at once, and with universal concurrence, at least without opposition or difficulty, in favor of the duke of ANJOU. By what has been observed, or hinted rather very shortly, and I fear a little confusedly, it is plain that reducing the power of France, and securing the whole Spanish succession to the house of Austria, were two points that king WILLIAM, at the head of the British and Dutch commonwealths and of the greatest confederacy Europe had seen, was obliged to give up. All the acquisitions that France cared to keep for the maintenance of her power were confirmed to her by the treaty of Ryswic: and king WILLIAM allowed, indirectly at least, the pretensions of the house of Bourbon to the Spanish succession, as LEWIS the fourteenth allowed, in the same manner, those of the house of Austria, by the treaties of partition. Strange situation! in which no expedient remained to prepare for an event, visibly so near, and of such vast importance as the death of the king of SPAIN, but a partition of his monarchy, without his consent, or his knowledge! If king WILLIAM had not made this partition, the emperor would have made one, and with as little regard to trade, to the barrier of the seven provinces, or to the general system of Europe, as had been shewed by him when he made the private treaty with France already mentioned, in one thousand six hundred and sixty eight. The ministers of Vienna were not wanting to insinuate to those of France overtures of a separate treaty, as more conducive to their common interests than the accession of his imperial majesty to that of partition. But the councils of Versailles judged very reasonably, that a partition made with England and Holland would be more effectual than any other, if a partition was to take place: and that such a partition would be just as effectual as one made with the emperor, to furnish arguments to the emissaries of France, and motives to the Spanish councils, if a will in favor of France could be obtained. I repeat it again; I cannot see what king WILLIAM could do in such circumstances as he found himself in after thirty years struggle, except what he did: neither can I see how he could do what he did, especially after the resentment expressed by the Spaniards, and the furious memorial presented by CANALES on the conclusion of the first treaty of partition, without apprehending that the consequence would be a will in favor of France. He was in the worst of all political circumstances, and that wherein no one good measure remains to be taken; and out of which he left the two nations, at the head of whom he had been so long, to fight and negotiate themselves and their confederates, as well as they could.

WHEN this will was made and accepted, LEWIS the fourteenth had succeeded, and the powers in opposition to him had failed, in all the great objects of interest and ambition, which they had kept in sight for more than forty years; that is, from the beginning of the present period. The actors changed their parts in the tragedy that followed. The power, that had so long and so cruelly attacked, was now to defend, the Spanish monarchy: and the powers, that had so long defended, were now to attack it. Let us see how this was brought about: and that we may see it the better, and make a better judgment of all that passed from the death of CHARLES the second to the peace of

Utrecht, let us go back to the time of his death, and confider the circumſtances that formed this complicated ſtate of affairs in three views; a view of right, a view of policy, and a view of power.

The right of ſucceeding to the crown of Spain would have been undoubtedly in the children of MARIA THERESA, that is, in the houſe of Bourbon; if this right had not been barred by the ſolemn renunciations ſo often mentioned. The pretenſions of the houſe of Auſtria were founded on theſe renunciations, on the ratification of them by the Pyrenean treaty, and the confirmation of them by the will of PHILIP the fourth. The pretenſions of the houſe of Bourbon were founded on a ſuppoſition, it was indeed no more, and a vain one too, that theſe renunciations were in their nature null. On this foot the diſpute of right ſtood during the life of CHARLES the ſecond, and on the ſame it would have continued to ſtand even after his death, if the renunciations had remained unſhaken; if his will, like that of his father, had confirmed them, and had left the crown, in purſuance of them, to the houſe of Auſtria. But the will of CHARLES the ſecond, annulling theſe renunciations, took away the ſole foundation of the Auſtrian pretenſions; for, however this act might be obtained, it was juſt as valid as his father's, and was confirmed by the univerſal concurrence of the Spaniſh nation to the new ſettlement he made of that crown. Let it be, as I think it ought to be, granted, that the true heirs could not claim againſt renunciations that were, if I may ſay ſo, conditions of their

birth: but CHARLES the second had certainly as
good a right to change the course of succession
agreeable to the order of nature and the constitution of that monarchy, after his true heirs were
born, as PHILIP the fourth had to change it contrary to this order and this constitution, before
they were born, or at any other time. He had
as good a right, in short, to dispense with the
Pyrenean treaty, and to set it aside in this respect,
as his father had to make it: so that the renunciations being annulled by that party to the
Pyrenean treaty who had exacted them, they
could be deemed no longer binding, by virtue of
this treaty, on the party who had made them.
The sole question that remained therefore between
these rival houses, as to right, was this, whether
the engagements taken by LEWIS the fourteenth
in the partition treaties obliged him to adhere to the
terms of the last of them in all events, and to
deprive his family of the succession which the king
of SPAIN opened, and the Spanish nation offered
to them; rather than to depart from a composition
he had made, on pretensions that were disputable
then, but were now out of dispute? It may be
said, and it was said, that the treaties of partition
being absolute, without any condition or exception
relative to any disposition the king of SPAIN had
made or might make of his succession, in favor of
Bourbon or Austria; the disposition made by his
will, in favor of the duke of ANJOU, could not
affect the engagements so lately taken by LEWIS
the fourteenth in these treaties, nor dispense with

a literal obfervation of them. This might be true on ftrict principles of juftice; but I apprehend that none of thefe powers, who exclaimed fo loudly againft the perfidy of France in this cafe, would have been more fcrupulous in a parallel cafe. The maxim 'fummum jus eft fumma injuria' would have been quoted, and the rigid letter of the treaties would have been foftened by an equitable interpretation of their fpirit and intention. His imperial majefty, above all, had not the leaft color of right to exclaim againft France on this occafion; for in general, if his family was to be ftripped of all the dominions they have acquired by breach of faith, and means much worfe than the acceptation of the will, even allowing all the invidious circumftances imputed to the conduct of France to be true, the Auftrian family would fink from their prefent grandeur to that low ftate they were in two or three centuries ago. In particular, the emperor, who had conftantly refufed to accede to the treaties of partition, or to fubmit to the difpofitions made by them, had not the leaft plaufible pretence to object to LEWIS the fourteenth, that he departed from them. Thus, I think, the right of the two houfes ftood on the death of CHARLES the fecond. The right of the Spaniards, an independent nation, to regulate their own fucceffion, or to receive the prince whom their dying monarch had called to it; and the right of England and Holland to regulate the fucceffion, to divide, and parcel out this monarchy in different lots, it would be equally foolish to go about to establish. One is too evident, the other too absurd, to admit of any proof. But enough has been said concerning a right, which was in truth little regarded by any of the parties concerned immediately or remotely in the whole course of these proceedings. Particular interests were alone regarded, and these were pursued as ambition, fear, resentment, and vanity directed: I mean the ambition of the two houses contending for superiority of power; the fear of England and Holland lest this superiority should become too great in either; the resentment of Spain at the dismemberment of that monarchy projected by the partition-treaties; and the vanity of that nation, as well as of the princes of the house of Bourbon: for as vanity mingled with resentment to make the will, vanity had a great share in determining the acceptation of it.

LET us now consider the same conjuncture in a view of policy. The policy of the Spanish councils was this. They could not brook that their monarchy should be divided: and this principle is expressed strongly in the will of CHARLES the second, where he exhorts his subjects not to suffer any dismemberment or diminution of a monarchy founded by his predecessors with so much glory. Too weak to hinder this dismemberment by their own strength, too well apprised of the little force and little views of the court of Vienna, and their old allies having engaged to procure this dismemberment even by force of arms; nothing remained for them to do, upon this principle, but to detach France from the engagements of the partition treaties, by giving their whole monarchy to a prince of the house of Bourbon. As much as may have been said concerning the negotiations of France to obtain a will in her favor, and yet to keep in reserve the advantages stipulated for her by the partition-treaties if such a will could not be obtained, and though I am persuaded that the marshal of HARCOURT, who helped to procure this will, made his court to LEWIS the fourteenth as much as the marshal of TALLARD, who negotiated the partitions; yet it is certain, that the acceptation of the will was not a measure definitively taken at Versailles when the king of SPAIN died. The alternative divided those councils, and, without entering at this time into the arguments urged on each side, adhering to the partitions seemed the cause of France, accepting the will that of the house of Bourbon.

It has been said by men of great weight in the councils of Spain, and was said at that time by men as little fond of the house of Bourbon, or of the French nation, as their fathers had been; that if England and Holland had not formed a confederacy and begun a war, they would have made PHILIP the fifth as good a Spaniard as any of the preceding PHILIPS, and not have endured the influence of French councils in the administration of their government: but that we threw them entirely into the hands of France when we began the war, because the fleets and armies of this crown being necessary to their defence, they could not avoid submitting to this influence as long as the same necessity continued; and, in fact, we have seen that the influence lasted no longer. But notwithstanding this, it must be confessed, that a war was unavoidable. The immediate securing of commerce and of barriers, the preventing an union of the two monarchies in some future time, and the preservation of a certain degree at least of equality in the scales of power, were points too important to England, Holland, and the rest of Europe, to be rested on the moderation of French, and the vigor of Spanish councils, under a prince of the house of France. If satisfaction to the house of Austria, to whose rights England and Holland shewed no great regard whilst they were better founded than they were since the will, had been alone concerned; 'a drop of blood spilt, or five shillings spent in the quarrel, would have been too much profusion. But this was properly the scale into which it became the common interest to throw all the weight that could be taken out of that of Bourbon. And therefore your lordship will find, that when negotiations with D'AVAUX were set on foot in Holland to prevent a war, or rather on our part to gain time to prepare for it, in which view the Dutch and we had both acknowledged PHILIP king of SPAIN; the great article we insisted on was, that reasonable satisfaction should be given the emperor, upon his pretensions founded on the treaty of partition. We could do no otherwise; and France, who offered to make the treaty of Ryswic the foundation of that treaty, could do no otherwise than refuse to consent that the treaty of partition should be so, after accepting the will, and thereby engaging to oppose all partition or difmemberment of the Spanish monarchy. I should mention none of the other demands of England and Holland, if I could neglect to point out to your lordship's obfervation, that the fame artifice was employed at this time, to perplex the more a negotiation that could not fucceed on other accounts, as we faw employed in the courfe of the war, by the English and Dutch minifters, to prevent the fuccefs of negotiations that might, and ought to have fucceeded. The demand I mean is that of " a liberty not only „ to explain the terms propofed, but to increafe „ or amplify them in the courfe of the negotiation." I do not remember the words, but this is the fenfe, and this was the meaning of the confederates in both cafes.

IN the former, king WILLIAM was determined to begin the war by all the rules of good policy; fince he could not obtain, nay fince France could not grant in that conjuncture, nor without being forced to it by a war, what he was obliged by thefe very rules to demand. He intended therefore nothing by this negotiation, if it may be called fuch, but to preferve forms and appearances, and perhaps, which many have fufpected, to have time to prepare, as I hinted juft now, both abroad and at home. Many things concurred to favor his preparations abroad. The alarm, that had been given by the acceptation of the will, was increafed by every ftep that France made to fecure the effect of it. Thus, for inftance, the furprifing and feizing the Dutch troops, in the fame night, and at the same hour, that were dispersed in the garrisons of the Spanish Netherlands, was not excused by the necessity of securing those places to the obedience of PHILIP, nor softened by the immediate dismission of those troops. The impression it made was much the same as those of the surprises and seizures of France in former usurpations. No one knew then, that the sovereignty of the ten provinces was to be yielded up to the elector of BAVARIA: and every one saw that there remained no longer any barrier between France and the seven provinces. At home, the disposition of the nation was absolutely turned to a war with France, on the death of king JAMES the second, by the acknowledgment LEWIS the fourteenth made of his son as king of England. I know what has been said in excuse for this measure, taken as I believe, on female importunity; but certainly without any regard to public faith, to the true interest of France in those circumstances, or to the true interest of the prince thus acknowledged, in any. It was said, that the treaty of Ryswic obliging his most christian majesty only not to disturb king WILLIAM in his possession, he might, without any violation of it, have acknowledged this prince as king of England; according to the political casuistry of the French, and the example of France, who finds no fault with the powers that treat with the kings of England, although the kings of England retain the title of kings of France; as well as the example of Spain, who makes no complaints that other states treat with the kings of France, although the kings of France retain the title of Navarre. But besides that the examples are not apposite, because no other powers acknowledge in form the king of England to be king of France, nor the king of France to be king of Navarre; with what face could the French excuse this measure? Could they excuse it by urging that they adhered to the strict letter of one article of the treaty of Ryfwic, against the plain meaning of that very article, and against the whole tenor of that treaty; in the same breath with which they justified the acceptation of the will, by pretending they adhered to the supposed spirit and general intention of the treaties of partition, in contradiction to the letter, to the specific engagements, and to the whole purport of those treaties? This part of the conduct of Lewis the fourteenth may appear justly the more surprising, because in most other parts of his conduct at the same time, and in some to his disadvantage, he acted cautiously, endeavoured to calm the minds of his neighbours, to reconcile Europe to his grandson's elevation, all to avoid all shew of beginning hostilities.

Though king William was determined to engage in a war with France and Spain, yet the same good policy, that determined him to engage, determined him not to engage too deeply. The engagement taken in the grand alliance of one thousand seven hundred and one is, " To procure „ an equitable and reasonable satisfaction to his „ imperial majesty for his pretension to the Spanish „ succession; and sufficient security to the king of

" ENGLAND, and the States General, for their dominions, and for the navigation and commerce of their subjects, and to prevent the union of the two monarchies of France and Spain." As king of England, as stateholder of Holland, he neither could, nor did engage any further. It may be disputed perhaps among speculative politicians, whether the balance of power in Europe would have been better preserved by that scheme of partition, which the treaties, and particularly the last of them, proposed, or by that which the grand alliance proposed to be the object of the war? I think there is little room for such a dispute, as I shall have occasion to say hereafter more expresly. In this place I shall only say, that the object of this war, which king WILLIAM meditated, and queen ANNE waged, was a partition, by which a prince of the house of Bourbon, already acknowledged by us and the Dutch as king of Spain, was to be left on the throne of that dismembered monarchy. The wisdom of those councils saw that the peace of Europe might be restored and secured on this foot, and that the liberties of Europe would be in no danger.

THE scales of the balance of power will never be exactly poized, nor in the precise point of equality either discernible or necessary to be discerned. It is sufficient in this, as in other human affairs, that the deviation be not too great. Some there will always be. A constant attention to these deviations is therefore necessary. When they are little, their increase may be easily prevented by early care and the precautions that good policy suggests. But when they become great for want of this care and these precautions, or by the force of unforeseen events, more vigor is to be exerted and greater efforts to be made. But even in such cases, much reflection is necessary on all the circumstances that form the conjuncture; lest, by attacking with ill success, the deviation be confirmed; and the power that is deemed already exorbitant become more so; and lest, by attacking with good success, whilst one scale is pillaged, too much weight of power be thrown into the other. In such cases, he who has considered, in the histories of former ages, the strange revolutions that time produces, and the perpetual flux and reflux of public as well as private fortunes, of kingdoms and states as well as of those who govern or are governed in them, will incline to think, that if the scales can be brought back by a war, nearly, though not exactly, to the point they were at before this great deviation from it, the rest may be left to accidents, and to the use that good policy is able to make of them.

When Charles the fifth was at the heighth of his power, and in the zenith of his glory, when a king of France and a pope were at once his prisoners; it must be allowed, that, his situation and that of his neighbours compared; they had as much at least to fear from him and from the house of Austria, as the neighbours of Lewis the fourteenth had to fear from him and from the house of Bourbon, when, after all his other success, one of his grandchildren was placed on the Spanish throne. And yet among all the conditions of the several leagues againſt Charles the fifth, I do not remember that it was ever ſtipulated, that " no „ peace should be made with him as long as he „ continued to be emperor and king of Spain; „ nor as long as any Auſtrian prince continued „ capable of uniting on his head the Imperial and „ Spanish crowns. "

If your lordship makes the application, you will find that the difference of ſome circumſtances does not hinder this example from being very appoſite, and ſtrong to the preſent purpoſe. Charles the fifth was emperor and king of Spain; but neither was Lewis the fourteenth king of Spain, nor Philip the fifth king of France. That had happened in one inſtance, which it was apprehended might happen in the other. It had happened, and it was reaſonably to be apprehended that it might happen again, and that the Imperial and Spaniſh crowns might continue, not only in the ſame family, but on the ſame heads; for meaſures were taken to ſecure the ſucceſſion of both to Philip the ſon of Charles. We do not find however that any confederacy was formed, any engagement taken, or any war made, to remove or prevent this great evil. The princes and ſtates of Europe contented themſelves to oppoſe the deſigns of Charles the fifth, and to check the growth of his power accaſionally, and as intereſt invited, or neceſſity forced them to do; not conſtantly. They did perhaps too little againſt him, and

ſometimes

sometimes too much for him: but if they did too little of one kind, time and accident did the rest. Distinct dominions, and different pretensions, created contrary interests in the house of Austria: and on the abdication of CHARLES the fifth, his brother succeeded, not his son, to the empire. The house of Austria divided into a German and a Spanish branch: and if the two branches came to have a mutual influence on one another and frequently a common interest, it was not till one of them had fallen from grandeur, and till the other was rather aiming at it, than in possession of it. In short PHILIP was excluded from the imperial throne by so natural a progression of causes and effects, arising not only in Germany but in his own family, that if a treaty had been made to exclude him from it in favor of FERDINAND, such a treaty might have been said very probably to have executed itself.

THE precaution I have mentioned, and that was neglected in this case without any detriment to the common cause of Europe, was not neglected in the grand alliance of one thousand seven hundred and one. For in that, one of the ends proposed by the war is, to obtain an effectual security against the contingent union of the crowns of France and Spain. The will of CHARLES the second provides against the same contingency: and this great principle of preventing too much dominion and power from falling to the lot of either of the families of Bourbon or Austria, seemed to be agreed on all sides; since in the partition-treaty

P

the same precaution was taken against an union of the Imperial and Spanish crowns. King WILLIAM was enough piqued against France. His ancient prejudices were strong and well founded. He had been worsted in war, over-reached in negotiation, and personally affronted by her. England and Holland were sufficiently alarmed and animated, and a party was not wanting, even in our island, ready to approve any engagements he would have taken against France and Spain, and in favor of the house of Austria; though we were less concerned, by any national interest, than any other power that took part in the war, either then, or afterwards. But this prince was far from taking a part beyond that which the particular interests of England and Holland, and the general interest of Europe, necessarily required. Pique must have no more a place than affection, in deliberations of this kind. To have engaged to dethrone PHILIP, out of resentment to LEWIS the fourteenth, would have been a resolution worthy of CHARLES the twelfth, king of Sweden, who sacrificed his country, his people, and himself at last, to his revenge. To have engaged to conquer the Spanish monarchy for the house of Austria, or to go, in favor of that family, one step beyond those that were necessary to keep this house on a foot of rivalry with the other, would have been, as I have hinted, to act the part of a vassal, not of an ally. The former pawns his state, and ruins his subjects, for the interest of his superior lord, perhaps for his lord's humor, or his passion: the latter goes no further than his own interest carries him; nor makes war for those of another, nor even for his own if they are remote and contingent, as if he fought pro aris et focis, for his religion, his liberty, and his property. Agreeably to these principles of good policy, we entered into the war that began on the death of CHARLES the second; but we soon departed from them, as I shall have occasion to observe in considering the state of things, at this remarkable juncture, in a view of strength.

LET me recall here what I have said somewhere else. They who are in the sinking scale of the balance of power do not easily, nor soon, come off from the habitual prejudices of superiority over their neighbours, nor from the confidence that such prejudices inspire. From the year one thousand six hundred and sixty seven, to the end of that century, France had been constantly in arms, and her arms had been successful. She had sustained a war, without any confederates against the principal powers of Europe confederated against her, and had finished it with advantage on every side, just before the death of the king of SPAIN. She continued armed after the peace, by sea and land. She increased her forces, while other nations reduced theirs, and was ready to defend, or to invade her neighbours, whilst, their confederacy being dissolved, they were in no condition to invade her, and in a bad one to defend themselves. Spain and France had now one common cause. The electors of BAVARIA and COLOGNE supported it in Germany, the duke of SAVOY was an ally, the duke of MANTUA a vaffal of the two crowns in Italy. In a word, appearances were formidable on that fide; and if a diftruft of ftrength, on the fide of the confederacy, had induced England and Holland to compound with France for a partition of the Spanish fucceffion, there feemed to be ftill greater reafon for this diftruft after the acceptation of the will, the peaceable and ready fubmiffion of the entire monarchy of Spain to PHILIP, and all the meafures taken to fecure him in this pof-feffion. Such appearances might well impofe. They did fo on many, and on none more than on the French themfelves, who engaged with great confidence and fpirit in the war; when they found it, as they might well expect it would be, unavoidable. The ftrength of France however, though great, was not fo great as the French thought it, nor equal to the efforts they undertook to make. Their engagement, to maintain the Spanish monarchy entire under the dominion of PHILIP, exceeded their ftrength. Our engagement, to procure fome out-skirts of it for the houfe of Auftria, was not in the fame difproportion to our ftrength. If I fpeak pofitively on this occafion, yet I cannot be accufed of prefumption; becaufe, how difputable foever thefe points might be when they were points of political fpeculation, they are fuch no longer, and the judgment I make is dictated to me by experience. France threw herfelf into the finking fcale, when she accepted the will. Her fcale continued to fink during the whole courfe of the war, and might have been kept by the peace as low as the true interest of Europe required. What I remember to have heard the duke of MARLBOROUGH say, before he went to take on him the command of the army in the Low Countries in one thousand seven hundred and two, proved true. The French misreckoned very much, if they made the same comparison between their troops and those of their enemies, as they had made in precedent wars. Those that had been opposed to them, in the last, were raw for the most part when it began, the British particularly: but they had been disciplined, if I may say so, by their defeats. They were grown to be veteran at the peace of Ryswic, and though many had been disbanded, yet they had been disbanded lately: so that even these were easily formed anew, and the spirit that had been raised continued in all. Supplies of men to recruit the armies were more abundant on the side of the confederacy, than on that of the two crowns: a necessary consequence of which it seemed to be, that those of the former would grow better, and those of the latter worse, in a long, extensive, and bloody war. I believe it proved so; and if my memory does not deceive me, the French were forced very early to send recruits to their armies, as they send slaves to their gallies. A comparison between those who were to direct their councils, and to conduct the armies on both sides, is a task it would become me little to undertake. The event shewed, that if France had had her CONDE, her TURENNE, or her

LUXEMBURG, to oppose to the confederates: the confederates might have opposed to her, with equal confidence, their EUGENE of Savoy, their MARLBOROUGH, or their STARENBERG. But there is one observation I cannot forbear to make. The alliances were concluded, the quotas were settled, and the season for taking the field approached, when king WILLIAM died. The event could not fail to occasion some consternation on one side, and to give some hopes on the other; for, notwithstanding the ill success with which he made war generally, he was looked upon as the sole centre of union that could keep together the great confederacy then forming: and how much the French feared, from his life, had appeared a few years before, in the extravagant and indecent joy they expressed on a false report of his death. A short time shewed how vain the fears of some and the hopes of others were. By his death, the duke of MARLBOROUGH was raised to the head of the army, and indeed of the confederacy: where he, a new, a private man, a subject, acquired by merit and by management a more deciding influence, than high birth, confirmed authority, and even the crown of Great Britain, had given to king WILLIAM. Not only all the parts of that vast machine, the grand alliance, were kept more compact and entire; but a more rapid and vigorous motion was given to the whole: and, instead of languishing out disastrous campaigns, we saw every scene of the war full of action. All those wherein he appeared, and many of those wherein he was not then an actor, but abettor however of their action, were crowned with the most triumphant success. I take with pleasure this opportunity of doing justice to that great man, whose faults I knew, whose virtues I admired; and whose memory, as the greatest general and as the greatest minister that our country or perhaps any other has produced, I honor. But besides this, the observation I have made comes into my subject, since it serves to point out to your lordship the proof of what I said above, that France undertook too much, when she undertook to maintain the Spanish monarchy entire in the possession of PHILIP: and that we undertook no more than what was proportionable to our strength, when we undertook to weaken that monarchy by dismembering it, in the hands of a prince of the house of Bourbon, which we had been disabled by ill fortune and worse conduct to keep out of them. It may be said that the great success of the confederates against France proves that their generals were superior to her's, but not that their forces and their national strength were so; that with the same force with which she was beaten, she might have been victorious; that if she had been so, or if the success of the war had varied, or been less decisive against her in Germany, in the Low Countries, and in Italy, as it was in Spain, her strength would have appeared sufficient, and that of the confederacy insufficient. Many things may be urged to destroy this reasoning: I content myself with one. France could not long have made even the unsuccessful efforts she did make, if England and Holland had done what it is undeniable they had strength to do; if besides pillaging, I do not say conquering, the Spanish West-Indies, they had hindered the French from going to the South Sea; as they did annually during the whole course of the war without the least molestation, and from whence they imported into France in that time as much silver and gold as the whole species of that kingdom amounted to. With this immense and constant supply of wealth France was reduced in effect to bankruptcy before the end of the war. How much sooner must she have been so, if this supply had been kept from her? The confession of France herself is on my side. She confessed her inability to support what she had undertaken, when she sued for peace as early as the year one thousand seven hundred and six. She made her utmost efforts to answer the expectation of the Spaniards, and to keep their monarchy entire. When experience had made it evident that this was beyond her power, she thought herself justified to the Spanish nation, in consenting to a partition, and was ready to conclude a peace with the allies on the principles of their grand alliance. But as France seemed to flatter herself, till experience made her desirous to abandon an enterprise that exceeded her strength; you will find, my lord, that her enemies began to flatter themselves in their turn, and to form designs and take engagements that exceeded theirs. Great Britain was drawn into these engagements little by little; for I do not remember any parliamentary declaration for continuing the war till PHILIP should be dethroned, before the year one thousand seven hundred and six: and then such a declaration was judged necessary to second the resolution of our ministers and our allies, in departing from the principles of the grand alliance, and in proposing not only the reduction of the French, but the conquest of the Spanish monarchy, as the objects of the war. This new plan had taken place, and we had begun to act upon it, two years before, when the treaty with Portugal was concluded, and the archduke CHARLES, now emperor, was sent into Portugal first, and into Catalonia afterwards, and was acknowledged and supported as king of Spain.

WHEN your lordship peruses the anecdotes of the times here spoken of, and considers the course and event of the great war which broke out on the death of the king of Spain, CHARLES the second, and was ended by the treaties of Utrecht and Rastat; you will find, that in order to form a true judgment on the whole you must consider very attentively the great change made by the new plan that I have mentioned; and compare it with the plan of the grand alliance, relatively to the general interest of Europe, and the particular interest of your own country. It will not, because it cannot, be denied, that all the ends of the grand alliance might have been obtained by a peace in one thousand seven hundred and six. I need not recall the events of that, and of the precedent years of the war. Not only the arms of France had been defeated on every side; but the inward state of that kingdom was already more exhausted than it had ever been. She went on indeed, but she staggered and reeled under the burden of the war. Our condition, I speak of Great Britain, was not quite so bad; but the charge of the war increased annually upon us. It was evident that this charge must continue to increase, and it was no less evident that our nation was unable to bear it without falling soon into such distress, and contracting such debts, as we have seen and felt, and still feel. The Dutch neither restrained their trade, nor over-loaded it with taxes. They soon altered the proportion of their quotas, and were deficient even after this alteration in them. But, however, it must be allowed that they exerted their whole strength; and they and we paid the whole charge of the war. Since therefore by such efforts as could not be continued any longer, without oppressing and impoverishing these nations to a degree that no interest except that of their very being, nor any engagement of assisting an alliance totis viribus can require, France was reduced, and all the ends of the war were become attainable; it will be worth your lordship's while to consider why the true use was not made of the success of the confederates against France and Spain, and why a peace was not concluded in the fifth year of the war. When your lordship considers this, you will compare in your thoughts what the state of Europe would have been, and that of your own country might have been, if the plan of the grand alliance had been purfued: with the poffible as well as certain, the contingent as well as neceffary, confequences of changing this plan in the manner it was changed. You will be of opinion, I think, and it feems to me, after more than twenty years of recollection, re-examination, and reflection, that impartial pofterity muft be of the fame opinion; you will be of opinion, I think, that the war was wife and juft before the change, becaufe neceffary to maintain that equality among the powers of Europe on which the public peace and common profperity depends: and that it was unwife and unjuft after this change, becaufe unneceffary to this end, and directed to other and to contrary ends. You will be guided by undeniable facts to difcover, through all the falfe colors which have been laid, and which deceived many at the time, that the war, after this change, became a war of paffion, of ambition, of avarice, and of private intereft; the private intereft of particular perfons and particular ftates; to which the general intereft of Europe was facrificed fo entirely, that if the terms infifted on by the confederates had been granted, nay if even thofe which France was reduced to grant, in one thoufand feven hundred and ten, had been accepted, fuch a new fyftem of power would have been created as might have expofed the balance of this power to deviations, and the peace of Europe to troubles, not inferior to thofe that the war was defigned, when it began, to prevent. Whilft you obferve this in general, you will find particular occafion to lament the fate of Great Britain, in the midft of triumphs that have been founded so high. She had triumphed indeed to the year one thousand seven hundred and six inclusively: but what were her triumphs afterwards? What was her success after she proceeded on the new plan? I shall say something on that head immediately. Here let me only say, that the glory of taking towns, and winning battles, is to be measured by the utility that results from those victories. Victories, that bring honor to the arms, may bring shame to the councils, of a nation. To win a battle, to take a town, is the glory of a general, and of an army. Of this glory we had a very large share in the course of the war. But the glory of a nation is to proportion the ends she proposes, to her interest and her strength; the means she employs to the ends she proposes, and the vigor she exerts to both. Of this glory, I apprehend, we have had very little to boast, at any time, and particularly in the great conjuncture of which I am speaking. The reasons of ambition, avarice, and private interest, which engaged the princes and states of the confederacy to depart from the principles of the grand alliance, were no reasons for Great Britain. She neither expected nor desired any thing more than what she might have obtained by adhering to those principles. What hurried our nation then, with so much spirit and ardor, into those of the new plan? Your lordship will answer this question to yourself, I believe: by the prejudices and rashness of party; by the influence that the first successes of the confederate arms gave to our ministers; and the popularity they gave, if I may say so, to the war; by ancient, and fresh refentments, which the unjuſt and violent uſurpations, in short the whole conduct of LEWIS the fourteenth for forty years together, his haughty treatment of other princes and ſtates, and even the ſtyle of his court, had created; and, to mention no more, by a notion, groundleſs but prevalent, that he was and would be maſter as long as his grandſon was king of Spain, and that there could be no effectual meaſure taken, though the grand alliance ſuppoſed that there might, to prevent a future union of the two monarchies, as long as a prince of the houſe of Bourbon ſat on the Spaniſh throne. That ſuch a notion should have prevailed, in the firſt confuſion of thoughts which the death and will of CHARLES the ſecond produced, among the generality of men, who ſaw the fleets and armies of France take poſſeſſion of all the parts of the Spaniſh monarchy, is not to be wondered at by thoſe that conſider how ill the generality of mankind are informed, how incapable they are of judging; and yet how ready to pronounce judgment; in fine, how inconſiderately they follow one another in any popular opinion which the heads of party broach, or to which the firſt appearances of things have given occaſion. But, even at this time, the councils of England and Holland did not entertain this notion. They acted on quite another, as might be ſhewn in many inſtances, if any other beſides that of the grand alliance was neceſſary. When theſe councils therefore ſeemed to entertain this notion afterwards, and acted and took engagements to act upon it, we muſt conclude that they had other motives. They could not have theſe; for they knew, that as the Spaniards had been driven by the two treaties of partition to give their monarchy to a prince of the houſe of Bourbon, ſo they were driven into the arms of France by the war that we made to force a third upon them. If we acted rightly on the principles of the grand alliance, they acted rightly on thoſe of the will: and if we could not avoid making an offenſive war, at the expence of forming and maintaining a vaſt confederacy, they could not avoid purchaſing the protection and aſſiſtance of France in a defenſive war, and eſpecially in the beginning of it, according to what I have ſomewhere obſerved already, by yielding to the authority and admitting the influence of that court in all the affairs of their government. Our miniſters knew therefore, that if any inference was to be drawn from the firſt part of this notion, it was for ſhortening, not prolonging, the war; for delivering the Spaniards as ſoon as poſſible from habits of union and intimacy with France; not for continuing them under the ſame neceſſity, till by length of time theſe habits ſhould be confirmed. As to the latter part of this notion, they knew that it was falſe and ſilly. GARTH the beſt natured ingenious wild man I ever knew, might be in the right when he ſaid, in ſome of his poems at that time,

" — An Auſtrian prince alone,
„ Is fit to nod upon a Spaniſh throne."

The ſetting an Auſtrian prince upon it was, no

doubt, the fureſt expedient to prevent an union of the two monarchies of France and Spain; juſt as ſetting a prince of the houſe of Bourbon on that throne was the fureſt expedient to prevent an union of the Imperial and Spaniſh crowns. But it was equally falſe to ſay, in either caſe, that this was the ſole expedient. It would be no paradox, but a propoſition eaſily proved, to advance, that if theſe unions had been effectually provided againſt, the general intereſt of Europe would have been little concerned whether PHILIP or CHARLES had nodded at Madrid. It would be likewiſe no paradox to ſay, that the contingency of uniting France and Spain under the ſame prince appeared more remote, about the middle of the laſt great war, when the dethronement of PHILIP in favor of CHARLES was made a condition of peace ſine qua non, than the contingency of an union of the Imperial and Spaniſh crowns. Nay, I know not whether it would be a paradox to affirm, that the expedient that was taken, and that was always obvious to be taken, of excluding PHILIP and his race from the ſucceſſion of France, by creating an intereſt in all the other princes of the blood, and by conſequence a party in France itſelf, for their excluſion, whenever the caſe ſhould happen, was not in its nature more effectual than any that could have been taken: and ſome muſt have been taken, not only to exclude CHARLES from the empire whenever the caſe ſhould happen that happened ſoon, the death of his brother JOSEPH without iſſue male, but his poſterity likewiſe in all future vacancies of the imperial throne. The expedient that was taken against PHILIP at the treaty of Utrecht, they who opposed the peace attempted to ridicule; but some of them have had occasion since that time to see, though the case has not happened, how effectual it would have been if it had: and he who should go about to ridicule it after our experience, would only make himself ridiculous. Notwithstanding all this, he, who transports himself back to that time, must acknowledge, that the confederated powers in general could not but be of GARTH's mind, and think it more agreeable to the common interest of Europe, that a branch of Austria, rather than a branch of Bourbon, should gather the Spanish succession, and that the maritime powers, as they are called impertinently enough with respect to the superiority of Great Britain, might think it was for their particular interest to have a prince, dependent for some time at least on them, king of Spain, rather than a prince whose dependence, as long as he stood in any, must be naturally on France. I do not say, as some have done, a prince whose family was an old ally, rather than a prince whose family was an old enemy; because I lay no weight on the gratitude of princes, and am as much persuaded that an Austrian king of Spain would have made us returns of that sort in no other proportion than of his want of us, as I am that PHILIP and his race will make no other returns of the same sort to France. If this affair had been entire, therefore, on the death of the king of SPAIN; if we had made no partition, nor

he

he any will, the whole monarchy of Spain would have been the prize to be fought for: and our wishes, and such efforts as we were able to make, in the most unprovided condition imaginable, must have been on the side of Auſtria. But it was far from being entire. A prince of the houſe of Auſtria might have been on the ſpot, before the king of Spain died, to gather his ſucceſſion; but inſtead of this a prince of the houſe of Bourbon was there ſoon afterwards, and took poſſeſſion of the whole monarchy, to which he had been called by the late king's will, and by the voice of the Spaniſh nation. The councils of England and Holland therefore preferred very wiſely, by their engagements in the grand alliance, what was more practicable though leſs eligible, to what they deemed more eligible; but ſaw become by the courſe of events, if not abſolutely impracticable, yet an enterpriſe of more length, more difficulty, and greater expence of blood and treaſure, than theſe nations were able to bear; or than they ought to bear, when their ſecurity and that of the reſt of Europe might be ſufficiently provided for at a cheaper rate. If the confederates could not obtain, by the force of their arms, the ends of the war, laid down in the grand alliance, to what purpoſe would it be to ſtipulate for more? And if they were able to obtain theſe, it was evident that, whilſt they diſmembered the Spaniſh monarchy they muſt reduce the power of France. This happened; the Low Countries were conquered; the French were driven out of Germany and Italy; and Lewis the

Q

fourteenth, who had so long and so lately set mankind at defiance, was reduced to sue for peace.

If it had been granted him in one thousand seven hundred and six, on what foot must it have been granted? The allies had already in their power all the states that were to compose the reasonable satisfaction for the emperor. I say, in their power; because though Naples and Sicily were not actually reduced at that time, yet the expulsion of the French out of Italy, and the disposition of the people of those kingdoms, considered, it was plain the allies might reduce them when they pleased. The confederate arms were superior till then in Spain, and several provinces acknowledged CHARLES the third. If the rest had been yielded to him by treaty, all that the new plan required had been obtained. If the French would not yet have abandoned PHILIP, as we had found that the Castilians would not even when our army was at Madrid, all that the old plan, the plan of the grand alliance required, had been obtained; but still France and Spain had given nothing to purchase a peace, and they were in circumstances not to expect it without purchasing it. They would have purchased it, my lord: and France, as well as Spain, would have contributed a larger share of the price, rather than continue the war, in her exhausted state. Such a treaty of peace would have been a third treaty of partition indeed, but vastly preferable to the two former. The great objection to the former was drawn from that considerable increase of dominion, which the crown of France, and not a branch of

the houfe of Bourbon, acquired by them. I know
what may be faid fpeciously enough to perfuade,
that fuch an increafe of dominion would not have
augmented, but would rather have weakened the
power of France, and what examples may be drawn
from hiftory to countenance fuch an opinion. I
know likewife, that the compact figure of France,
and the contiguity of all her provinces, make a
very effential part of the force of her monarchy.
Had the defigns of CHARLES the eighth, LEWIS
the twelfth, FRANCIS the firft, and HENRY the
fecond, fucceeded, the dominions of France would
have been more extenfive, and I believe the ftrength
of her monarchy would have been lefs. I have
fometimes thought that even the lofs of the battle
of St. Quentin, which obliged HENRY the fecond
to recal the duke of GUISE with his army out of
Italy, was in this refpect no unhappy event. But
the reafoning which is good, I think, when applied
to thofe times, will not hold when applied to ours,
and to the cafe I confider here; the ftate of France,
the ftate of her neighbours, and the whole confti-
tution of Europe being fo extremely different. The
objection therefore to the two treaties of partition
had a real weight. The power of France, deemed
already exorbitant, would have been increafed by
this acceffion of dominion, in the hands of LEWIS
the fourteenth: and the ufe he intended to make
of it by keeping Italy and Spain in awe, appears
in the article that gave him the ports on the
Tufcan coaft, and the province of Guipufcoa. This
king WILLIAM might, and, I queftion not, did

see; but that prince might think too, that for this very reason LEWIS the fourteenth would adhere, in all events, to the treaty of partition: and that these consequences were more remote, and would be less dangerous, than those of making no partition at all. The partition, even the worst that might have been made, by a treaty of peace in one thousand seven hundred and six, would have been the very reverse of this. France would have been weakened, and her enemies strengthened, by her concessions on the side of the Low Countries, of Germany, and Savoy. If a prince of her royal family had remained in possession of Spain and the West-Indies, no advantage would have accrued to her by it, and effectual bars would have been opposed to an union of the two monarchies. The house of Austria would have had a reasonable satisfaction for that shadow of right, which a former partition gave her. She had no other after the will of CHARLES the second; and this may be justly termed a shadow, since England, Holland, and France could confer no real right to the Spanish succession, nor to any part of it. She had declined acceding to that partition, before France departed from it, and would have preferred the Italian provinces, without Spain and the West-Indies, to Spain and the West-Indies without the Italian provinces. The Italian provinces would have fallen to her share by this partition. The particular demands of England and Holland would have suffered no difficulty, and those that we were obliged by treaty to make for others would have been easy to adjuſt. Would not this have been enough, my lord, for the public ſecurity, for the common intereſt, and for the glory of our arms? To have humbled and reduced, in five campaigns, a power that had diſturbed and inſulted Europe almoſt forty years; to have reſtored, in ſo short a time, the balance of power in Europe to a ſufficient point of equality, after it had been more than fifty years, that is from the treaty of Weſtphalia, in a gradual deviation from this point; in short to have retrieved, in one thouſand ſeven hundred and ſix, a game that was become deſperate at the beginning of the century. To have done all this before the war had exhauſted our ſtrength, was the utmoſt ſure that any man could deſire who intended the public good alone: and no honeſt reaſon ever was, nor ever will be given, why the war was protracted any longer; why we neither made peace after a short, vigorous, and ſuccefsful war, nor put it entirely out of the power of France to continue at any rate a long one. I have ſaid, and it is true, that this had been entirely out of her power, if we had given greater interruption to the commerce of Old and New Spain, and if we had hindered France from importing annually, from the year one thouſand ſeven hundred and two, ſuch immenſe treaſures as she did import by the ships she ſent, with the permiſſion of Spain, to the South Sea. It has been advanced, and it is a common opinion, that we were reſtrained by the jealouſy of the Dutch from making uſe of the liberty given by treaty to them and us, and which, without his imperial majesty's leave, since we entered into the war, we might have taken, of making conquests the Spanish West-Indies. Be it so. But to go to the South Seas, to trade there if we could, to pillage the West-Indies without making conquests if we could not, and, whether we traded or whether we pillaged, to hinder the French from trading there; was a measure that would have given, one ought to think, no jealousy to the Dutch, who might, and it is to be supposed would, have taken their part in these expeditions; or if it had given them jealousy, what could they have replied when a British minister had told them: " That it little „ became them to find fault that we traded with „ or pillaged the Spaniards in the West-Indies to „ the detriment of our common enemy, whilst we „ connived at them who traded with this enemy to „ his and their great advantage, against our remon- „ strances, and in violation of the condition upon „ which we had given the first augmentation of „ our forces in the Low Countries?" We might have pursued this measure notwithstanding any engagement that we took by the treaty with Portugal, if I remember that treaty right: but instead of this, we wasted our forces, and squandered millions after millions in supporting our alliance with this crown, and in pursuing the chimerical project which was made the object of this alliance. I call it chimerical, because it was equally so, to expect a revolution in favor of CHARLES the third on the slender authority of such a trifler as the admiral of Castile; and, when this failed us, to hope to conquer Spain by the assistance of the Portuguefe, and the revolt of the Catalans. Yet this was the foundation upon which the new plan of the war was built, and fo many ruinous engagements were taken.

THE particular motives of private men, as well as of princes and ftates, to protract the war, are partly known, and partly guefled, at this time. But whenever that time comes, and I am perfuaded it will come, when their fecret motives, their fecret defigns, and intrigues, can be laid open, I prefume to fay to your lordfhip that the moft confufed fcene of iniquity, and folly, that it is poffible to imagine, will appear. In the mean while, if your lordfhip confiders only the treaty of barrier, as my lord TOWNSHEND figned it, without, nay in truth, againft orders; for the duke of MARLBOROUGH, though joint plenipotentiary, did not: if you confider the famous preliminaries of one thoufand feven hundred and nine, which we made a mockshew of ratifying, though we knew that they would not be accepted; for fo the marquis of TORCY had told the penfionary before he left the Hague, as the faid marquis has affured me very often fince that time: if you enquire into the anecdotes of Gertruydenberg, and if you confult other authentic papers that are extant, your lordfhip will fee the policy of the new plan, I think, in this light. Though we had refufed, before the war began, to enter into engagements for the conqueft of Spain, yet as foon as it began, when the reafon of things was ftill the fame, for the fuccefs of our firft campaign cannot be faid to have altered it, we entered into these very engagements. By the treaty wherein we took these engagements first, Portugal was brought into the grand alliance; that is, she consented to employ her formidable forces against PHILIP, at the expence of England and Holland, provided we would debar ourselves from making any acquisitions, and the house of Austria promise, that she should acquire many important places in Spain, and an immense extent of country in America. By such bargains as this, the whole confederacy was formed, and held together. Such means were indeed effectual to multiply enemies to France and Spain; but a project so extensive and so difficult as to make many bargains of this kind necessary, and necessary for a great number of years, and for a very uncertain event, was a project into which, for this very reason, England and Holland should not have entered. It is worthy your observation, my lord, that these bad bargains would not have been continued, as they were almost to our immediate ruin, if the war had not been protracted under the pretended necessity of reducing the whole Spanish monarchy to the obedience of the house of Austria. Now, as no other confederate except Portugal was to receive his recompence by any dismemberment of dominions in Old or New Spain, the engagements we took to conquer this whole monarchy had no visible necessary cause, but the procuring the accession of this power, that was already neuter, to the grand alliance. This accession, as I have said before, served only to make us neglect immediate and certain advantages, for remote and uncertain hopes; and chufe to attempt the conqueſt of the Spanish nation at our own vaſt expence, whom we might have ſtarved, and by ſtarving reduced both the French and them, at their expence.

I CALLED the neceſſity of reducing the whole Spanish monarchy to the obedience of the houſe of Auſtria, a pretended neceſſity: and pretended it was, not real, without doubt. But I am apt to think your lordship may go further, and find ſome reaſons to ſuſpect, that the opinion itſelf of this neceſſity was not very real, in the minds of thoſe who urged it: in the minds I would ſay of the able men among them; for that it was real in ſome of our zealous Britiſh politicians, I do them the juſtice to believe. Your lordship may find reaſons to ſuſpect perhaps, that this opinion was ſet up rather to occaſion a diverſion of the forces of France, and to furniſh pretences for prolonging the war for other ends.

BEFORE the year one thouſand ſeven hundred and ten, the war was kept alive with alternate ſucceſs in Spain; and it may be ſaid therefore, that the deſign of conquering this kingdom continued, as well as the hopes of ſucceeding. But why then did the States General refuſe, in one thouſand ſeven hundred and nine, to admit an article in the barrier-treaty, by which they would have obliged themſelves to procure the whole Spaniſh monarchy to the houſe of Auſtria, when that zealous politician my lord TOWNSHEND preſſed them to it? If their opinion of the neceſſity of carrying on the war, till this point could be obtained, was real; why did they rifque the immenfe advantages given them with fo much profufe generofity by this treaty, rather than confent to an engagement that was fo conformable to their opinion?

AFTER the year one thoufand feven hundred and ten, it will not be faid, I prefume, that the war could be fupported in Spain with any profpect of advantage on our fide. We had fufficiently experienced how little dependence could be had on the vigor of the Portuguefe; and how firmly the Spanifh nation in general, the Caftilians in particular, were attached to PHILIP. Our armies had been twice at Madrid, this prince had been twice driven from the capital, his rival had been there, none ftirred in favor of the victorious, all wifhed and acted for the vanquifhed. In fhort the falshood of all thofe lures, by which we had been enticed to make war in Spain, had appeared fufficiently in one thoufand feven hundred and fix; but was fo grosly evident in one thoufand feven hundred and ten, that Mr. CRAGGS, who was fent towards the end of that year by Mr. STANHOPE into England, on commiffions which he executed with much good fenfe and much addrefs, owned to me, that, in Mr. STANHOPE's opinion, and he was not apt to defpond of fuccefs, efpecially in the execution of his own projects, nothing could be done more in Spain, the general attachment of the people to PHILIP, and their averfion to CHARLES confidered: that armies of twenty or thirty thoufand men might walk about that country till dooms-day, fo he expreffed himfelf, without effect: that wherever they came, the people would fubmit to CHARLES the third out of terror, and, as foon as they were gone, proclaim PHILIP the fifth again out of affection: that to conquer Spain required a great army; and to keep it, a greater.

WAS it poffible, after this, to think in good earneft of conquering Spain, and could they be in good earneft who continued to hold the fame language, and to infift on the fame meafures? Could they be fo in the following year, when the emperor JOSEPH died? CHARLES was become then the fole furviving male of the houfe of Auftria, and fucceeded to the empire as well as to all the hereditary dominions of that family. Could they be in earneft who maintained, even in this conjuncture, that "no peace could be fafe, honorable, ,, or lafting, fo long as the kingdom of Spain ,, and the Weft-Indies remained in the poffeffion ,, of any branch of the houfe of Bourbon?" Did they mean that CHARLES should be emperor and king of Spain? In this project they would have had the allies againft them. Did they mean to call the duke of SAVOY to the crown of Spain, or to beftow it on fome other prince? In this project they would have had his Imperial majefty againft them. In either cafe the confederacy would have been broken: and how then would they have continued the war? Did they mean nothing, or did they mean fomething more than they owned;

something more than to reduce the exorbitant power of France, and to force the whole Spanish monarchy out of the houfe of Bourbon?

BOTH thefe ends might have been obtained at Gertruydenberg. Why were they not obtained? Read the preliminaries of one thoufand feven hundred and nine, which were made the foundation of this treaty. Inform yourfelf of what paffed there, and òbferve what followed. Your lordship will remain aftonished. I remain fo every time I reflect upon them, though I faw thefe things at no very great diftance, even whilft they were in tranfaction; and though I know moft certainly that France loft, two years before, by the little skill and addrefs of her principal * minifter, in anfwering overtures made during the fiege of Lisle by a principal perfon among the allies, fuch an opportunity, and fuch a correfpondence, as would have removed fome of the obftacles that lay now in her way, have prevented others, and have procured her peace. An equivalent for the thirty-feventh article of the preliminaries, that is, for the ceffion of Spain and the Weft-Indies, was the point to be difcuffed at Gertruydenberg. Naples and Sicily, or even Naples and Sardinia would have contented the French, at leaft they would have accepted them as the equivalent. BUYS and VANDERDUSSEN, who treated with them, reported this to the minifters of the allies: and it was upon this occafion that the duke of MARLBOROUGH, as BUYS himfelf told me, took immediately the lead, and congratulated the affembly on the near ap-

* CHAMILLARD.

proach* of a peace; said, that since the French were in this disposition, it was time to consider what further demands should be made upon them, according to the liberty observed in the preliminaries; and exhorted all the ministers of the allies to adjust their several ulterior pretensions, and to prepare their demands.

THIS proceeding, and what followed, put me in mind of that of the Romans with the Carthaginians. The former were resolved to consent to no peace till Carthage was laid in ruins. They set a treaty however on foot, at the request of their old enemy, imposed some terms, and referred them to their generals for the rest. Their generals pursued the same method, and, by reserving still a right of making ulterior demands, they reduced the Carthaginians at last to the necessity of abandoning their city, or of continuing the war after they had given up their arms, their machines, and their fleet, in hopes of peace.

FRANCE saw the snare, and resolved to run any risque rather than to be caught in it. We continued to demand, under pretence of securing the cession of Spain and the West-Indies, that LEWIS the fourteenth should take on him to dethrone his grandson in the space of two months; and, if he did not effect it in that time, that we should be at liberty to renew the war without restoring the places that were to be put into our hands according to the preliminaries; which were the most important places France possessed on the side of the Low Countries. LEWIS offered to abandon his grandson; and, if he could not prevail on him to resign, to furnish money to the allies, who might at the expence of France force him to evacuate Spain. The proposition made by the allies had an air of inhumanity: and the rest of mankind might be shocked to see the grandfather obliged to make war on his grandson. But Lewis the fourteenth had treated mankind with too much inhumanity in his prosperous days, to have any reason to complain even of this proposition. His people indeed, who are apt to have great partiality for their kings, might pity his distress. This happened, and he found his account in it. Philip must have evacuated Spain, I think, notwithstanding his own obstinacy, the spirit of his queen, and the resolute attachment of the Spaniards, if his grandfather had insisted, and been in earnest to force him. But if this expedient was, as it was, odious, why did we prefer to continue the war against France and Spain, rather than accept the other? Why did we neglect the opportunity of reducing, effectually and immediately, the exorbitant power of France, and of rendering the conquest of Spain practicable? both which might have been brought about, and consequently the avowed ends of the war might have been answered, by accepting the expedient that France offered. " France " it was said, „ was not sincere: she meant nothing more than „ to amuse, and divide." This reason was given at the time; but some of those who gave it then, I have seen ashamed to insist on it since. France was not in a condition to act the part she had acted in former treaties: and her diſtreſs was no bad pledge of her ſincerity on this occaſion. But there was a better ſtill. The ſtrong places that she muſt have put into the hands of the allies, would have expoſed her, on the leaſt breach of faith, to ſee, not her frontier alone, but even the provinces that lie behind it, deſolated: and prince EUGENE might have had the ſatisfaction, it is ſaid, I know not how truly, he deſired, of marching with the torch in his hand to Verſailles.

YOUR lordship will obſerve, that the conferences at Gertruydenberg ending in the manner they did, the inflexibility of the allies gave new life and ſpirit to the French and Spanish nations, diſtreſſed and exhauſted as they were. The troops of the former withdrawn out of Spain, and the Spaniards left to defend themſelves as they could, the Spaniards alone obliged us to retreat from Madrid, and defeated us in our retreat. But your lordship may think perhaps, as I do, that if LEWIS the fourteenth had bound himſelf by a ſolemn treaty to abandon his grandſon, had paid a ſubſidy to dethrone him, and had conſented to acknowledge another king of Spain, the Spaniards would not have exerted the ſame zeal for PHILIP; the actions of Almenara and Saragoſſa might have been deciſive, and thoſe of Brihuega and Villa Vicioſa would not have happened. After all theſe events, how could any reaſonable man expect that a war should be ſupported with advantage in Spain, to which the court of Vienna had contributed nothing from the firſt, ſcarce bread to their archduke; which Portugal waged faintly and with deficient quotas; and which the Dutch had in a manner renounced, by neglecting to recruit their forces? How was CHARLES to be placed on the Spanish throne, or PHILIP at least to be driven out of it? by the success of the confederate arms in other parts. But what success sufficient to this purpose, could we expect? This question may be answered best, by shewing what success we had.

PORTUGAL and Savoy did nothing before the death of the emperor JOSEPH; and declared in form, as soon as he was dead, that they would carry on the war no longer to set the crown of Spain on the head of CHARLES, since this would be to fight against the very principle they had fought for. The Rhine was a scene of inaction. The sole efforts, that were to bring about the great event of dethroning PHILIP, were those which the duke of MARLBOROUGH was able to make. He took three towns in one thousand seven hundred and ten, Aire, Bethune, and St. Venant; and one, Bouchain, in one thousand seven hundred and eleven. Now this conquest being in fact the only one the confederates made that year, Bouchain may be said properly and truly to have cost our nation very near seven millions sterling; for your lordship will find, I believe, that the charge of the war for that year amounted to no less. It is true that the duke of MARLBOROUGH had proposed a very great project, by which incursions would have been made during the winter into France;

France; the next campaign might have been opened early on our side; and several other great and obvious advantages might have been obtained; but the Dutch refused to contribute, even less than their proportion, for the queen had offered to take the deficiency on herself, to the expence of barraks and forage; and disappointed by their obstinacy the whole design.

We were then amused with visionary schemes of marching our whole army, in a year or two more, and after a town or two more were taken, directly to Paris, or at least into the heart of France. But was this so easy or so sure a game? The French expected we would play it. Their generals had visited the several posts they might take, when our army should enter France, to retard, to incommode, to distress us in our march, and even to make a decisive stand and to give us battle. I take what I say here from indisputable authority, that of the persons consulted and employed in preparing for this great distress. Had we been beaten, or had we been forced to retire towards our own frontier in the Low Countries, after penetrating into France, the hopes on which we protracted the war would have been disappointed, and, I think, the most sanguine would have then repented refusing the offers made at Gertruydenberg. But if we had beaten the French; for it was scarce lawful in those days of our presumption to suppose the contrary, would the whole monarchy of Spain have been our immediate and certain prize? Suppose, and I suppose it on good grounds, my lord, that the French had refolved to defend their country inch by inch, and that LEWIS the fourteenth had determined to retire with his court to Lions or elfewhere, and to defend the paſſage of the Loire, when he could no longer defend that of the Seine, rather than fubmit to the terms impofed on him: what should we have done in this cafe? Muſt we not have accepted fuch a peace as we had refufed; or have protracted the war till we had conquered France firſt, in order to conquer Spain afterwards? Did we hope for revolutions in France? We had hoped for them in Spain: and we should have been bubbles of our hopes in both. That there was a fpirit raifed againſt the government of LEWIS the fourteenth, in his court, nay in his family, and that ſtrange fchemes of private ambition were formed and forming there, I cannot doubt: and fome effects of this fpirit produced perhaps the greateſt mortifications that he fuffered in the latter part of his reign.

A SLIGHT inſtance of this fpirit is all I will quote at this time. I fupped, in the year one thoufand feven hundred and fifteen, at a houfe in France, where two * perfons of no fmall figure, who had been in great company that night, arrived very late. The converfation turned on the events of the precedent war, and the negotiations of the late peace; in the procefs of the converfation, one of them † broke loofe, and faid, directing his

---

* The dukes de LA FEUILLADE and MORTEMAR.
† LA FEUILLADE.

discourse to me, "Vous auriez pu nous écraser dans ce tems là: pourquoi ne l'avez-vous pas fait?" I answered him coolly, "Par ce que dans ce tems-là nous n'avons plus craint votre puissance." This anecdote, too trivial for history, may find its place in a letter, and may serve to confirm what I have admitted, that there were persons even in France, who expected to find their private account in the distress of their country. But these persons were a few, men of wild imaginations and strong passions, more enterprizing than capable, and of more name than credit. In general the endeavours of LEWIS the fourteenth, and the sacrifices he offered to make in order to obtain a peace, had attached his people more than ever to him: and if LEWIS had determined not to go farther than he had offered at Gertruydenberg, in abandoning his grandson, the French nation would not have abandoned him.

BUT to resume what I have said or hinted already; the necessary consequences of protracting the war in order to dethrone PHILIP, from the year one thousand seven hundred and eleven inclusively, could be no other than these: our design of penetrating into France might have been defeated, and have become fatal to us by a reverse of fortune: our first success might not have obliged the French to submit; and we might have had France to conquer, after we had failed in our first attempt to conquer Spain, and even in order to proceed to a second: the French might have submitted, and the Spaniards not; and whilst the former had been employed to force the latter, according to the scheme of the allies; or whilst, the latter submitting likewise, PHILIP had evacuated Spain, the high allies might have gone together by the ears about dividing the spoil, and disposing of the crown of Spain. To these issues were things brought by protracting the war; by refusing to make peace, on the principles of the grand alliance at worst, in one thousand seven hundred and six; and by refusing to grant it, even on those of the new plan, in one thousand seven hundred and ten. Such contingent events as I have mentioned stood in prospect before us. The end of the war was removed out of sight; and they, who clamoured rather than argued for the continuation of it, contented themselves to affirm, that France was not enough reduced, and that no peace ought to be made as long as a prince of the house of Bourbon remained on the Spanish throne. When they would think France enough reduced, it was impossible to guess. Whether they intended to join the Imperial and Spanish crowns on the head of CHARLES, who had declared his irrevocable resolution to continue the war till the conditions insisted upon at Gertruydenberg were obtained: whether they intended to bestow Spain and the Indies on some other prince: and how this great alteration in their own plan should be effected by common consent: how possession should be given to CHARLES, or to any other prince, not only of Spain but of all the Spanish dominions out of Europe, where the attachment to PHILIP was at least as strong as in Castile, and where it would not be so easy, the distance and extent of these dominions considered, to oblige the Spaniards to submit to another government: These points, and many more equally necessary to be determined, and equally difficult to prepare, were neither determined nor prepared; so that we were reduced to carry on the war, after the death of the emperor JOSEPH, without any positive scheme agreed to, as the scheme of the future peace, by the allies. That of the grand alliance we had long before renounced: that of the new plan was become ineligible; and, if it had been eligible, it would have been impracticable, because of the division it would have created among the allies themselves: several of whom would not have consented, notwithstanding his irrevocable resolution, that the emperor should be king of Spain. I know not what part the protractors of the war, in the depth of their policy, intended to take. Our nation had contributed, and acted so long under the direction of their councils, for the grandeur of the house of Austria, like one of the hereditary kingdoms usurped by that family, that it is lawful to think their intention might be to unite the Imperial and Spanish crowns. But I rather think they had no very determinate view, beyond that of continuing the war as long as they could. The late lord OXFORD told me, that my lord SOMERS being pressed, I know not on what occasion nor by whom, on the unnecessary and ruinous continuation of the war, instead of giving reasons to shew the necessity of it, contented himself to reply, that he had been bred up in a hatred of France. This was a strange reply for a wise man: and yet I know not whether he could have given a better then, or whether any of his pupils could give a better now.

The whig party in general acquired great and just popularity, in the reign of our CHARLES the second, by the clamor they raised against the conduct of that prince in foreign affairs. They who succeeded to the name rather than the principles of this party, after the revolution, and who have had the administration of the government in their hands with very little interruption ever since, pretending to act on the same principle, have run into an extreme as vicious and as contrary to all the rules of good policy, as that which their predecessors exclaimed against. The old whigs complained of the inglorious figure we made, whilst our court was the bubble, and our king the pensioner of France; and insisted that the growing ambition and power of LEWIS the fourteenth should be opposed in time. The modern whigs boasted, and still boast, of the glorious figure we made, whilst we reduced ourselves, by their councils, and under their administrations, to be the bubbles of our pensioners, that is of our allies; and whilst we measured our efforts in war, and the continuation of them, without any regard to the interests and abilities of our own country, without a just and sober regard, such an one as contemplates objects in their true light and sees them in their true magnitude, to the general system of power in Europe; and, in short, with a principal regard merely to particular interests at home and abroad. I say at home and abroad; because it is not less true, that they have sacrificed the wealth of their country to the forming and maintaining a party at home, than that they have done so to the forming and maintaining, beyond all pretences of necessity, alliances abroad. These general assertions may be easily justified without having recourse to private anecdotes, as your lordship will find when you consider the whole series of our conduct in the two wars; in that which preceded, and that which succeeded immediately the beginning of the present century, but above all the last of them. In the administrations that preceded the revolution, trade had flourished, and our nation had grown opulent: but the general interest of Europe had been too much neglected by us; and slavery, under the umbrage of prerogative, had been well nigh established among us. In those that have followed, taxes upon taxes, and debts upon debts have been perpetually accumulated, till a small number of families have grown into immense wealth, and national beggary has been brought upon us; under the specious pretences of supporting a common cause against France, reducing her exorbitant power, and poising that of Europe more equally in the public balance: laudable designs no doubt, as far as they were real, but such as, being converted into mere pretences, have been productive of much evil; some of which we feel and have long felt, and some will extend it's consequences to our latest posterity. The reign of prerogative was short: and the evils and the dangers, to which we were exposed by it, ended with it. But the reign of false and squandering policy has lasted long, it lasts still, and will finally complete our ruin. Beggary has been the consequence of slavery in some countries: slavery will be probably the consequence of beggary in ours; and if it is so, we know at whose door to lay it. If we had finished the war in one thousand seven hundred and six, we should have reconciled, like a wise people, our foreign and our domestic interests as nearly as possible: we should have secured the former sufficiently, and not have sacrificed the latter as entirely as we did by the prosecution of the war afterwards. You will not be able to see without astonishment, how the charge of the war encreased yearly upon us from the beginning of it; nor how immense a sum we paid in the course of it to supply the deficiencies of our confederates. Your astonishment, and indignation too, will increase, when you come to compare the progress that was made from the year one thousand seven hundred and six exclusively, with the expence of more than thirty millions, I do not exaggerate though I write upon memory, that this progress cost us, to the year one thousand seven hundred and eleven inclusively. Upon this view, your lordship will be persuaded that it was high time to take the resolution of making peace, when the queen thought fit to change her ministry, towards the end of the year one thousand seven hundred and ten. It was high time indeed to save our country from absolute insolvency and bankruptcy, by putting an end to a scheme of conduct, which the prejudices of a party, the whimsy of some particular men, the private interest of more, and the ambition and avarice of our allies, who had been invited as it were to a scramble by the preliminaries of one thousand seven hundred and nine, alone maintained. The persons therefore, who came into power at this time, hearkened, and they did well to hearken, to the first overtures that were made them. The disposition of their enemies invited them to do so, but that of their friends, and that of a party at home who had nursed, and been nursed by the war, might have deterred them from it, for the difficulties and dangers, to which they must be exposed in carrying forward this great work, could escape none of them. In a letter to a friend it may be allowed me to say, that they did not escape me: and that I foresaw, as contingent but not improbable events, a good part of what has happened to me since. Though it was a duty therefore that we owed to our country, to deliver her from the necessity of bearing any longer so unequal a part in so unnecessary a war, yet was there some degree of merit in performing it. I think so strongly in this manner, I am so incorrigible, my lord, that if I could be placed in the same circumstances again, I would take the same resolution, and act the same part. Age and experience might enable me to act with more ability, and greater skill; but all I have suffered since the death of the queen should not hinder me from acting. Notwithstanding this, I shall not be surprised if you think that the peace of Utrecht was not answerable to the success of the war, nor to the efforts made in it. I think so myself, and have always owned, even when it was making and made, that I thought so. Since we had committed a successful folly, we ought to have reaped more advantage from it than we did: and, whether we had left PHILIP, or placed another prince on the throne of Spain, we ought to have reduced the power of France, and to have strengthened her neighbours, much more than we did. We ought to have reduced her power for generations to come, and not to have contented ourselves with a momentary reduction of it. France was exhausted to a great degree of men and money, and her government had no credit: but they, who took this for a sufficient reduction of her power, looked but a little way before them, and reasoned too superficially. Several such there were however; for as it has been said, that there is no extravagancy which some philosopher or other has not maintained, so your experience, young as you are, must have shewn you, that there is no absurd extreme, into which our party-politicians of Great Britain are not prone to fall, concerning the state and conduct of public affairs. But if France was exhausted: so were we, and so were the Dutch. Famine rendered her condition much more miserable than ours, at one time, in appearance and in reality too. But as soon as this accident, that had distressed the French and frightened LEWIS the fourteenth to the utmost degree, and the immediate consequences of it were over; it was obvious to observe, though few made the observation, that whilst we were unable to raise in a year, by some millions at least, the expences of the year, the French were willing and able to bear the imposition of the tenth over and above all the other taxes that had been laid upon them. This observation had the weight it deserved; and sure it deserved to have some among those who made it, at the time spoken of, and who did not think that the war was to be continued as long as a parliament could be prevailed on to vote money. But supposing it to have deserved none, supposing the power of France to have been reduced as low as you please, with respect to her inward state; yet still I affirm, that such a reduction could not be permanent, and was not therefore sufficient. Whoever knows the nature of her government, the temper of her people, and the natural advantages she has in commerce over all the nations that surround her, knows, that an arbitrary government, and the temper of her people enable her on particular occasions to throw off a load of debt much more easily, and with consequences much less to be feared, than any of her neighbours can: that although, in the general course of things, trade be cramped and industry vexed by this arbitrary government, yet neither one nor the other is oppressed; and the temper of the people, and the natural advantages of the country, are such, that how great soever her diſtreſs be at any point of time, twenty years of tranquility ſuffice to re-eſtabliſh her affairs, and to enrich her again at the expence of all the nations of Europe. If any one doubts of this, let him conſider the condition in which this kingdom was left by Lewis the fourteenth; the ſtrange pranks the late duke of Orleans played, during his regency and adminiſtration, with the whole ſyſtem of public revenue, and private property; and then let him tell himſelf, that the revenues of France, the tenth taken off, exceed all the expences of her government by many millions of livres already, and will exceed them by many more in another year.

Upon the whole matter, my lord, the low and exhauſted ſtate to which France was reduced, by the laſt great war, was but a momentary reduction of her power: and whatever real and more laſting reduction the treaty of Utrecht brought about in ſome inſtances, it was not ſufficient. The power of France would not have appeared as great as it did, when England and Holland armed themſelves and armed all Germany againſt her, if ſhe had lain as open to the invaſions of her enemies, as her enemies lay to her's. Her inward ſtrength was great; but the ſtrength of thoſe frontiers which Lewis the fourteenth was almoſt forty years in forming, and which the folly of all his neighbours in their turns ſuffered him to form, made this ſtrength as formidable as it became. The true reduction of the exorbitant power of France, I take no notice of chimerical projects about changing her government, confifted therefore in difarming her frontiers, and fortifying the barriers againſt her, by the ceſſion and demolition of many more places than fhe yielded up at Utrecht; but not of more than fhe might have been obliged to facrifice to her own immediate relief, and to the future fecurity of her neighbours. That fhe was not obliged to make thefe facrifices, I affirm was owing folely to thofe who oppofed the peace: and I am willing to put my whole credit with your lordship, and the whole merits of a caufe that has been fo much contefted, on this iffue. I fay a caufe that has been fo much contefted; for in truth, I think, it is no longer a doubt any where, except in British pamphlets, whether the conduct of thofe who neither declined treating, as was done in one thoufand feven hundred and fix; nor pretended to treat without a defign of concluding, as was done in one thoufand feven hundred and nine and ten, but carried the great work of the peace forward to its confummation; or the conduct of thofe who oppofed this work in every ſtep of its progrefs, faved the power of France from a greater and a fufficient reduction at the treaty of Utrecht. The very minifters, who were employed in this fatal oppofition, are obliged to confefs this truth. How should they deny it? Thofe of Vienna may complain that the emperor had not the entire Spanish monarchy, or thofe of Holland that the States were not made mafters directly and indirectly of the whole Low Countries. But neither they, nor any one elfe that has any fenfe of fhame about him, can deny that the late queen, though she was resolved to treat because she was resolved to finish the war, yet was to the utmost degree desirous to treat in a perfect union with her allies, and to procure them all the reasonable terms they could expect; and much better than those they reduced themselves to the necessity of accepting, by endeavouring to wrest the negotiation out of her hands. The disunion of the allies gave France the advantages she improved. The sole question is, Who caused this disunion? and that will be easily decided by every impartial man, who informs himself carefully of the public anecdotes of that time. If the private anecdotes were to be laid open as well as those, and I think it almost time they should, the whole monstrous scene would appear, and shock the eye of every honest man. I do not intend to descend into many particulars at this time: but whenever I, or any other person as well informed as I, shall descend into a full deduction of such particulars, it will become undeniably evident, that the most violent opposition imaginable, carried on by the Germans and the Dutch in league with a party in Britain, began as soon as the first overtures were made to the queen; before she had so much as begun to treat: and was therefore an opposition not to this or that plan of treaty, but in truth to all treaty; and especially to one wherein Great Britain took the lead, or was to have any particular advantage. That the Imperialists meant no treaty, unless a preliminary, and impracticable condition of it was to set the crown of Spain on the emperor's head, will appear from this; that prince EUGENE, when he came into England, long after the death of JOSEPH and the elevation of CHARLES, upon an errand most unworthy of so great a man, treated always on this suppofition: and I remember with how much inward impatience I affifted at conferences held with him concerning quotas for renewing the war in Spain, in the very fame room, at the cockpit, where the queen's minifters had been told in plain terms, a little before, by thofe of other allies, " that their mafters would not confent „ that the Imperial and Spanish crowns should „ unite on the fame head." That the Dutch were not averfe to all treaty, but meant none wherein Great Britain was to have any particular advantage, will appear from this; that their minifter declared himfelf ready and authorifed to ftop the oppofition made to the queen's meafures, by prefenting a memorial, wherein he would declare, " that his „ mafters entered into them, and were refolved „ not to continue the war for the recovery of „ Spain, provided the queen would confent that „ they should garrifon Gibraltar and Port-mahon „ jointly with us, and share equally the Affiento, „ the South Sea ship, and whatever should be „ granted by the Spaniards to the queen and her „ fubjects." That the whigs engaged in this league with foreign powers againft their country, as well as their queen, and with a phrenfy more unaccountable than that which made and maintained the folemn league and covenant formerly, will appear from this; that their attempts were directed not only to wreſt the negotiations out of the queen's hands, but to oblige their country to carry on the war, on the ſame unequal foot that had coſt her already about twenty millions more than she ought to have contributed to it. For they not only continued to abet the emperor, whoſe inability to ſupply his quota was confeſſed; but the Dutch likewiſe, after the States had refuſed to ratify the treaty their miniſter ſigned at London towards the end of the year one thouſand ſeven hundred and eleven, and by which the queen united herſelf more cloſely than ever to them; engaging to purſue the war, to conclude the peace, and to guaranty it, when concluded, jointly with them; " provided they would keep „ the engagements they had taken with her, and „ the conditions of proportionate expence under „ which our nation had entered into the war." Upon ſuch ſchemes as theſe was the oppoſition to the treaty of Utrecht carried on: and the means employed, and the means projected to be employed, were worthy of ſuch ſchemes; open, direct, and indecent defiance of legal authority, ſecret conſpiracies againſt the ſtate, and baſe machinations againſt particular men, who had no other crime than that of endeavouring to conclude a war, under the authority of the queen, which a party in the nation endeavoured to prolong, againſt her authority. Had the good policy of concluding the war been doubtful, it was certainly as lawful for thoſe, who thought it good, to adviſe it, as it had been for thofe, who thought it bad, to advife the contrary: and the decifion of the fovereign on the throne ought to have terminated the conteft. But he who had judged by the appearances of things on one fide, at that time, would have been apt to think, that putting an end to the war, or to Magna Charta, was the fame thing; that the queen on the throne had no right to govern independently of her fucceffor; nor any of her fubjects a right to adminifter the government under her, though called to it by her, except thofe whom she had thought fit to lay afide. Extravagant as thefe principles are, no other could juftify the conduct held at that time by thofe who oppofed the peace: and as I faid juft now, that the phrenfy of this league was more unaccountable than that of the folemn league and covenant, I might have added, that it was not very many degrees lefs criminal. Some of thofe, who charged the queen's minifters, after her death, with imaginary treafons, had been guilty during her life of real treafons: and I can compare the folly and violence of the fpirit that prevailed at that time, both before the conclufion of the peace, and, under pretence of danger to the fucceffion, after it, to nothing more nearly than to the folly and violence of the fpirit that feized the tories foon after the acceffion of GEORGE the firft. The latter indeed, which was provoked by unjuft and impolitic perfecution, broke out in open rebellion; the former might have done fo, if the queen had lived a little longer. But to return.

THE obstinate adherence of the Dutch to this league, in opposition to the queen, rendered the conferences of Utrecht, when they were opened, no better than mock conferences. Had the men who governed that commonwealth been wise and honest enough to unite, at least then, cordially with the queen, and, since they could not hinder a congress, to act in concert with her in it; we should have been still in time to maintain a sufficient union among the allies, and a sufficient superiority over the French. All the specific demands that the former made, as well as the Dutch themselves, either to incumber the negotiation, or to have in reserve, according to the artifice usually employed on such occasions, certain points from which to depart in the course of it with advantage, would not have been obtained: but all the essential demands, all in particular that were really necessary to secure the barriers in the Low Countries and of the four circles against France, would have been so: for France must have continued, in this case, rather to sue for peace, than to treat on an equal foot. The first dauphin, son of LEWIS the fourteenth, died several months before this congress began: the second dauphin, his grandson, and the wife and the eldest son of this prince, died soon after it began, of the same unknown distemper, and were buried together in the same grave. Such family misfortunes, following a long series of national misfortunes, made the old king, though he bore them with much seeming magnanimity, desirous to get out of the war at any tolerable rate, that he might not run the rifque of leaving a child of five years old, the prefent king, engaged in it. The queen did all that was morally poffible, except giving up her honor in the negotiation, and the interefts of her fubjects in the conditions of peace, to procure this union with the ftates general. But all she could do was vain; and the fame phrenfy, that had hindered the Dutch from improving to their and to the common advantage the public misfortunes of France, hindered them from improving to the fame purpofes the private misfortunes of the houfe of Bourbon. They continued to flatter themfelves that they should force the queen out of her meafures, by their intrigues with the party in Britain who oppofed thefe meafures, and even raife an infurrection againft her. But thefe intrigues, and thofe of prince EUGENE, were known and difappointed; and monfieur BUYS had the mortification to be reproached with them publicly, when he came to take leave of the lords of the council, by the earl of OXFORD; who entered into many particulars that could not be denied, of the private transactions of this fort, to which BUYS had been a party, in compliance with his inftructions, and, as I believe, much againft his own fenfe and inclinations. As the feafon for taking the field advanced, the league propofed to defeat the fuccefs of the congrefs by the events of the campaign; but inftead of defeating the fuccefs of the congrefs, the events of the campaign ferved only to turn this fuccefs in favor of France. At the beginning of the year, the queen and the States, in concert, might have given the law to friend and foe, with great advantage to the former, and with such a detriment to the latter, as the causes of the war rendered just, the events of it reasonable, and the objects of it necessary. At the end of the year, the allies were no longer in a state of giving, nor the French of receiving the law; and the Dutch had recourse to the queen's good offices, when they could oppose and durst insult her no longer. Even then, these offices were employed with zeal, and with some effect for them.

Thus the war ended, much more favorably to France than she expected, or they who put an end to it designed. The queen would have humbled and weakened this power. The allies who opposed her would have crushed it, and have raised another as exorbitant on the ruins of it. Neither one nor the other succeeded, and they who meant to ruin the French power preserved it, by opposing those who meant to reduce it.

Since I have mentioned the events of the year one thousand seven hundred and twelve, and the decisive turn they gave to the negotiations in favor of France, give me leave to say something more on this subject. You will find that I shall do so with much impartiality. The disastrous events of this campaign in the Low Countries, and the consequences of them, have been imputed to the separation of the British troops from the army of the allies. The clamor against this measure was great at that time, and the prejudices which this clamor raised are great still among some men. But as clamor raised these prejudices, other prejudices gave birth to this clamor: and it is no wonder they should do so among persons bent on continuing the war; since I own very freely, that when the first step that led to this separation came to my knowledge, which was not an hour, by the way, before I writ by the queen's order to the duke of ORMOND, in the very words in which the order was advised and given, " that he should not engage in any „ siege, nor hazard a battle, till further order," I was surprised and hurt; so much, that if I had had an opportunity of speaking in private to the queen, after I had received monsieur DE TORCY's letter to me on the subject, and before she went into the council, I should have spoken to her, I think, in the first heat, against it. The truth is, however, that the step was justifiable at that point of time in every respect, and therefore that the consequences are to be charged to the account of those who drew them on themselves, not to the account of the queen, nor of the minister who advised her. The step was justifiable to the allies surely, since the queen took no more upon her, no not so much by far, in making it, as many of them had done by suspending, or endangering, or defeating operations in the heat of the war, when they declined to send their troops, or delayed the march of them, or neglected the preparations they were obliged to make, on the most frivolous pretences. Your lordship will find in the course of your enquiries many particular instances of what is here pointed out in general. But I cannot help descending into some few of those that regard the emperor and the States General, who cried the loudest and with the most effect, though they had the least reason, on account of their own conduct, to complain of the queen's. With what face could the emperor, for instance, presume to complain of the orders sent to the duke of ORMOND? I say nothing of his deficiencies, which were so great, that he had at this very time little more than one regiment that could be said properly to act against France and Spain at his sole charge; as I affirmed to prince EUGENE before the lords of the council, and demonstrated upon paper the next day. I say nothing of all that preceded the year one thousand seven hundred and seven, on which I should have much to say. But I desire your lordship only to consider, what you will find to have passed after the famous year one thousand seven hundred and six. Was it with the queen's approbation, or against her will, that the emperor made the treaty for the evacuation of Lombardy, and let out so great a number of French regiments time enough to recruit themselves at home, to march into Spain, and to destroy the British forces at Almanza? Was it with her approbation, or against her will, that, instead of employing all his forces and all his endeavours, to make the greatest design of the whole war, the enterprise on Toulon, succeed, he detached twelve thousand men to reduce the kingdom of Naples, that must have fallen of course? and that an opportunity of ruining the whole maritime force of France, and of ruining or subduing her provinces on that side, was lost, merely by this unnecessary diversion, and by the conduct of prince EUGENE, which left no room to doubt that he gave occasion to this fatal disappointment on purpose, and in concert with the court of Vienna?

TURN your eyes, my lord, on the conduct of the States, and you will find reason to be astonished at the arrogance of the men who governed in them at this time, and who presumed to exclaim against a queen of Great Britain, for doing what their deputies had done more than once in that very country, and in the course of that very war. In the year one thousand seven hundred and twelve, at the latter end of a war, when conferences for treating a peace were opened, when the least sinister event in the field would take off from that superiority which the allies had in the congress, and when the past success of the war had already given them as much of this superiority as they wanted to obtain a safe, advantageous, honorable, and lasting peace, the queen directed her general to suspend till further order the operations of her troops. In one thousand seven hundred and three, in the beginning of a war, when something was to be risqued or no success to be expected, and when the bad situation of affairs in Germany and Italy required, in a particular manner, that efforts should be made in the Low Countries, and that the war should not languish there whilst it was unsuccessful every where else; the duke of MARLBOROUGH determined to attack the French, but the Dutch deputies would not suffer their troops to go on; defeated his design in the very moment of it's execution, if I remember well, and gave no other reason for their proceeding than that which is a reason against every battle, the possibility of being beaten. The circumstance of proximity to their frontier was urged, I know, and it was said, that their provinces would be exposed to the incursions of the French if they lost the battle. But besides other answers to this vain pretence, it was obvious that they had ventured battles as near home as this would have been fought, and that the way to remove the enemy farther off was by action, not inaction. Upon the whole matter, the Dutch deputies stopped the progress of the confederate army at this time, by exercising an arbitrary and independent authority over the troops of the States. In one thousand seven hundred and five, when the success of the preceding campaign should have given them an entire confidence in the duke of MARLBOROUGH's conduct, when returning from the Moselle to the Low Countries he began to make himself and the common cause amends, for the disappointment which pique and jealousy in the prince of BADEN, or usual sloth and negligence in the Germans, had occasioned just before, by forcing the French lines; when he was in the full pursuit of this advantage, and when he was marching to attack an enemy half defeated, and more than half-dispirited; nay when he had made his dispositions for attacking, and part of his troops had paſſed the Dyle — the deputies of the States once more tied up his hands, took from him an opportunity too fair to be loſt; for theſe, I think, were ſome of the terms of his complaint: and in ſhort the confederacy received an affront at leaſt, where we might have obtained a victory. Let this that has been ſaid ſerve as a ſpecimen of the independency on the queen, her councils, and her generals, with which theſe powers acted in the courſe of the war; who were not aſhamed to find fault that the queen, once, and at the latter end of it, preſumed to ſuſpend the operations of her troops till farther order. But be it that they foreſaw what this farther order would be. They foreſaw then, that as ſoon as Dunkirk ſhould be put into the queen's hands, ſhe would conſent to a ſuſpenſion of arms for two months, and invite them to do the ſame. Neither this foreſight, nor the ſtrong declaration which the biſhop of BRISTOL made by the queen's order at Utrecht, and which ſhewed them that her reſolution was not taken to ſubmit to the league into which they had entered againſt her, could prevail on them to make a right uſe of theſe two months, by endeavouring to renew their union and good underſtanding with the queen; though I can ſay with the greateſt truth, and they could not doubt of it at the time, that ſhe would have gone more than half-way to meet them, and that her miniſters would have done their utmoſt to bring it about. Even then we might have reſumed the ſuperiority we began to loſe in the congreſs; for, the queen and the

States uniting, the principal allies would have united with them: and, in this cafe, it would have been fo much the intereft of France to avoid any chance of feeing the war renewed, that she muft, and she would, have made fure of peace, during the fufpenfion, on much worfe terms for herfelf and for Spain, than she made it afterwards. But the prudent and fober States continued to act like froward children, or like men drunk with refentment and paffion; and fuch will the conduct be of the wife governments in every circumftance, where a fpirit of faction and of private intereft prevails, among thofe who are at the head, over reafon or ftate. After laying afide all decency in their behaviour towards the queen, they laid afide all caution for themfelves. They declared " they „ would carry on the war without her." Landrecy feemed, in their efteem, of more importance than Dunkirk; and the opportunity of wafting fome French provinces, or of putting the whole event of the war on the decifion of another battle, preferable to the other meafure that lay open to them; that, I mean, of trying in good earneft, and in an honeft concert with the queen, during the fufpenfion of arms, whether fuch terms of peace, as ought to fatisfy them and the other allies might not be impofed on France.

If the confederate army had broke into France, the campaign before this, or in any former campaign; and if the Germans and the Dutch had exercifed then the fame inhumanity, as the French had exercifed in their provinces in former wars; if they had burnt Verfailles, and even Paris, and if they had disturbed the ashes of the dead princes that repose at Saint Denis, every good man would have felt the horror, that such cruelties inspire: no man could have said that the retaliation was unjust. But in one thousand seven hundred and twelve, it was too late, in every respect, to meditate such projects. If the French had been unprepared to defend their frontier, either for want of means, or in a vain confidence that the peace would be made, as our king CHARLES the second was unprepared to defend his coast at the latter end of his first war with Holland, the allies might have played a sure game in satisfying their vengeance on the French, as the Dutch did on us in one thousand six hundred and sixty seven; and imposing harder terms on them, than those they offered, or would have accepted. But this was not the case. The French army was, I believe, more numerous than the army of the allies, even before separation, and certainly in a much better condition than two or three years before, when a deluge of blood was spilt to dislodge them, for we did no more, at Malplaquet. Would the Germans and the Dutch have found it more easy to force them at this time, than it was at that? Would not the French have fought with as much obstinacy to save Paris, as they did to save Mons? and, with all the regard due to the duke of ORMOND and to prince EUGENE, was the absence of the duke of MARLBOROUGH of no consequence? Turn this affair every way in your thoughts, my lord, and you will find that the Germans and the

Dutch had nothing in theirs, but to break, at any rate, and at any risque, the negotiations that were begun, and to reduce Great Britain to the necessity of continuing, what she had been too long, a province of the confederacy. A province indeed, and not one of the best treated; since the confederates assumed a right of obliging her to keep her pacts with them, and of dispensing with their obligations to her, of exhausting her, without rule, or proportion, or measure, in the support of a war, to which she alone contributed more than all of them, and in which she had no longer an immediate interest, nor even any remote interest that was not common, or, with respect to her, very dubious; and, after all this, of complaining that the queen presumed to hearken to overtures of peace, and to set a negotiation on foot, whilst their humor and ambition required that the war should be prolonged for an indefinite time, and for a purpose that was either bad or indeterminate.

The suspension of arms, that began in the Low Countries, was continued, and extended afterwards by the act I signed at Fontainebleau. The fortune of the war turned at the same time: and all those disgraces followed, which obliged the Dutch to treat, and to desire the assistance of the queen, whom they had set at defiance so lately. This assistance they had, as effectually as it could be given in the circumstances, to which they had reduced themselves, and the whole alliance: and the peace of Great Britain, Portugal, Savoy, Prussia, and the States General, was made, without his imperial majesty's concurrence, in the spring of one thousand seven hundred and thirteen; as it might have been made, much more advantageously for them all, in that of one thousand seven hundred and twelve. Less obstinacy on the part of the States, and perhaps more decisive resolutions on the part of the queen, would have wound up all these divided threads in one, and have finished this great work much sooner and better. I say, perhaps more decisive resolutions on the part of the queen; because, although I think that I should have conveyed her orders for signing a treaty of peace with France, before the armies took the field, much more willingly, than I executed them afterwards in signing that of the cessation of arms; yet I do not presume to decide, but shall desire your lordship to do so, on a review of all circumstances, some of which I shall just mention.

THE league made for protracting the war having opposed the queen to the utmost of their power, and by means of every sort, from the first appearances of a negotiation; the general effect of this violent opposition, on her and her ministers was, to make them proceed by slower and more cautious steps: the particular effect of it was, to oblige them to open the eyes of the nation, and to inflame the people with a desire of peace, by shewing, in the most public and solemn manner, how unequally we were burdened, and how unfairly we were treated by our allies. The first gave an air of diffidence and timidity to their conduct, which encouraged the league, and gave vigor to the opposition. The second irritated the Dutch particularly; for the emperor and the other allies had the modesty at least, not to pretend to bear any proportion in the expence of the war: and thus the two powers, whose union was the most essential, were the most at variance, and the queen was obliged to act in a closer concert with her enemy who desired peace, than she would have done if her allies had been less obstinately bent to protract the war. During these transactions, my lord OXFORD, who had his correspondencies apart, and a private thread of negotiation always in his hands, entertained hopes that PHILIP would be brought to abandon Spain in favor of his father-in-law, and to content himself with the states of that prince, the kingdom of Sicily, and the preservation of his right of succession to the crown of France. Whether my lord had any particular reasons for entertaining these hopes, besides the general reasons founded on the condition of France, on that of the Bourbon family, and on the disposition of LEWIS the fourteenth, I doubt very much. That LEWIS, who sought, and had need of seeking peace, almost at any rate, and who saw that he could not obtain it, even of the queen, unless PHILIP abandoned immediately the crown of Spain, or abandoned immediately, by renunciation and a solemn act of exclusion, all pretension to that of France. That LEWIS was desirous of the former, I cannot doubt; that PHILIP would have abandoned Spain with the equivalents that have been mentioned, or either of them, I believe likewise;

if the prefent king of FRANCE had died, when his father, mother, and eldeft brother did: for they all had the fame diftemper. But LEWIS would ufe no violent means to force his grandfon; the queen would not continue the war to force him; PHILIP was too obftinate, and his wife too ambitious, to quit the crown of Spain, when they had difcovered our weaknefs, and felt their own ftrength in that country, by their fuccefs in the campaign of one thoufand feven hundred and ten: after which my lord STANHOPE himfelf was convinced that Spain could not be conquered, nor kept, if it was conquered, without a much greater army, than it was poffible for us to fend thither. In that fituation it was wild to imagine, as the earl of OXFORD imagined, or pretended to imagine, that they would quit the crown of Spain, for a remote and uncertain profpect of fucceeding to that of France, and content themfelves to be, in the mean time, princes of very fmall dominions. PHILIP therefore, after ftruggling long that he might not be obliged to make his option till the fucceffion of France lay open to him, was obliged to make it, and made it, for Spain. Now this, my lord, was the very crifis of the negotiation: and to this point I apply what I faid above of the effect of more decifive refolutions on the part, of the queen. It was plain, that, if she made the campaign in concert with her allies, she could be no longer miftrefs of the negotiations, nor have almoft a chance for conducting them to the iffue she propofed. Our ill fuccefs in the field would have rendered the French lefs tractable in the congrefs: our good fuccefs there would have rendered the allies fo. On this principle the queen fufpended the operations of her troops, and then concluded the ceffation.

COMPARE now the appearances and effect of this meafure, with the appearances and effect that another meafure would have had. In order to arrive at any peace, it was neceffary to do what the queen did, or to do more: and, in order to arrive at a good one, it was neceffary to be prepared to carry on the war, as well as to make a shew of it; for she had the hard task upon her, of guarding againft her allies, and her enemies both. But in that ferment, when few men confidered any thing coolly, the conduct of her general, after he took the field, though he covered the allies in the fiege of Quefnoy, correfponded ill, in appearance, with the declarations of carrying on the war vigorously, that had been made, on feveral occafions, before the campaign opened. It had an air of double dealing; and as fuch it paffed among thofe, who did not combine in their thoughts all the circumftances of the conjuncture, or who were infatuated with the notional neceffity of continuing the war. The clamor could not have been greater, if the queen had figned her peace feparately: and, I think, the appearances might have been explained as favorably in one cafe, as in the other. From the death of the emperor JOSEPH, it was neither our intereft, nor the common intereft, well underftood, to fet the crown of Spain on the prefent emperor's head. As foon therefore as PHILIP had made his option, and if she had taken this refolution early, his option would have been fooner made, I prefume that the queen might have declared, that she would not continue the war an hour longer to procure Spain for his Imperial majefty; that the engagements, she had taken whilft he was archduke, bound her no more; that, by his acceffion to the empire, the very nature of them was altered; that she took effectual meafures to prevent, in any future time, an union of the crowns of France and Spain, and, upon the fame principle, would not confent, much lefs fight, to bring about an immediate union of the Imperial and Spanish crowns; that they, who infifted to protract the war, intended this union; that they could intend nothing elfe, fince they ventured to break with her, rather than to treat, and were fo eager to put the reafonable fatisfaction, that they might have in every other cafe without hazard, on the uncertain events of war; that she would not be impofed on any longer in this manner, and that she had ordered her minifters to fign her treaty with France, on the furrender of Dunkirk into her hands; that she pretended not to prefcribe to her allies, but that she had infifted, in their behalf, on certain conditions, that France was obliged to grant to thofe of them, who should fign their treaties at the fame time as she did, or who should confent to an immediate ceffation of arms, and during the ceffation treat under her mediation. There had been more frankness, and more dignity in this proceeding, and the effect must have been more advantageous. France would have granted more for a separate peace, than for a cessation: and the Dutch would have been more influenced by the prospect of one, than of the other: especially since this proceeding would have been very different from theirs at Munster, and at Nimeghen, where they abandoned their allies, without any other pretence than the particular advantage they found in doing so. A suspension of the operations of the queen's troops, nay a cessation of arms between her and France, was not definitive; and they might, and they did, hope to drag her back under their, and the German yoke. This therefore was not sufficient to check their obstinacy, nor to hinder them from making all the unfortunate haste they did make to get themselves beaten at Denain. But they would possibly have laid aside their vain hopes, if they had seen the queen's ministers ready to sign her treaty of peace, and those of some principal allies ready to sign at the same time; in which case the mischief, that followed, had been prevented, and better terms of peace had been obtained for the confederacy: a prince of the house of Bourbon, who could never be king of France, would have sat on the Spanish throne, instead of an emperor: the Spanish scepter would have been weakened in the hands of one, and the Imperial scepter would have been strengthened in those of the other: France would have had no opportunity of recovering from former blows, nor of finishing a long unsuccessful war by two successful campaigns: her ambition, and her power, would have declined with her old king, and under the minority that followed: one of them at least might have been so reduced by the terms of peace, if the defeat of the allies in one thousand seven hundred and twelve, and the loss of so many towns as the French took in that and the following year, had been prevented, that the other would have been no longer formidable, even supposing it to have continued; whereas I suppose that the tranquillity of Europe is more due, at this time, to want of ambition, than to want of power, on the part of France. But, to carry the comparison of these two measures to the end, it may be supposed that the Dutch would have taken the same part, on the queen's declaring a separate peace, as they took on her declaring a cessation. The preparations for the campaign in the Low countries were made; the Dutch, like the other confederates, had a just confidence in their own troops, and an unjust contempt for those of the enemy; they were transported from their usual sobriety and caution by the ambitious prospect of large acquisitions, which had been opened artfully to them; the rest of the confederate army was composed of Imperial and German troops: so that the Dutch, the Imperialists, and the other Germans, having an interest to decide which was no longer the interest of the whole confederacy, they might have united against the queen in one case, as they did in the other; and the mischief, that followed to them and the common cause, might not have been prevented. This might have been the case, no doubt. They might have flattered themselves that they should be able to break into France, and to force PHILIP, by the distress brought on his grandfather, to resign the crown of Spain to the emperor, even after Great Britain, and Portugal, and Savoy too perhaps, were drawn out of the war; for these princes desired as little, as the queen, to see the Spanish crown on the emperor's head. But, even in this case, though the madness would have been greater, the effect would not have been worse. The queen would have been able to serve these confederates as well by being mediator in the negotiations, as they left it in her power to do, by being a party in them: and Great Britain would have had the advantage of being delivered so much sooner from a burden, which whimsical and wicked politics had imposed, and continued upon her till it was become intolerable. Of these two measures, at the time when we might have taken either, there were persons who thought the last preferable to the former. But it never came into public debate. Indeed it never could; too much time having been lost in waiting for the option of PHILIP, and the suspension and cessation having been brought before the council rather as a measure taken, than a matter to be debated. If your lordship, or any one else, should judge, that, in such circumstances as those of the confederacy in the beginning of one thousand seven hundred and twelve, the latter measure ought to have been taken, and the Gordian knot to have been cut, rather than to suffer a mock treaty to languish on, with so much advantage to the French as the disunion of the allies gave them; in short, if slowness, perplexity, inconsistency, and indecision should be objected, in some instances, to the queen's councils at that time; if it should be said particularly, that she did not observe the precise moment when the conduct of the league formed against her, being exposed to mankind, would have justified any part she should have taken (though she declared, soon after the moment was passed, that this conduct had set her free from all her engagements) and when she ought to have taken that of drawing, by one bold measure, her allies out of the war, or herself out of the confederacy, before she lost her influence on France: if all this should be objected, yet would the proofs brought to support these objections shew, that we were better allies than politicians, that the desire the queen had to treat in concert with her confederates, and the resolution she took not to sign without them,' made her bear what no crowned head had ever born before; and that where she erred, she erred principally by the patience, the compliance, and the condescension she exercised towards them, and towards her own subjects in league with them. Such objections as these may lie to the queen's conduct, in the course of this great affair; as well as objections of human infirmity to that of those persons employed by her in the transactions of it; from which neither those who preceded, nor thofe who fucceeded, have, I prefume, been free. But the principles on which they proceeded were honeft, the means they ufed were lawful, and the event they propofed to bring about was juft. Whereas the very foundation of all the oppofition to the peace was laid in injuftice and folly: for what could be more unjuft, than the attempt of the Dutch and the Germans, to force the queen to continue a war for their private intereft and ambition, the difproportionate expence of which oppreffed the commerce of her fubjects, and loaded them with debts for ages yet to come? A war, the object of which was fo changed, that from the year one thoufand feven hundred and eleven she made it not only without any engagement, but againft her own, and the common intereft? What could be more foolish; you will think that I foften the term too much, and you will be in the right to think fo: what could be more foolish; than the attempt of a party in Britain, to protract a war fo ruinous to their country, without any reafon that they durft avow, except that of wreaking the refentments of Europe on France, and that of uniting the Imperial and Spanish crowns on an Auftrian head? one of which was to purchafe revenge at a price too dear; and the other was to expofe the liberties of Europe to new dangers, by the conclufion of a war which had been made to affert and fecure them.

I HAVE dwelt the longer on the conduct of thofe who promoted, and of thofe who oppofed, the negotiations of the peace made at Utrecht, and on the comparison of the measure pursued by the queen with that which she might have pursued, because the great benefit we ought to reap from the study of history, cannot be reaped unless we accustom ourselves to compare the conduct of different governments, and different parties, in the same conjunctures, and to observe the measures they did pursue, and the measures they might have pursued, with the actual consequences that followed one, and the possible, or probable consequences, that might have followed the other. By this exercise of the mind, the study of history anticipates, as it were, experience, as I have observed in one of the first of these letters, and prepares us for action. If this consideration should not plead a sufficient excuse for my prolixity on this head, I have one more to add that may. A rage of warring possessed a party in our nation till the death of the late queen: a rage of negotiating has possessed the same party of men, ever since. You have seen the consequences of one: you see actually those of the other. The rage of warring confirmed the beggary of our nation, which began as early as the revolution; but then it gave, in the last war, reputation to our arms, and our councils too. For though I think, and must always think, that the principle, on which we acted after departing from that laid down in the grand alliance of one thousand seven hundred and one, was wrong: yet must we confess that it was pursued wisely, as well as boldly. The rage of negotiating has been a chargeable rage likewise, at least as chargeable in it's proportion. Far from paying our debts, contracted in war, they continue much the same, after three and twenty years of peace. The taxes that oppress our mercantile interest the most are still in mortgage; and those that oppress the landed interest the most, instead of being laid on extraordinary occasions, are become the ordinary funds for the current service of every year. This is grievous, and the more so to any man, who has the honor of his country, as well as her prosperity at heart, because we have not, in this case, the airy consolation we had in the other. The rage of negotiating began twenty years ago, under pretence of consummating the treaty of Utrecht: and, from that time to this, our ministers have been in one perpetual maze. They have made themselves and us, often, objects of aversion to the powers on the continent: and we are become at last objects of contempt, even to the Spaniards. What other effect could our absurd conduct have? What other return has it deserved? We came exhausted out of long wars; and, instead of pursuing the measures necessary to give us means and opportunity to repair our strength and to diminish our burdens, our ministers have acted, from that time to this, like men who sought pretences to keep the nation in the same exhausted condition, and under the same load of debt. This may have been their view perhaps; and we could not be surprised if we heard the same men declare national poverty necessary to support the present government, who have so frequently declared corruption and a standing army to be so. Your good sense, my lord, your virtue, and your love of your country, will always determine you to oppose such vile schemes, and to contribute your utmost towards the cure of both these kinds of rage; the rage of warring, without any proportionable interest of our own, for the ambition of others; and the rage of negotiating, on every occasion, at any rate, without a sufficient call to it, and without any part of that deciding influence which we ought to have. Our nation inhabits an island, and is one of the principal nations of Europe; but, to maintain this rank, we must take the advantages of this situation, which have been neglected by us for almost half a century: we must always remember, that we are not part of the continent, but we must never forget that we are neighbours to it. I will conclude, by applying a rule, that HORACE gives for the conduct of an epic or dramatic poem, to the part Great Britain ought to take in the affairs of the continent, if you allow me to transform Britannia into a male divinity, as the verse requires.

Nec Deus intersit, nisi dignus vindice nodus Inciderit.

If these reflections are just, and I should not have offered them to your lordship had they not appeared both just and important to my best understanding, you will think that I have not spent your time unprofitably in making them, and exciting you by them to examine the true intereſt of your country relatively to foreign affairs; and to compare it with thoſe principles of conduct, that I am perſuaded, have no other foundation than party-deſigns, prejudices, and habits; the private intereſt of ſome men and the ignorance and raſhneſs of others.

My letter is grown ſo long, that I ſhall ſay nothing to your lordſhip, at this time concerning the ſtudy of modern hiſtory, relatively to the intereſts of your country in domeſtic affairs; and I think there will be no need to do ſo at any other. The Hiſtory of the rebellion by your great grandfather, and his private memorials, which your lordſhip has in manuſcript, will guide you ſurely as far as they go: where they leave you, your lordſhip muſt not expect any hiſtory; for we have more reaſon to make this complaint, " abeſt enim hiſtoria literis noſtris," than TULLY had to put it into the mouth of ATTICUS, in his firſt book of laws. But where hiſtory leaves you, it is wanted leaſt: the traditions of this century, and of the latter end of the laſt, are freſh. Many, who were actors in ſome of theſe events, are alive; and many who have converſed with thoſe that were actors in others. The public is in poſſeſſion of ſeveral collections and memorials, and ſeveral there are in private hands. You will want no materials to form true notions of tranſactions ſo recent. Even pamphlets, writ on different ſides and on different occaſions in our party diſputes, and hiſtories of no more authority than pamphlets, will help you to come at truth. Read them with fuspicion, my lord, for they deserve to be suspected: pay no regard to the epithets given, nor to the judgments passed; neglect all declamation, weigh the reasoning, and advert to fact. With such precautions, even BURNET's history may be of some use. In a word, your lordship will want no help of mine to discover, by what progression the whole constitution of our country, and even the character of our nation, has been altered: nor how much a worse use, in a national sense, though a better in the sense of party politicks, the men called Whigs have made of long wars and new systems of revenue, since the revolution; than the men called Tories made, before it, of long peace, and stale prerogative. When you look back three or four generations ago, you will see that the English were a plain, perhaps a rough, but a good-natured hospitable people, jealous of their liberties, and able as well as ready to defend them, with their tongues, their pens, and their swords. The restoration began to turn hospitality into luxury, pleasure into debauch, and country peers and country commoners into courtiers and men of mode. But whilst our luxury was young, it was little more than elegance: the debauch of that age was enlivened with wit, and varnished over with gallantry. The courtiers and the men of mode knew what the constitution was, respected it, and often asserted it. Arts and sciences flourished, and, if we grew more trivial, we were not become either grossly ignorant, or openly profligate. Since the revolution, our kings have been reduced indeed to a seeming annual dependance on parliament; but the business of parliament, which was esteemed in general a duty before, has been exercised in general as a trade since. The trade of parliament, and the trade of funds, have grown universal. Men, who stood forward in the world, have attended to little else. The frequency of parliaments, that increased their importance, and should have increased the respect of them, has taken off from their dignity: and the spirit that prevailed, whilst the service in them was duty, has been debased since it became a trade. Few know, and scarce any respect, the British constitution: that of the church has been long since derided; that of the State as long neglected; and both have been left at the mercy of the men in power, whoever those men were. Thus the Church, at least the hierarchy, however sacred in it's origin or wise in it's institution, is become an useless burden on the State: and the State is become, under ancient and known forms, a new and undefinable monster; composed of a king without monarchical splendor, a senate of nobles without aristocratical independency, and a senate of commons without democratical freedom. In the mean time, my lord, the very idea of wit, and all that can be called taste, has been lost among the great; arts and sciences are scarce alive; luxury has been increased but not refined; corruption has been established, and is avowed. When governments are worn out, thus it is: the decay appears in every inftance. Public and private virtue, public and private fpirit, fcience and wit, decline all together.

That you, my lord, may have a long and glorious share in reftoring all thefe, and in drawing our government back to the true principles of it, I wish moft heartily. Whatever errors I may have committed in public life, I have always loved my country: whatever faults may be objected to me in private life, I have always loved my friend: whatever ufage I have received from my country, it shall never make me break with her: whatever ufage I have received from my friends, I never shall break with one of them, while I think him a friend to my country. Thefe are the fentiments of my heart. I know they are thofe of your lordship's: and a communion of fuch fentiments is a tie that will engage me to be, as long as I live,

My lord,

Your moft faithful fervant.

A PLAN

FOR A

General History of Europe.

LETTER IX.

I SHALL take the liberty of writing to you a little oftener than the three or four times a year, which, you tell me, are all you can allow yourself to write to those you like best: and yet I declare to you with great truth, that you never knew me so busy in your life, as I am at present. You must not imagine from hence that I am writing memoirs of myself. The subject is too slight to descend to posterity, in any other manner, than by that occasional mention which may be made of any little actor in the history of our age. SYLLA, CAESAR, and others of that rank, were, whilst they lived, at the head of mankind: their story was in some sort the story of the world, and as such might very properly be transmitted under their names to future generations. But for those who have acted much inferior parts, if they publish the piece, and call it after their own names, they are impertinent; if they publish only their own share in it, they inform mankind by halves, and neither give much inftruction, nor create much attention. France abounds with writers of this fort, and, I think, we fall into the other extreme. Let me tell you, on this occafion, what has fometimes come into my thoughts.

THERE is hardly any century in hiftory which began by opening fo great a fcene, as the century wherein we live, and shall I fuppofe, die. Compare it with others, even the moft famous, and you will think fo. I will sketch the two laft, to help your memory.

THE lofs of that balance which LAURENCE of Medicis had preferved, during his time, in Italy; the expedition of CHARLES the eighth to Naples; the intrigues of the duke of MILAN, who fpun, with all the refinements of art, that net wherein he was taken at laft himfelf; the fuccefsful dexterity of FERDINAND the Catholic, who built one pillar of the Auftrian greatnefs in Spain, in Italy, and in the Indies; as the fucceffion of the houfe of Burgundy, joined to the Imperial dignity and the hereditary countries, eftablished another in the upper and lower Germany: thefe caufes, and many others, combined to form a very extraordinary conjuncture; and, by their confequences, to render the fixteenth century fruitful of great events, and of aftonishing revolutions.

THE beginning of the feventeenth opened still a greater and more important fcene. The Spanish yoke was well-nigh impofed on Italy by the famous triumvirate, TOLEDO at Milan, OSSUNA at Naples, and LA CUEVA at Venice. The distractions of France, as well as the state-policy of the queen mother, seduced by Rome, and amused by Spain; the despicable character of our JAMES the first, the rashness of the elector Palatine, the bad intelligence of the princes and states of the league in Germany, the mercenary temper of JOHN GEORGE of Saxony, and the great qualities of MAXIMILIAN of Bavaria, raised FERDINAND the second to the Imperial throne; when, the males of the elder branch of the Austrian family in Germany being extinguished at the death of MATTHIAS, nothing was more desirable, nor perhaps more practicable, than to throw the empire into another house. Germany ran the same risque as Italy had done: FERDINAND seemed more likely, even than CHARLES the fifth had been, to become absolute master; and, if France had not furnished the greatest minister, and the North the greatest captain, of that age, in the same point of time, Vienna and Madrid would have given the law to the western world.

As the Austrian scale sunk, that of Bourbon rose. The true date of the rise of that power, which has made the kings of France so considerable in Europe, goes up as high as CHARLES the seventh, and LEWIS the eleventh. The weakness of our HENRY the sixth, the loose conduct of EDWARD the fourth, and perhaps the oversights of HENRY the seventh, helped very much to knit that monarchy together, as well as to enlarge it. Advantage might have been taken of the divisions which

which religion occafioned; and fupporting the proteftant party in France would have kept that crown under reftraints, and under inabilities, in fome meafure equal to thofe which were occafioned anciently by the vaft alienations of its demefnes, and by the exorbitant power of its vaſſals. But JAMES the firſt was incapable of thinking with fenſe, or acting with ſpirit. CHARLES the firſt had an imperfect glimpſe of his true intereft, but his uxorious temper, and the extravagancy of that madman BUCKINGHAM; gave RICHELIEU time to finish a great part of his project: and the miseries, that followed in England, gave MAZARINE time and opportunity to complete the fyftem. The laft great act of this cardinal's adminiftration was the Pyrenean treaty.

HERE I would begin, by reprefenting the face of Europe fuch as it was at that epocha, the interefts and the conduct of England, France, Spain, Holland, and the empire. A fummary recapitulation should follow of all the fteps taken by France, during more than twenty years, to arrive at the great object fhe had propofed to herfelf in making this treaty: the moft folemn article of which the minifter, who negotiated it, defigned should be violated; as appears by his letters, writ from the Island of Pheafants, if I miftake not. After this, another draught of Europe should have it's place according to the relations, which the feveral powers ſtood in, one towards another, in one thouſand fix hundred and eighty eight: and the alterations which the revolution in England made in the politicks of Europe. A summary account should follow of the events of the war that ended in one thousand six hundred and ninety seven, with the different views of king WILLIAM the third, and LEWIS the fourteenth, in making the peace of Ryswic; which matter has been much canvassed, and is little understood. Then the dispositions made by the partition-treaties, and the influences and consequences of these treaties; and a third draught of the state of Europe at the death of CHARLES the second of Spain. All this would make the subject of one or two books, and would be the most proper introduction imaginable to an history of that war with which our century began, and of the peace which followed.

THIS war, foreseen for above half a century, had been, during all that time, the great and constant object of the councils of Europe. The prize to be contended for was the richest that ever had been staked, since those of the Persian and Roman empires. The union of two powers, which separately, and in opposition, had aimed at universal monarchy, was apprehended. The confederates therefore engaged in it, to maintain a balance between the two houses of Austria and Bourbon, in order to preserve their security, and to assert their independence. But with the success of the war they changed their views: and, if ambition began it on the side of France, ambition continued it on the other. The battles, the sieges, the surprising revolutions, which happened in the course of this war, are not to be paralleled in any period of the same compass. The motives, and the measures, by which it was protracted, the true reasons why it ended in a manner, which appeared not proportionable to it's success; and the new political state into which Europe was thrown by the treaties of Utrecht and Baden, are subjects on which few persons have the necessary informations, and yet every one speaks with assurance, and even with passion. I think I could speak on them with some knowledge, and with as much indifference as POLYBIUS does of the negotiations of his father LYCORTAS, even in those points where I was myself an actor.

I WILL even confess to you, that I should not despair of performing this part better than the former. There is nothing in my opinion so hard to execute, as those political maps, if you will allow me such an expression, and those systems of hints, rather than relations of events, which are necessary to connect and explain them; and which must be so concise, and yet so full; so complicate, and yet so clear. I know nothing of this sort well done by the ancients. SALLUST's introduction, as well as that of THUCYDIDES, might serve almost for any other piece of the Roman or Greek story, as well as for those which these two great authors chose. POLYBIUS does not come up, in his introduction, to this idea neither. Among the moderns, the first book of MACHIAVEL's History of Florence is a noble original of this kind: and perhaps father PAUL's History of Benefices is, in the same kind of composition, inimitable.

THESE are a few of those thoughts, which come into my mind when I consider how incumbent it is on every man, that he should be able to give an account even of his leisure; and, in the midst of solitude, be of some use to society.

I KNOW not whether I shall have courage enough to undertake the task I have chalked out: I distrust my abilities with reason, and I shall want several informations, not easy, I doubt, for me to obtain. But, in all events, it will not be possible for me to go about it this year; the reasons of which would be long enough to fill another letter, and I doubt that you will think this grown too bulky already.

Adieu.

www.ingramcontent.com/pod-product-compliance
Lightning Source LLC
Chambersburg PA
CBHW022050230426
43672CB00008B/1129